YOUNG PEOPLE'S PARTICIPATION

Revisiting Youth and Inequalities in Europe

Edited by
Maria Bruselius-Jensen, Ilaria Pitti and
E. Kay M. Tisdall

P

First published in Great Britain in 2022 by

Policy Press, an imprint of
Bristol University Press
University of Bristol
1-9 Old Park Hill
Bristol
BS2 8BB
UK
t: +44 (0)117 374 6645
e: bup-info@bristol.ac.uk

Details of international sales and distribution partners are available at
policy.bristoluniversitypress.co.uk

British Library Cataloguing in Publication Data
A catalogue record for this book is available from the British Library

ISBN 978-1-4473-4541-1 hardcover
ISBN 978-1-4473-4542-8 paperback
ISBN 978-1-4473-4544-2 ePub
ISBN 978-1-4473-4543-5 ePdf

Cover design: Robin Hawes
Front cover image: iStock-1160644769

Contents

List of figures and tables   v

Notes on contributors   vii

Acknowledgements   xiii

1   Revisiting young people's participation: an introduction   1
Maria Bruselius-Jensen, E. Kay M. Tisdall and Ilaria Pitti

PART I: Young people's experiences of participation and engagement

2   Cultural activism against inequalities: the experience of   17
Quaderni Urbani in Bologna
Alessio La Terra

3   It's okay to think freely: how participation changed us   29
Christina McMellon, Katherine Dempsie and Myada Eltiraifi

4   Frontrunners Against Inequality: the stories of Darpan   43
and Barwago
Darpan Raj Gautam and Barwago Jama Hussein

PART II: Current state and conditions for young people's participation: critiques and trends

5   Bounded agency and social participation: how   53
socioeconomic situation and experiences influence
young people's way of engaging in society
Sabine Israel, Jo Deakin, Renata Franc, Anna Markina,
Rein Murakas and Markus Quandt

6   From ideology to strategic engagement   77
Jonas Lieberkind

7   Digital participation and digital divides in a former   99
socialist country
Airi-Alina Allaste and David Cairns

8   The participation project: how projects shape young   119
people's participation
Maria Bruselius-Jensen and Anne Mette W. Nielsen

PART III: Broadening participation: young people's own approaches to participation

9   Young Italians and the crisis: emerging trends in   139
     activism and self-organisation
     Ilaria Pitti and Nicola De Luigi

10   Justifying self-organisation: between inequality and critique 157
     Anne-Lene Sand

11   Advocacy and participation: young people with autism   175
     spectrum disorder and their experiences with statutory
     casework
     Cecilie K. Moesby-Jensen

12   Young people seeking asylum: voice and activism in a   195
     'hostile environment'
     Gráinne McMahon and Rhetta Moran

PART IV: New opportunities for young people's participation: facilitating new forms of youth participation

13   Meaningful, effective and sustainable? Challenges for   217
     children and young people's participation
     E. Kay M. Tisdall

14   Journey mapping as a method to make sense of   235
     participation
     Anne Mette W. Nielsen and Maria Bruselius-Jensen

15   Playful walks: a methodological approach for analysing   255
     the embodied citizenship of young people in the
     countryside
     Claire Levy

16   Transformative participation in the lifeworlds of   275
     marginalised youth: learning for change
     Mette Bladt and Barry Percy-Smith

17   Revisiting young people's participation and looking   293
     ahead: concluding remarks
     E. Kay M. Tisdall, Ilaria Pitti and Maria Bruselius-Jensen

Index   305

List of figures and tables

Figures

4.1	Barwago's map of her participatory journey	44
4.2	Darpan's map of his participatory journey	48
5.1	Social position effect on efficacy	62
5.2	Social experiences effect on efficacy	62
5.3	Personal efficacy effect on activism, everyday engagement and helping	63
5.4	Perceived income effect on activism, everyday engagement and helping	64
5.5	Social exclusion effect on activism, everyday engagement and helping	65
5.6	Discrimination effect on activism, everyday engagement and helping	65
5.7	Education effect on activism, everyday engagement and helping	66
5.8	Activity status effect on activism, everyday engagement and helping	66
5.9	Local connection effect on activism, everyday engagement and helping	67
5.10	Social trust effect on activism, everyday engagement and helping	67
5.11	Police contact effect on activism, everyday engagement and helping	68
6.1	Political trust and reflexivity	85
6.2	Conventional and unconventional political participation	88
6.3	Unconventional political participation	89
10.1	A young man rehearsing violin under the bridge	164
10.2	Young people assemble before a concert on the periphery of the city	164
10.3	At night, bands play on a 'stage' comprising a podium between the concrete pillars of a bridge	165
10.4	A sign on the ground directed at users of a public outdoor skateboarding park in Denmark	169
14.1	The first four frames of Sofie's journey map	241
14.2	Last frame of Sofie's journey map	243
14.3	Isaam's journey map	244

14.4	Examples of small, project-defined communities. Danish text says: 1. Courage, happiness, unity, common cause. 2. Meet new young people	246
14.5	Examples of larger, local communities. Danish text says: 1. Welcome to a ghetto, welfare support, Islam, immigrants, integration, crime. 2. Help other young people – make a difference	247
14.6	Examples of big, societal communities	248
15.1	Walking along the canal, August 2017	259
15.2	Visual methods	262
15.3	Walking	263
15.4	Lucy running, August 2017	265
15.5	Map making, August 2017	267

Tables

5.1	Overview of the positive and negative effect of social position and life experiences on agency	70
6.1	ICCS test, European average scores for civic knowledge	84
6.2	ICCS items, conventional and unconventional political participation	88
6.3	An outline of empirical findings	94
7.1	Dimensions of participation in Estonia in the MYPLACE study	106
15.1	Table of activity	261

Notes on contributors

Airi-Alina Allaste is Professor of Sociology at Tallinn University, Estonia. Her research, publications and teaching have concentrated on youth studies. She has coordinated several projects on youth cultures, lifestyles and participation, and has edited seven books/special journal issues. Her research focuses mainly on the analyses of the meanings that young people themselves attribute to their lives. Her most recent publication, written jointly with Kari Saari, was 'Social media and participation in different socio-political contexts', which appeared in 2020 in the journal *YOUNG*.

Mette Bladt is Associate Professor at University College Copenhagen, Denmark, working in the field of action research with young offenders. Her research focuses on participation as a key factor in challenging inequality structures, in particular how the institutional welfare system could be developed to accommodate marginalised young people and therefore extend and enhance their life opportunities.

Maria Bruselius-Jensen is Associate Professor at the Centre for Youth Research, Department of Culture and Learning, Aalborg University, Denmark. She has a general research interest in youth civic engagement with particular experience with both methodological and theoretical approaches to young people's facilitated participation. Recent work includes studies of social communities, new trends in voluntary engagement and project-based facilitated youth participation.

David Cairns is Principal Researcher at the Centre for Research and Studies in Sociology, ISCTE-University of Lisbon, Portugal. He has published extensively in the areas of youth, mobility, political participation and education, including seven books and articles in journals including *YOUNG*, *Journal of Youth Studies*, *Children's Geographies*, *Social and Cultural Geography* and *International Migration*. He is currently working on a project exploring precariousness in the careers of scientists in Portugal.

Jo Deakin is Senior Lecturer in Criminology at the University of Manchester, UK. Her research, situated at the intersection between youth work, justice and social policy, focuses on youth inclusion and exclusion in community and institutional settings. Specifically, her research addresses young people's responses to aspects of criminalisation, social control and stigma. She is a multi-methods researcher with a particular interest in participatory arts-based methods and peer research with young and sometimes vulnerable populations.

Katherine Dempsie, 19, lives in Edinburgh and has been a part of Young Edinburgh Action since it began. She loves travel and drinking tea.

Myada Eltiraifi, 18, studies social sciences at college in Edinburgh and hopes to study international relations at university. She is involved in Young Edinburgh Action and is a youth adviser with the TRIUMPH research network based at University of Glasgow, UK.

Renata Franc is a senior scientific adviser and team leader at the Ivo Pilar Institute of Social Sciences in Zagreb, Croatia, and Professor of Social and Political Psychology, University of Zagreb, Croatia. Her research interests include youth, social and political attitudes and values, political and social participation, intergroup relations and quality of life. She has particular expertise in survey research and quantitative data analyses. Currently she works on two European Union (EU) Horizon 2020 projects focused on youth: CHIEF (Cultural Heritage and Identities of Europe's Future) and DARE (Dialogue about Radicalisation and Equality).

Darpan Raj Gautam is a student of international studies at Roskilde University, Denmark. He moved to Denmark at the age of ten and has been living there for ten years. As he is interested in development work, he works in a youth club, where his main focus is the development and engagement of young people in activities to help divert them from criminality and destructive choices.

Barwago Jama Hussein is a student of political science at Aarhus University, Denmark. She used to live in Tingbjerg, a social housing area outside Copenhagen. She is a founding member of Tingbjerg Youth Community, an organisation that aims to change the public view of young people living in this area.

Sabine Israel is a PhD researcher and data analyst at GESIS Leibniz Institute for the Social Sciences in Cologne, Germany. Her most recent work within the EU Horizon 2020 project PROMISE focused on unequal social participation opportunities of young people. With an MSc in public policy from the Maastricht Graduate School of

Governance and a PhD focusing on poverty and social inequalities in Europe, her interest lies in evidence-based policy evaluation at the intersection between political structure and living conditions.

Alessio La Terra is a philosopher and political activist. He graduated from the University of Bologna, Italy, with an MA in philosophy in 2017 and is currently studying to become a high school teacher in philosophy and history. His research interests focus on contemporary central European philosophy and on the history of scientific thought. His MA thesis has been published under the title *I Limiti Terreni dello Spirito [The Earthly Limits of the Spirit]* (Il Capitello del Sole, 2018).

Claire Levy is a PhD researcher at Goldsmiths, University of London, UK and Senior Lecturer in Film at Bath Spa University, UK. Her research focuses on participatory methodologies and the embodied ways young people engage with their locality. She is a documentary film-maker and her work often focuses on experiences of young people. She is also editor of *Streetsigns*, an online magazine published by the Centre for Urban and Community Research at Goldsmiths, University of London.

Jonas Lieberkind is Associate Professor of Educational Sociology at the Danish School of Education, Aarhus University, Denmark. His research is based on both theoretical and empirical studies of society, politics and citizenship education. In particular, he has focused on current tendencies among young people, their attitudes towards society, and research questions concerning students' political socialisation. He is part of the Danish research team that conducts the International Civic and Citizen Education Study.

Nicola De Luigi is Associate Professor of Sociology at the University of Bologna, Italy. His research activities focus on two main fields – youth studies and social policy – addressing the following issues: gender inequalities in the transition from education to the labour market, educational processes and labour market changes, youth politics and participation in urban spaces. He is the author of many journal articles and works with research institutes and networks at both national and international levels.

Anna Markina is a researcher in the School of Law, University of Tartu, Estonia. Her research focuses on youth delinquency, the juvenile justice system, youth imprisonment and intervention programmes. She has conducted qualitative research with young people on probation and parole, in prisons and reformatories, addressing the rights of the child, the effectiveness of interventions and young people's response to them. She is a member of the steering committee of the International Self-Report Delinquency Study.

Gráinne McMahon is a feminist academic at the University of Huddersfield, UK. She researches feminism and human rights activism and social movements, and young people's social, political and civic participation. Her work centres voice and experience in challenging the patriarchal, elitist and racist structures that oppress, in particular, women and people of colour. She is the research lead and a trustee for RAPAR, a human rights organisation in Manchester, UK, and is active on social media: @grainnemcmahon.

Christina McMellon is a researcher and youth worker currently based at the Universities of Edinburgh and Glasgow, UK. She is committed to exploring meaningful ways for young people to participate in all research and particularly research related to mental and sexual health. She loves travel, the sea and good stories.

Cecilie K. Moesby-Jensen is Assistant Professor of Social Work and Disability at the Department of Sociology and Social Work, University of Aalborg, Denmark. Her research field is social work with vulnerable children and young people, and she is currently involved in a study on the meetings between statutory caseworkers and children and young people with autism spectrum disorders and their families. She lives in Copenhagen and is vice-chair of a non-governmental organisation dedicated to encouraging children with disabilities to join sport clubs.

Rhetta Moran is a praxivist, most interested in creating and sustaining people and things – initiatives, projects and organisations – in ways that are always alive to the relationship between theory and practice. As a writer and action researcher, she has over 30 years' experience of working from local to global, across all sectors, to centralise the involvement of vulnerable people in the development of constructive changes and solution making. In 2001, she initiated RAPAR (www.rapar.co.uk).

Rein Murakas works as a consultant researcher and an analyst for Estonian and international research projects. His main research fields include youth problems, inequality, financial behaviour, entrepreneurship, social policy, health, methodology and the use of social science data sources.

Anne Mette W. Nielsen is Assistant Professor at the Centre for Youth Research, Aalborg University, Denmark. Her research interests include young people's participation and agency in education, community projects and cultural institutions. She is currently engaged in research about young people on the edge of society and their participation in formal and informal arenas.

Barry Percy-Smith is Professor of Childhood Youth and Participatory Practice at the University of Huddersfield, UK. He has extensive experience in the theory and practice of youth participation and has published widely on these issues, including *A Handbook of Children and Young People's Participation: Perspectives from Theory and Practice* (co-edited with Nigel Thomas, Routledge, 2010). His main interests are in children and young people as active agents of change, and participatory approaches to learning and change in organisations and communities.

Ilaria Pitti is Senior Assistant Professor at the University of Bologna, Italy, and Vice-President (Southern Europe) of the International Sociological Association's Research Committee 34 Sociology of Youth. Her research is located at the crossroad between youth and social movement studies, focusing on the analysis of young people's participation in social movements and subcultures. She is also interested in the effects of precariousness on youth conditions and on young people's individual and collective reaction to precariousness.

Markus Quandt is a senior researcher and team leader at GESIS Leibniz Institute for the Social Sciences in Cologne, Germany. His research is based on quantitative surveys in cross-country comparative settings. Substantive interests are in political and social participation, as collective goods problems in individualising and rapidly changing societies. Methodological interests concern the comparability and validity of survey-based measures of attitudes and values. He is affiliated to the group conducting the European Values Study.

Anne-Lene Sand is a postdoctoral researcher at the Design School Kolding, Department for Design for Play. She holds an MSc in educational anthropology and a PhD in education. For the past nine years her research has been centred on young people's self-organised and semi-organised urban practices, using a variety of sensory and visual methods in order to uncover the perspective of young people.

E. Kay M. Tisdall is Professor of Childhood Policy at the University of Edinburgh, UK. She is part of the Childhood and Youth Studies Research Group at the Moray House School of Education and Sport. She has developed a collaborative programme on children and young people's participation, both domestically and with cross-national partners. She is author of a range of policy and academic publications, and has editing experience of both books and special journal issues, including *Global Studies of Childhood* and *International Journal of Human Rights*.

Acknowledgements

The editors would like to thank the VELUX FOUNDATIONS for providing funding for the work of the European Network of Multi-Disciplinary Research in Youth and Participation that has led to this edited book. Also thanks to all the members of the network for engaging in important explorations of the concept, practice and future of youth participation in Europe and for taking part in the intricate and time-demanding process of writing this book. We are grateful to have all your contributions in the book. Thanks to Policy Press for believing in the relevance of the publication even while it was in the making. Finally, a profound thanks to all the young people across Europe who have voiced their experiences with engaging in participatory processes. Without you this book would have no merit.

1

Revisiting young people's participation: an introduction

Maria Bruselius-Jensen, E. Kay M. Tisdall and Ilaria Pitti

Over 30 years after the United Nations Convention on the Rights of the Child (UNCRC) was ratified by the United Nations (UN) General Assembly in 1989, young people's active citizenship and participation rights have gained increased attention in both academia, policy and practice (Westwood et al, 2014; Gal and Duramy, 2015; McMellon and Tisdall, 2020). In particular, young people's civic participation is promoted at local, national and regional levels through such organisations as the European Union, UNICEF and international non-governmental organisations (NGOs). Young people's participation has become a major rights issue and one gaining increasing policy and practice importance.

While the UNCRC addresses the human rights of children under the age of 18, attention to participation also extends to older young people. Political institutions, research and society are concerned about young people's societal engagement, carried by fears that new generations of European youth are unengaged and disinterested in politics and have lost trust in democratic institutions (Loncle et al, 2012), and that this will lead to a crisis in democracy. Such a deficit perspective has been counteracted by recent research, which demonstrates that young people are often not uninvolved but they use forms and means other than formal participation to engage in society and to influence politics (Quintelier, 2007; Pohl et al, 2020). Whether constructing youth participation as in crisis or changing, institutions from social work to education are investing in supporting, facilitating and educating young people to be engaged societally as the 'citizens of tomorrow' (Walther et al, 2020).

Young people of recent generations have grown up not only with the right to be consulted, but also with multiple initiatives to support their democratic education and facilitate their engagement (Taru et al, 2014). Key actors such as municipalities, institutions and NGOs advocate giving 'voice' to young people and consulting them on matters that concern their lives (Kjellander et al, 2016). However, professionals can be unsure about how to include young people in change and decision making, while institutional structures may create barriers as well as opportunities (Tisdall et al, 2014). With participation activities proliferating, the book is timely in assessing the ways in which young people experience such activities, their transformative potential both personally and for society, and the ways in which adults and organisations do or do not support such participation.

This book comes at a time of considerable upheaval and change for young people in Europe. The 2008 global financial crisis has led to a rise of youth unemployment in many European countries, while the challenges fostered by massive migrations and climate change are putting pressure on political and economic systems. This complexity is further exacerbated by the outbreak of the COVID-19 pandemic. While young people have so far been relatively spared from serious illness, the long-term effects of this new crisis on the European economies and labour markets are likely to hit them harder, primarily in terms of accessing stable jobs and social security. The pandemic crisis could foster another global economic crisis. In turn, this could lead national governments to adopt austerity measures similar to those enacted in response to the 2008 global financial crisis, limiting education, youth work and other social services that could support young people.

The current scenario results in uncertainty for young people, but it also creates spaces for experimentation and innovation through participation.

This book showcases original research evidence and analysis, arising from a network of European social science researchers from childhood and youth studies. It revisits how, under what conditions and for what purpose young people[1] – in different contexts – participate in making decisions and foster changes on issues that concern them and their communities. It does so by drawing on research undertaken after the 2008 financial crisis but before the COVID-19 pandemic. The chapters are aligned by a shared focus on the interplay between the concepts of youth, participation and inequality. The book provides an opportunity to update these three long-standing and central concepts for young people's participation, and to critically consider them in the current environment. Thus, the book both contributes new insights for contemporary young people's participation and strengthens the core concepts for participatory research and practice. The following sections further explore the concepts of participation, youth and inequality and their application in this book.

Participation

To promote young people's participation, formal structures have been established in numerous countries, from pupil councils within schools (Cross et al, 2014) to children's or youth parliaments (Cushing and van Vliet, 2017). Examples abound of young people being invited to comment on community, service and policy developments, at local, regional and national levels; sometimes their involvement goes further, in forms of co-design and co-production (Tisdall et al, 2014). Participation projects and activities have proliferated, from young people influencing their local contexts (for example, care-experienced young people influencing local authority services[2]), to young people speaking to international decision makers on issues ranging from child marriage to equal opportunities.[3] The recent profile of young people's activism in climate change, including Greta Thunberg's speech to the UN General Assembly[4] and the widespread marches of school children and youth (Sengupta, 2019), have gripped the public imagination and flooded both traditional and social media. Young people's participation is now high profile for the public, as well as being of policy, practice and research interest.

Despite or perhaps because of its popularity, participation as a concept is used widely but differently, with no consensus across literatures, research and policies on its definition. A very basic definition of 'participation' – for example, 'the fact that you take part or become involved in something' in the *Cambridge English Dictionary*[5] – is very generalised, lacks links to decision making and impact, and thus provides only a starting point from a rights perspective. Inspired by Cotta (1979), the concept of participation is defined here as having two interconnected meanings. On the one hand, participation does refer to 'taking part' in something and particularly to taking part in civic and political activities. On the other hand, participation refers to 'being part' of something, included in a society with a series of rights and possibilities. Through a wide variety of case examples, this book demonstrates how the two dimensions of participation are interconnected in young people's possibilities of being part of and taking part in different welfare societies.

Youth

As a second focus, the book interrogates the conditions of 'youth' and 'being young' in contemporary Europe and how these impact on young people's practices and possibilities of participation. The book starts from the premise that 'youth' is first and foremost a social category (Bourdieu, 1993) whose boundaries and contents are continuously defined and redefined in the evolving interactions between structural forces and individual agency (Archer, 2003). Further, 'being young' is conceptualised as a status that entails specific opportunities, constraints and expectations of behaviour that emerge from and are negotiated in the interactions between young individuals and their surrounding social contexts (Furlong, 2009; Kelly and Kamp, 2014).

Social sciences have analysed youth through different theoretical frameworks. The transition perspective (Furlong, 2009) has understood youth as a life stage traditionally meant to prepare young individuals to acquire adult roles in society through a series of 'modern' rites of passage that young people have to face: namely – for Western societies – completing education, finding a job, moving out of the family home and starting a family of their own (Woodman and Bennet, 2015). Transition analyses have highlighted how growing social mobility has increased the transitions young people go through and the speed by which they take place (Furlong et al, 2011; Rosa, 2013). A generational perspective recognises certain similarities across young people in different societies but also how individual young people can experience these differently in their particular contexts (Woodman and Wyn, 2015). Lastly, the cultural perspective highlights not only the variety of youth cultures, but also the cultural practices and strategies through which young people cope with and make sense of their positions in society (Hall and Jefferson, 1975; Woodman and Bennet, 2015). Despite their differences, these three perspectives within youth studies point out how youth must be understood in relation to the young person's specific life conditions and surrounding social contexts. With that in mind, the book has sought to give space to diversity among young people. Contributions depict an array of different youth conditions: for example, young people with disabilities, young asylum seekers, and young people living in rural areas. The stories consider the multifaceted and differentiated meanings that 'being young' can have to young people and how differences in conditions can affect young people's participation.

The 'adult world' intervenes to shape youth through definitions and discourses. Legal definitions can define the passages from youth to adulthood, with implications for young people's participation opportunities: for example, a minimum age for voting rights. Adults' understandings of youth can define the appropriateness of a young person's participation. Such definitions are part of an intergenerational struggle, where young people and their expressions are often portrayed in negative terms, such as being passive, unengaged and self-centred or dangerous and threatening (Pickard and Bessant, 2019; Walther et al, 2020). The book therefore pays attention to how youth participation is formed in the interactions between young people, adults and institutions. Chapters consider how particular understandings and discourses of 'youth' shape what counts and is discounted as young people's participation. They consider what spaces young people are invited to engage with, which ones they are excluded from, and which ones young people carve out for themselves.

Inequality

The third concept scaffolding this book is inequality. A long tradition in social sciences and related studies has grappled with the concept and manifestations of inequality (Castel, 2003; Dorling, 2015). For this book, inequality is the structuring of advantaged and disadvantaged life chances and is the effect of an uneven distribution of opportunities among the members of a given society (Rawls, 1971; Nussbaum, 1995). The unequal distribution of life chances within a given society produces social hierarchies and different degrees of integration for its members, who can occupy more 'central' or more 'peripheral' positions in relation to civil, political and social spheres (Castel, 2003). When it comes to youth, social sciences have analysed structural disparities in young people's possibilities to meet basic needs such as food and housing (Green, 2017), in access to education (Heathfield and Fusco, 2016), and in health and other services (Alemán-Díaz et al, 2016). Research shows how dimensions of class (Threadgold, 2017), gender (Thompson, 2011), ethnicity (Harris, 2012) and place (Cuervo and Miranda, 2019) interact with age in creating more or less 'marginal youths'.

When studying youth and participation, the intergenerational dimension is central (Bates and Riseborough, 1993; Furlong, 2009; Woodman and Leccardi, 2015) and underlines the unequal distribution of resources between co-existing adult and youth generations. Indeed, studies indicate that in Western contexts young people born after 1980 might become the first generation who can expect to attain lower economic living standards than previous generations (Bessant et al, 2018). Thus, the intergenerational perspective recognises the systematic disparities in the distribution of economic resources and political power between generations (Pickard and Bessant, 2019).

While the distribution of material resources represents the most visible form of inequality, disparities also occur in relation to the different possibilities that individuals and groups have to participate – both to take part in and being part of their societies. From this perspective, inequality refers to a set of systematic disparities in an individual's or group's abilities: to receive recognition; to influence others' behaviours in order to produce advantages for themselves and the groups they belong to; and to have control of the choices concerning their present and their future (Saraceno, 2006). Adopting this perspective of inequality facilitates consideration of both 'traditional' and 'emerging' disparities in young people's participation.

The perduring effect that factors such as class, education and gender have in structuring young people's possibilities of participation have been extensively demonstrated by literature. Young people with lower-class backgrounds systematically show lower levels of participation in both institutional and unconventional forms of participation (Marien et al, 2010) and experience difficulties in obtaining recognition based on their modes of expression (Pitti et al, 2020). This also seems to be the case for young people from ethnic minorities (Harris, 2008). Many of the chapters included in this book contribute to the analysis of these traditional effects of social inequalities on youth participation. However, attention is also given to less explored forms of inequalities in the participatory sphere. Literature has shown how spatial dimensions are relevant in shaping young people's capabilities to participate (Holloway et al, 2018). Several studies have highlighted the different possibilities of engagement accessible to urban and rural young people (Farrugia, 2019), while temporal aspects are relevant in explaining young people's involvement (Feixa et al, 2016), especially in relation to forms of engagement that require a relevant investment of time to be fulfilled (such as volunteering or activism) (Pitti, 2018). The book explores the relationships between participation and both traditional and emerging forms of inequality.

Participation can be a means through which young people seek to cope with the different forms of inequality they encounter in their lives (Loncle et al, 2012). However, some practices and logics of youth participation produce and reproduce forms of inequality that hinder young people's full engagement and their rights to participate (Batsleer et al, 2020). The book provides a critical assessment of how specific ways of structuring and promoting youth participation can create 'hierarchies of engagement' and systematic forms of exclusion, and accentuate certain inequalities. It also examines participation's possibilities for inclusion, innovation and change.

Outline of the book

This book arose out of network meetings in 2018 and 2019 with scholars across Europe and from different fields in the social sciences, who shared a strong interest in strengthening young people's inclusion, recognition and participation on issues that matter to them. With evidenced examples and substantive research from these authors, the book challenges current policies and practices on young people's participation and asks, as a result, how young people can be supported to take part in social change and decision making and what can be learnt from young people's own initiatives.

The first part of the book contains three chapters written by and with young people who explore the experiences and the outcomes of their own participation. Chapter 2 is written by Alessio La Terra, a young activist involved in the leftist social movement organisation Làbas, based in Bologna. The chapter considers the story of Quaderni Urbani, a self-organised cultural project that, through art, is seeking to develop and share radical messages and political activism on migration, housing and other social issues. The chapter focuses on the practice of 'cultural activism' and discusses the opportunities and challenges of combining radical political activism and cultural engagement. Chapter 3 learns from experiences in Scotland, where young people involved with Young Edinburgh Action (YEA), the city of Edinburgh's youth participation strategy, undertook participatory action projects and, subsequently, went on to co-produce a UK-wide network to improve young people's mental health (TRIUMPH). The chapter is co-authored by Katherine Dempsie and Myada Eltiraifi, two young people involved in first YEA and then TRIUMPH, along with Christina McMellon, who supported their involvement throughout. Chapter 4 is written by Darpan Raj Gautam and Barwago Jama Hussein, who took part in a project entitled Part of the Community, organised by the NGO Action Aid Denmark. The project aimed to develop fora for young people in deprived neighbourhoods, so young people could share their experiences of inequality and, together, gain influence and democratic experiences. These three chapters provide insights into the forms of and motivations for young people's engagement, as well as some of the difficulties these young people encountered in their participation journeys.

In Part II, four chapters revisit youth participation and inequality by investigating contemporary conditions and forms of youth participation. The section examines how young people's participation has been affected and shaped by broader changes in the economy, technological innovation, regimes and policies. Chapter 5 develops a context-based definition of social participation, to then consider the diverse forms of participation and factors that influence young people's agency and ability to engage. The authors find that experiencing inequalities seems to spur, rather than dissuade, young people's engagement. Chapter 6 revisits young people's political engagement, taking a historical perspective from the 1970s on youth rebellions and reflecting on surveys with young people via the International Civic and Citizenship Education Study. Chapter 7 focuses on young people's digital citizenship. Drawing on cross-European quantitative data and qualitative findings from Estonia, it explores how young people become informed, take a stand and take action through digital participation. The authors discuss how digital participation can also create inequalities of participation between groups of young people. Chapter 8 introduces the term 'project regime' to demonstrate how young people's participation is often facilitated and organised as projects, and how the managerial orders and logics of projects profoundly affect the conditions for young people's participation. Drawing on two case studies, the authors shows how the orders and logics of project organisation decide which, how and to what aims young people can participate in change and decision making within these project-based spaces for participation.

In Part III, chapters focus on how young people's participation takes different forms in different contexts. Each chapter is based on a study or project with a specific group of young people, where young people seek to make changes for their lives and others. Chapter 9 considers five cases of youth activism in political squats, to demonstrate how young people's activism aims to counteract austerity measures and economic crisis in Italy. The chapter focuses on young people's collective reactions to inequality through self-organisation and prefigurative actions. Chapter 10 likewise looks at young people's self-organisation in public spaces. The author explores how young people seek to turn abandoned urban spaces into spaces of participation and the accompanying challenges for the young people when they self-organise. In Chapter 11, the space for participation changes from a public to an individual and institutional space, with an analysis of how young people diagnosed with autism spectrum disorder struggle in their meetings with their statutory caseworkers. The study shows the young people's struggles to be considered active participants in decision making concerning crucial matters in their lives. Chapter 12 describes how young asylum seekers in the UK worked collectively to make their experiences heard and visible within a hostile and alienating public space.

Part IV addresses how young people's participation can be supported through specific approaches and methodologies within research and practice. Research on young people's participation has a strong tradition of developing methodologies that seek to enable young people to express and explore their views (Pink, 2007). This section builds on that tradition, to consider which methodologies appear effective in supporting young people's participation – and potential innovations. Chapter 13 reviews the pernicious challenges for young people's participation activities, such as tokenism, lack of impact on decision making, and criticisms that the young people involved are unrepresentative. It then explores examples of youth-led research, which address many of these challenges, due to young people being recognised as generators of knowledge, with legitimacy and credibility. Chapters 14 and 15 both present and explore new methodological approaches to support young people's participation in research. Chapter 14 discusses the methodology 'journey mapping' and illustrate how the methodology can support young people to form and share their often multifaceted experiences when taking part in participatory projects. Chapter 15 explores how film making can provide a playful framework for young people to express their non-verbal, embodied and visual experiences living in rural settings. Finally, Chapter 16 draws on the methodologies of participatory action research and critical utopian action research to argue for transformative learning to be central to participation processes for young people at risk of marginalisation. The chapter underlines that participatory processes necessitate reciprocal learning for both the young people and adults involved and that this, in turn, redresses power imbalances and engenders co-inquiry and mutual reciprocity in relationships of respect. The editors' concluding remarks in Chapter 17 complete the book.

Notes

[1] Broadly, the book address young people between the ages of 12 and 24 (see www.unesco.org/new/en/social-and-human-sciences/themes/youth/youth-definition and www.un.org/esa/socdev/documents/youth/fact-sheets/youth-definition.pdf [Accessed 18 January 2019]).

[2] See www.lifechangestrust.org.uk/care-experienced-young-people/champions-boards [Accessed 11 December 2019].

[3] See www.un.org/development/desa/youth/news/2019/10/youth-delegates

[4] See www.youtube.com/watch?v=11FCyUB81rI [Accessed 11 December 2019].

[5] See https://dictionary.cambridge.org/dictionary/english/participation [Accessed 31 January 2020].

References

Alemán-Díaz, A.Y., Toczydlowska, E., Mazur, J., Frasquilho, D., Melkumova, M. and Holmqvist, G. (2016) *Why Income Inequalities Matter for Young People's Health: A Look at the Evidence*, Innocenti Working Paper 2016-06, Florence: UNICEF Office of Research.

Archer, M. (2003) *Structure, Agency and the Internal Conversation*, Cambridge: Cambridge University Press, doi: 10.1017/CBO9781139087315

Bates, I. and Riseborough, G. (1993) *Youth and Inequality*, Buckingham: Open University.

Batsleer, J., Walther, A. and Lüküslü, D. (2020) 'Struggle over participation: towards a grounded theory of youth participation', in A. Walther, J. Batsleer, P. Loncle and A. Pohl (eds) (2020) *Young People and the Struggle for Participation: Contested Practices, Power and Pedagogies in Public Spaces*, Abingdon: Routledge, pp 119–218, https://doi.org/10.4324/9780429432095

Bessant, J., Farthing, R. and Watts, R. (2018) *The Precarious Generation: A Political Economy of Young People*, London: Routledge.

Bourdieu, P. (1993) '"Youth" is just a word', in P. Bourdieu (ed) *Sociology in Question*, Thousand Oaks, CA: Sage Publications, pp 94–10.

Castel, R. (2003) *Transformation of the Social Question*, Piscataway, NJ: Transaction Publishers.

Cotta, M. (1979) 'Il concetto di partecipazione politica: linee di un inquadramento teorico', [The concept of political participation: A theoretical framework], *Italian Political Science Review*, 9(2): 193–227.

Cross, B., Hulme, M. and McKinney, S. (2014) 'The last place to look: the place of pupil councils within citizen participation in Scottish schools', *Oxford Review of Education*, 40(5): 628–48.

Cuervo, H. and Miranda, A. (2019) *Youth, Inequality and Social Change in the Global South*, Singapore: Springer.

Cushing, D.F. and van Vliet, W. (2017) 'Children's right to the city: the emergence of youth councils in the United States', *Children's Geographies*, 15(3): 319–33.

Dorling, D. (2015) *Injustice: Why Social Inequality Still Persists*, Bristol: Policy Press.

Farrugia, D. (2019) *Spaces of Youth: Work, Citizenship and Culture in a Global Context*, London: Routledge.

Feixa, C., Leccardi, C. and Nilan, P. (eds) (2016) *Youth, Space and Time: Agoras and Chronotopes in the Global City*, Leiden: Brill.

Furlong, A. (2009) *Handbook of Youth and Young Adulthood*, London: Routledge.

Furlong, A., Woodman, D. and Wyn, J. (2011) 'Changing times, changing perspectives: reconciling "transition" and "cultural" perspectives on youth and young adulthood', *Journal of Sociology*, 47(4): 355–370, doi: 10.1177/1440783311420787

Gal, T. and Duramy, B.F. (eds) (2015) *International Perspectives and Empirical Findings on Child Participation*, Oxford: Oxford University Press.

Green, A. (2017) *The Crisis for Young People: Generational Inequalities in Education, Work, Housing and Welfare*, Cham: Palgrave Macmillan.

Hall, S. and Jefferson, T. (1975) *Resistance Through Rituals: Youth Subcultures in Post-War Britain*, Working Papers in Cultural Studies No. 7/8.

Harris, A. (ed) (2008) *Next Wave Cultures: Feminism, Subcultures, Activism*, Abingdon: Routledge.

Heathfield, M. and Fusco, D. (eds) (2016) *Youth and Inequality in Education: Global Actions in Youth Work*, New York, NY: Routledge.

Holloway, S.L., Holt, L. and Mills, S. (2018) 'Questions of agency: capacity, subjectivity, spatiality and temporality', *Progress in Human Geography*, 43(3): 458–77.

Irwin, S. and Nielsen, A. (eds) (2018) *Transitions to Adulthood Through Recession: Youth and Inequality in a European Comparative Perspective*, London: Routledge.

Kelly, P. and Kamp, A. (2014) *A Critical Youth Studies for the 21st Century*, Boston, MA: Brill.

Kjellander, T., Jørgensen, N.B., Westrum-Rein, J. and Ministerråd, N. (2016) *Do Rights!: Nordic Perspectives on Child and Youth Participation*, Copenhagen: Nordisk Ministerråd.

Loncle, P., Jackson, G. and Muniglia, V. (2012) *Youth Participation in Europe: Beyond Discourses, Practices and Realities*, Bristol: Policy Press.

Marien, S., Hooghe, M. and Quintelier, E. (2010) 'Unconventional participation and the problem of inequality: a comparative analysis', in E. Amnå (ed) *New Forms of Citizen Participation: Normative Implications*, Baden-Baden: Nomos Verlag, pp 131–46.

McMellon, C. and Tisdall, E.K.M. (2020) 'Children and young people's participation rights: looking backwards and moving forwards', *International Journal of Children's Rights*, 28(1): 157–82.

Nussbaum, M. (1995) 'Human capabilities, female human beings', in M. Nussbaum and J. Glover (eds) *Women, Culture, and Development: A Study of Human Capabilities*, Oxford: Clarendon Press.

Pickard, S. and Bessant, J. (2019) *Young People Regenerating Politics in Times of Crisis*, Cham: Palgrave Macmillan.

Pink, S. (2007) *Doing Visual Ethnography*, London: Sage Publications.

Pitti, I. (2018) *Youth and Unconventional Political Engagement*, Cham: Palgrave Macmillan.

Pitti, I., Mengilli, Y., Martelli, A. and Loncle, P. (2020) 'Participation and everyday life: emerging meanings in youth cultural practices', in A. Walther, J. Batsleer, A. Pohl and P. Loncle (eds) *Young People and the Struggle for Participation: Contested Practices, Power and Pedagogies in Public Spaces*, Abingdon: Routledge, pp 130–45.

Pohl, A., Batsleer, J., Loncle, P. and Walther, A. (2020) 'Contested practices, power and pedagogies of young people in public spaces', in A. Walther, J. Batsleer, A. Pohl and P. Loncle (eds) *Young People and the Struggle for Participation: Contested Practices, Power and Pedagogies in Public Spaces*, Abingdon: Routledge, pp 1–12.

Quintelier, E. (2007) 'Differences in political participation between young and old people', *Contemporary Politics*, 13(2): 165–80, doi: 10.1080/13569770701562658

Rawls, J. (1971) *A Theory of Justice*, Cambridge, MA: Belknap.

Rosa, H. (2013) *Social Acceleration: A New Theory of Modernity*, New York, NY: Columbia University Press.

Saraceno, C. (2006) 'Poverty and poverty discourses in Italy in comparative perspective', in M. Petmesidou and C. Papatheodorou (eds) *Poverty and Social Deprivation in the Mediterranean*, London: Zed Books, pp 95–115.

Sengupta, S. (2019) 'Protesting climate change, young people take to streets in a global strike', *The New York Times*, [online] 20 September. Available from: www.nytimes.com/2019/09/20/climate/global-climate-strike.html [Accessed 25 February 2020].

Taru, M., Coussée, F. and Williamson, H. (2014) *The History of Youth Work in Europe: Volume 4*, Strasbourg: Council of Europe Publishing.

Thompson, R. (2011) *Unfolding Lives: Youth, Gender and Change*, Bristol: Policy Press.

Threagold, S. (2017) *Youth, Class and Everyday Struggles*, New York, NY: Routledge.

Tisdall, E.K.M., Hinton, R., Gadda, A.M. and Butler, U.M. (2014) 'Introduction: children and young people's participation in collective decision-making', in E.K.M. Tisdall, A.M. Gadda and U.M. Butler (eds) *Children and Young People's Participation and its Transformative Potential: Learning from Across Countries*, Basingstoke: Palgrave Macmillan.

Walther, A., Batsleer, J., Loncle, P. and Pohl, A. (2020) *Young People and the Struggle for Participation: Contested Practices, Power and Pedagogies in Public Spaces*, Abingdon: Routledge.

Westwood, J., Larkins, C., Moxon, D., Perry, Y. and Thomas, N. (eds) (2014) *Participation, Citizenship and Intergenerational Relations in Children and Young People's Lives: Children and Adults in Conversation*, Basingstoke: Palgrave Macmillan.

Woodman, D. and Bennet, A. (2015) *Youth Cultures, Transitions, and Generations: Bridging the Gap in Youth Research*, Basingstoke: Palgrave Macmillan.

Woodman, D. and Leccardi, C. (2015) 'Generations, transitions and culture as practice: a temporal approach to youth studies', in D. Woodman and A. Bennett (eds) *Youth Cultures, Transitions, and Generations: Bridging the Gap in Youth Research*, Basingstoke: Palgrave Macmillan, pp 56–68.

Woodman, D. and Wyn, J. (2015) *Youth and Generation: Rethinking Continuity and Change in the Lives of Young People*, London: Sage Publications.

PART I

Young people's experiences of participation and engagement

2

Cultural activism against inequalities: the experience of Quaderni Urbani in Bologna

Alessio La Terra

Project history

How can an individual play a part in changing the existing order of things? This was the very simple question that, as a young Italian university student, I asked myself, in the years when an unprecedented economic crisis affected the most vulnerable strata of the economy of my country, showing its effects in terms of poverty, social marginality and socio-cultural disorientation. My generation has been named the 'generation of the crisis': a cohort psychologically scarred by precariousness experienced as an existential condition and yet aware of having been deviously deprived of the right to freely imagine its own future. The frustration with the institutions that enacted the austerity measures of 'tears and blood' that exasperated misery and inequality led many of us to experience feelings of surrender and passivity. However, among others it also stimulated new desires for direct intervention in the emerging social problems and the development of a political conscience no longer supported by ideologies and party structures. Starting from this critical awareness about the present in which I lived, I began to feel a burning need for commitment and the need to practically enact my convictions by going beyond the purely theoretical terrain of my studies. At first, I started to volunteer in some reception centres for migrants, homeless people, drug users and other marginalised groups run by the municipality of Bologna. However, it was only when I met the political collective of Làbas that I found a space of engagement that was compatible with my idea of participation. In Làbas, it was for me finally possible to reconcile my ideas about what political engagement should be with practical actions.

Làbas was born in 2012 from the occupation of a former military barracks that the activists tried to save from degradation and turn into an 'urban commons'. Within the barracks the political collective had set up a self-managed social shelter for migrants. In an environment 'immunised' from any form of racial, religious or cultural discrimination, migrants and asylum seekers were directly involved in the management of the shelter and supported in their strenuous process of social integration. These goals were pursued while trying not to replicate the logics of benevolence and welfarism of institutional services. On the contrary, the organisation of an Italian language school, of occupational workshops, and of events where migration policies and laws were explained were intended as measures to stimulate the direct activation of the hosted migrants on the social problems they were experiencing. These activities were inspired by the mutualistic logic of action adopted by the political collective of Làbas and aimed at promoting a real transformation of society. Alongside these projects aimed at ensuring a dignified reception to migrants, several other projects were developed to raise awareness of the issues of housing and migrant reception and to create a network between the local population of Bologna and the political activities of Làbas.

It took me some time to fully understand the complexity of the political community in which I had landed, but I could immediately recognise and appreciate the real freedom of engagement that was guaranteed to anyone approaching Làbas. Members were, of course, expected to share the basic values of anti-fascism, anti-racism and anti-sexism, but everyone was asked for an effort going beyond their own skills, attitudes and inclinations. This allowed me to put my skills at the service of a cause with which I fully identified. Among the many possibilities of activation existing within Làbas, I chose to channel my efforts into the cultural offer of the space and, together with other activists, I worked for the foundation of the self-managed social library of Làbas, which was created thanks to the donation of thousands of books by private citizens.

Within the library we started to experiment with a form of social activism centred on cultural issues. Indeed, the purpose of the project was not only to open an easily accessible reading room in the city centre nor to just make the procedures for lending books more flexible and less bureaucratic than in other libraries. The deepest intention was to use 'culture' as a channel to convey our ethical and political messages: the presentation of a book, the setting up of a photographic exhibition or the screening of a documentary became a means to denounce social injustices or to incite people actively to participate through self-representation and self-organisation.

The library was daily 'lived' by the activists and by a diverse population of users (for example, local inhabitants, migrants and students). This fostered the necessity to go beyond the often static and rigid organisational logics of traditional libraries: Làbas' self-managed library was intended as a meeting spot where occasions of dialogue and exchange of ideas were promoted and where alternative forms to voice our dissent towards institutional approaches to migration and other social issues were explored. Our methods, practices and topics were, hence, already 'political' and the political nature of our cultural project emerged even more clearly when it became necessary to abandon the places where that experience had sprung up, following the eviction of Làbas from the occupied barracks in August 2017.

The absence of a physical space in which to follow up on the work already done with the library represented, even more than an obstacle, an opportunity to rethink and further reflect on the role of culture in our political activism. We started thus a reflection on the forms that our project could adopt in order to promote a cultural transformation of society while facing the lack of a fixed venue for hosting our events. The imaginative effort that the resolution of these difficulties required led a small group of eight people previously involved in the library to gathered around a table and found a new artistic-literary and editorial project. While maintaining our connection with Làbas, we wanted this new project to engage more with the city and to become a recognised actor in the local environment. In these circumstances the project of Quaderni Urbani (Urban Notebooks) took flight.

Theoretical assumptions, purposes and methodologies of the project

> To speak of culture was always contrary to culture. Culture as a common denominator already contains in embryo that schematisation and process of cataloguing and classification which bring culture within the sphere of administration. (Horkheimer and Adorno, 1947, p 104)

From the start, Quaderni Urbani had the ambition to combine cultural commitment with social conflict. This seemingly belligerent goal, however, was not conditioned by ideological prejudices, but simply emerged from the experience of the obvious distortions of our surrounding social environment. The theoretical assumptions guiding our project were never explicitly discussed in the group, probably because they are considered a common and taken-for-granted cultural heritage for anyone who practises political activism. However, if asked to identify the most direct influences on our project, I would certainly find them in the Frankfurt School's critique of the 'cultural industry' and in the theories on socio-cultural reproduction of inequalities elaborated – within the Marxist tradition – by the French sociologists Bourdieu and Passeron.

In the first half of the 20th century, the critical theory of the Frankfurt School understood that the reproduction of artworks made possible by new technologies (film and photography) (see also Benjamin, 1935) would place culture in a relationship of dependence on the newly emerging 'cultural industry' and the economic interests that drove it. The reifying logic of the factory, now applied to cultural products, would transform these latter into proper 'goods'. The concept of cultural industry was coined to describe a process of mass production of cultural products, which after being 'banalised' by advertising communication, would be 'administered' to an audience no longer composed of passionate lovers of the arts, but of consumers. The dependence of the cultural work on the mass production system would have as a logical consequence, the emptying of that cultural work from any content that might be hostile to the interests of that system. Mass-produced cultural products would tend to be basic uniformity; they are 'invariable entities' (Horkheimer and Adorno, 1947, p 131) that have no creative subjectivity and that encourage the acritical adoption of the consumeristic lifestyle. The power of control over consumers is exercised through entertainment, the quintessence of industrially reproduced culture: the fun and frivolity of the content sold by the cultural industry aim to dull the critical conscience of users in order to socially disengage them and to imprison them in indifference. The alienation from one's own critical consciousness and the cultural homogenisation imposed by the cultural industry foster in individuals the conviction that the existing social order is 'natural' and 'unmodifiable'. The removal of any resistance against a cultural system that reduces the work of art to a good of consumption and the removal of any claim against a social system based on class privilege that idolises profit are the ultimate goals of the cultural industry (Horkheimer and Adorno, 1947, p 164).

The reflections of the Frankfurt School dialogue harmoniously with the study of the mechanisms of social and cultural reproduction conducted by Bourdieu and Passeron in the 1970s. Although the authors focused their analysis on the reproduction of inequalities within the context of formal education, their study (Bourdieu and Passeron,

1970) shed light on broader social processes. Bourdieu and Passeron stressed how the logic of action of both the educational institutions and the cultural industry entails a tendency towards acculturation that reproduces and crystallises the existing social order, while maintaining the inequalities that are structural to it. This reproduction of inequalities is achieved also with the help of devices of selection and censorships (advertisements, funding agencies, large editorial cartels) that are able to decide what is 'culture' and what is not. The culture that emerges from this process of selection has thus an arbitrary and partial character and mirrors the ideas of the ruling classes. It is a culture that legitimates only certain meanings, conceals the relationships of strength imposed by the system, acts as a symbolic and violent reinforcement of those relationships (Bourdieu and Passeron, 1970) and crystallises their alleged inevitability.

Although aware of the schematic synthesis of these reconstructions, I believe that for the activists of Quaderni Urbani, these theoretical assumptions maintain an indisputable validity in relation to cultural activism. From them we draw an historical and sociological lesson: that a considerable part of the cultural production of a society has always pursued the aim of reflecting the established order, then of reproducing and perpetuating in the arts, literature and in movies, a given model of society along with all its injustice and lack of equality. This awareness implies the recognition of culture as a label behind which there is often an ideological opportunism that is concerned with the preservation of the existing social order. The intention to enhance the ability of art and culture to be means through which to foster social change and question hegemonic thinking became the main purpose of Quaderni Urbani. In an historical period in which populist forces started to openly call for inhumanity, and closure of ports and borders, we worked towards a politicisation of culture. In so doing, we aimed to dismantle the alleged neutrality of dominant discourses, and to reveal their emptiness and their complicity with a system of structural inequalities. In this scenario, it became clear that the key element of our commitment should be the promotion of a counterculture and the support to those *engagé* cultural actors who intended to question and change the existing social order through their art. We turned our attention to independent publishers and artists, collectives of writers, and autonomous theatre companies, with whom we engaged in cooperation and mutual training, so as to create networks and extend in breadth and scope our cultural activism.

Decisions concerning the practices were crucial too. We wanted our political principles to show in the contents of our activities, but also in the practices and forms adopted by our project. We sought to avoid those organisational models in which cultural contents are merely unilaterally 'transmitted' from the artist to a passively receiving audience, as is mostly the case in school or academic contexts. Instead, we opted for activities where culture is collectively constructed, debated and resignified. This decision brought us to the organisation of open workshops ending in moments of final restitution in the form of collective exhibitions, readings or performances.

Our cultural activities were usually focused on a given topic (for example, the right to the city, migration policy) chosen from among those of greatest impact on the city and its residents or suggested by specific collaborations with artists or other cultural groups. Every decision on the work to be carried out is collectively taken, through weekly assemblies. The assemblies of Quaderni Urbani are self-managed and horizontal: this approach seeks to facilitate interaction and allows activists of heterogeneous cultural formation to 'contaminate' and enrich each other. Finally, we strive to avoid the elitist ultra-specialism that often distinguishes academic cultural events and we seek to maintain our activities free of charge so to ensure an immediate and extensive access to the cultural contents we create and share. In order to meet the necessary costs, we self-finance our activities by selling self-produced goods (such as hand-made notebooks) and by organising dinners based on a 'pay-as-you-wish/can' principle.

Since 2017, Quaderni Urbani has organised dozens of cultural events. Often, they have taken place in our spaces, but sometimes they have been organised elsewhere, even outside of Bologna. The horizontal structure of these events has encouraged the development of a critical and political knowledge among the participants and the creation of an authentically independent and free cultural offer. More specifically, we were able to group the organised events into three main types of activities:

- Open workshops: series of meetings through which the participants engage in a collective research/reflection aimed at critically assessing the complexity of a given social issue (for example, housing problems). This phase of collective reflection informs a subsequent practical phase of cultural and artistic self-production culminating in a final moment of open restitution of the results.
- Thematic readings: performative readings of classic and self-produced texts and poems on a given topic of political relevance.
- External collaborations: co-organisation of theatrical performances, presentation of books in the presence of authors, staging of artistic exhibitions in shared curatorship.

In the following section, a description of some of the events organised by Quaderni Urbani is used to exemplify these different practices.

Project work and its social impact

Metropolitan Snapshots (open workshop, May 2018)

In the past five years the city of Bologna has undergone a process of massive touristification. Investing in the food economy and in the transport sectors (and particularly in the expansion of the airport), the local government is trying to make Bologna an increasingly attractive destination for tourists. In so doing, the municipality has given ample room for manoeuvre to businesses ready to profit from the city's transformation. However, no attention has been paid to the fact that an unmanaged tourist flow causes a radical alteration of the physical and social morphology of the city. In Bologna, in particular, this uncontrolled tourism has produced, in addition to the proliferation of countless boutiques and megastores where local food products are sold at embarrassingly high prices, a housing crisis of devastating impact. It is the city centre that has been mainly affected and particularly the student population, which is now struggling to find affordable housing due to the conversion into Airbnb lets of about 1,700 apartments (Gentile et al, 2018).

The open workshop Metropolitan Snapshots was Quaderni Urbani's response to this housing crisis. The workshop aimed at being an opportunity to reflect on the ability of mass tourism to change the face of the city and to make an explicit call to act in the opposite direction. We found social photography to be the most incisive artistic medium for denouncing the transformation of the city, as well as the most effective means to win back the authentic soul of the city. We divided the work into three moments. First, we organised an initial briefing, in which we debated the narrative criteria of street photography, as well as its ability to portray the surrounding environment. Second, we organised a ten-day 'photographic relay', which saw the participants share and pass from one to another some analogue cameras. These were used to portray, in their neighbourhoods, places and people with a significant social or historical value. Finally, we created an exhibition of the shots that were also placed on a map of the centre of Bologna with the aim of revealing an alternative cartography of the city where the places of greatest social importance were highlighted.

The external participation in our first workshop and its results went well beyond our expectations. In fact, the workshop not only fostered the rediscovery of Bologna and its social composition, but also stimulated a collective process of awareness of the implications of our living together in a multi-ethnic and plural urban space. The ultimate message that our work aspired to convey? That travelling in already planned and standardised tourist routes means becoming part of a mechanism working for the profit of a few, as well as harming those who inhabit and animate the city every day.

Voices for Mediterranea (thematic reading, April 2019)

Over the past two years, every government that has ruled Italy has pursued migration policies centred on rejection of migrants and closures of borders. The adopted institutional policies have also promoted a criminalisation of humanitarian intervention. The numerous non-governmental organisations (NGOs) that have helped to mitigate the already dramatic death toll of the migrants crossing the Mediterranean Sea have been threatened with financial penalties and criminal measures. This has led to the almost total disappearance of NGOs in the central Mediterranean, thereby exacerbating the humanitarian catastrophe we have witnessed over the past decade.

In this context, Làbas and Quaderni Urbani have become co-funders of the courageous operation of Mediterranea Saving Humans (Mediterranea). This operation arose from the indignation fostered in us by the repressive and racist measures enacted by political institutions. Mediterranea was born as an enlarged umbrella association of different political groups and civic associations. Through international crowdfunding, the project has brought two boats back into the Mediterranean. Having an Italian flag, the two boats are partially spared from the restrictive measures applied to NGOs' boats. In the span of eight months, Mediterranea's boats have been involved in seven patrol missions in the Strait of Sicily. To date, the operation has rescued 237 people. The beginning of this mission led Quaderni Urbani to enlist in what we have called the 'land crew'. The land crew of Mediterranea has the task of spreading as much as possible the message of the project, of raising funds, and of empowering civil society to recognise the value of humanity. Although simple and basic, this value has assumed traits of heroism in a time marked by an increasing barbarisation of the public debate.

Taking advantage of our previous experience with the social library, we first took care of the management of a private library that was donated to us. The books of this library were sold to finance the mission. We organised a weekly 'book banquet' aimed at selling as well as collecting books and magazines. Through the resources obtained by selling the books we have brought a considerable economic contribution to Mediterranea and the banquet has also been an opportunity to talk about the operation and activate new forces around it.

We also sought to amplify the narrative power of the operation, by organising public thematic readings of some texts that our comrades had written. The reading Voices for Mediterranea gathered two types of texts: 'logbooks', that is, testimonies of direct experiences of navigation and rescue in the Strait of Sicily, and 'land journals', written by comrades who, like ourselves, had participated in the land crew.

The success of the event was huge. During 2019 we were asked to organise this thematic reading more than four times and the logbooks and journals of Mediterranea will soon published by Quaderni Urbani. It is not intended for these texts to be simply a literary exercise. On the contrary, they are born to witness and to communicate the personal efforts and political intentions entailed in a mission aimed at saving human lives from death at sea. In this way a wonderful and powerful interweaving of action and art is realised. This form of art gives recognition to the generous effort of those who jeopardise their physical and legal safety to fight against inhumanity and disengagement. Through these readings we thus ambitiously sought to turn our voices into megaphones.

Examples of external collaborations (2018–19)

Over the years, Quaderni Urbani has managed to create and diffuse an independent and free cultural offering, also thanks to the collaborations developed with other artistic and political groups animated by the same values. We have asked each of our collaborators to take an unequivocal position with respect to the issues we consider decisive, such as the anti-sexist and anti-racist nature of our activities.

In relation to these external collaborations, a particularly interesting example is that of the meetings with students of the Academy of Fine Arts, which have allowed an exchange of information and mutual training on the difficulties experienced by those who wish to make a living through art. By using our spaces within Làbas as an 'open atelier', we have sought to meet the needs of young emerging artists of the city of Bologna by enabling them to use the open atelier as a free exhibition space. Through the open atelier we have sought to spare art from commodification and to open up opportunities for critical discussion on the problems of independent culture.

During the event Avant-Punk, organised in partnership with the group LaZecca (a political and cultural collective working mostly through music), we promoted an unusual meeting between the surrealist movement and underground music. Through this event, we sought to give visibility to female surrealist artists, such as Nancy Cunard and Anaïs Nin, authors of a fervent literary counter-narrative permeated by the recusal of the dominant values and declined in terms of feminist and anti-fascist militancy. In addition to the public reading of their writings, some of which were translated into Italian for the first time by our group, the event included the exhibition of surrealist thematic posters and the screening of some short movies by Luis Buñuel, with simultaneous musical accompaniment. From a rebellious and eccentric subculture was thus born a seductive and dreamlike crossover of genres, in an evening that was a memorable experience of a riot of lights, sounds, colours and poetic verses.

Continuing our reflection on gender issues and in preparation for the global strike of the trans-feminist movement of NonUnaDiMeno, we developed a collaboration with the independent theatre company Ortika. This collaboration has led to the staging of a show on the topic of femicide. Femicide is an abomination that is still very prevalent in Italy and that needs to be addressed also changing narratives and discourses on violence against women. Indeed, our group will soon author a play script written collectively on the issue of gender-based violence. It is superfluous to continue enumerating the many events that have taken place in addition to those already mentioned: the history of Quaderni Urbani, although brief, already includes a rich haul of experience and achievements.

Conclusions: on sustainability and the role of militancy

A hungry belly has no ears.

(Jean de la Fontaine)

It is impossible for a call for justice to sprout in ground suffering from severe material scarcity, and in economically deprived contexts. This is the problem to which cultural activism remains exposed. Those who work through the arts or through knowledge must be aware that those who are receptive to cultural inputs are not the entire population but, on the contrary, represent a small privileged minority. Next to them, there is an endless multitude of people whose life has the appearance of a daily struggle for survival. Anyone who advocates the cause of social transformation only through culture and education is unaware that these same means can be used to achieve the opposite purpose, that is, they can be used as instruments of the reproduction of a system of inequalities. Culture can educate to the indifferent acceptance of injustice and to voluntary servitude too. This 'culture' hides from the more deprived groups the material conditions that could allow them to empower and emancipate themselves. This culture, like every attempt to make knowledge the prerogative of the few, entails ill-concealed authoritarian tendencies.

As I have previously argued, this is not the kind of culture that interests the political activist. The principles that inspire cultural activism are exactly opposite. It is truly worthy of us only when it is good for everyone, and knowledge becomes a form of oppression when it is not understood as collective achievement. The experience of Quaderni Urbani can represent a model of activism in which intellectual work is placed at the service of the community and where the horizontal sharing of knowledge gives rise to a commitment to social equality. However, the ultimate goal of liberation from inequality, in order to be achieved, requires that this commitment should not remain only at the intellectual level. This commitment must be translated into practices aimed at the concrete deconstruction of the system of inequality. True cultural activism must entail a two-fold emancipatory aim: cultural activism should work towards the liberation of bodies, no less than of the spirits. Only then, following Mayakovski's invitation, can we avoid art being simply a mirror that reflects the world, and allow it to become the hammer through which the world can be forged.

References

Benjamin, W. (1935) 'Das Kunstwerk im Zeitalter seiner technischen Reproduzierbarkeit' [The work of art in the age of mechanical reproduction] in *Walter Benjamin Schriften*, Frankfurt am Main: Suhrkamp Verlag.

Bourdieu, P. and Passeron, J. (1970) *La Reproduction: Éléments pour une Théorie du Système d'Enseignement* [Reproduction in Education, Society and Culture], Paris: Les Éditions de Minuit.

Gentile, A., Tassinari, F. and Zoboli, A. (2018) *Indagine sul Mercato degli Alloggi in Locazione nel Comune di Bologna* [Inquiry on Housing in Bologna's Municipality], Bologna: Instituto Carlo Cattaneo. Available from: www.cattaneo.org/wp-content/uploads/2018/04/Indagine-sul-mercato-degli-alloggi-in-locazione-Bo.pdf

Horkheimer, M. and Adorno, T.W. (1947) *Dialektik der Aufklärung: Philosophische Fragmente* [Dialectic of Enlightenment: Philosophical Fragments], Frankfurt am Main: Fischer Verlag GmBH.

3

It's okay to think freely: how participation changed us

Christina McMellon, Katherine Dempsie and Myada Eltiraifi

Introduction

While there is a significant literature exploring the theory and practice of young people's participation, there is less written about young people's experiences of taking part in participation activities. This chapter, co-written by two young people who volunteer with a project called Young Edinburgh Action (YEA) and a member of staff who used to work with YEA, provides a rich exploration of such experiences. The chapter comprises a 'story' written by each individual author detailing their time with the project. The stories do not have a common structure but rather reflect the aspects of the individual's experiences that they consider to be the most important and meaningful.[1] After the three stories there is a discussion section that was generated from a group discussion between the three authors about the commonalities and differences between the three stories (see also Chapter 13 in this book).

Box 3.1 Young Edinburgh Action

Young Edinburgh Action (YEA) was established in 2013 as an innovative approach to implementing the city's participation strategy.

Action research groups are at the heart of YEA's approach and enable a core group of young people to explore a topic and research the views of other young people in Edinburgh. Three topics for action research groups are chosen by young people each year.

A 'Conversation for Action' is convened at the end of each action research process and is an important interface where young people and senior decision makers

---

invited by the young people come together to discuss the topic and develop an action plan. Young people present their learning, ideas and recommendations in order to facilitate meaningful dialogue between young people and relevant policy makers and senior officers.

More information about YEA is available from: https://era.ed.ac.uk/bitstream/handle/1842/16875/CRFR%20briefing%2085.pdf?sequence=1&isAllowed=y

Myada's story

I remember not really wanting to join YEA; my mum just wanted to get me out of the house and she said, "Oh there's this thing at the council, I've signed you up for it, you have to go." I don't remember much about the event except there was food there and I enjoyed it! I remember giving them my phone number and then very quickly I was going to up to three different meetings every week.

Everyone in the groups was from different backgrounds and everyone had a different story and I really liked that. I liked how crazy and fun it was. We'd be doing stupid stuff all the time but it was okay to be stupid. I didn't like high school and I didn't have a lot of friends there, so it was nice to be in an environment where people didn't know me already and I could just be myself and people liked me for me. I could talk about things that were important to me with people my own age and no fear of getting in trouble or being judged like at school or at home.

I didn't feel that strongly about politics when I joined YEA, but through going to the meetings I started thinking, "Actually, yeah, 16-year-olds should have the vote." I really started to feel passionate about the subject, and then that's what sparked my interest in politics and stuff.

The Conversation for Action for the Votes at 16 Action Research Group was in one of the rooms in the city chambers. I remember showing the video that we'd made and then I remember feeling kind of stupid about the video and thinking, "They won't understand our inside jokes and maybe they won't take us seriously." But then I remember that we talked and got our points across and then I remember leaving and thinking like, "Yes! We just did that, that was really cool." But it was frustrating because we said, "What are you guys going to do about this?" and they said, "We'll get back to you about that 'cos we need to speak to our superiors and we need to have another meeting to talk about it" but nothing happened.

At the time I was very curious about the world; I was questioning all these things and the more I learned about the world and the more

I became friends with these people and learned about their experiences and things they'd done I was like, "Oh I wanna do that", but then I'd realise that, "Actually no I can't do that because of my parents or because this goes against my religion or this goes against my culture." My parents didn't like that I was questioning our community and how traditional it is. It annoyed me because I wasn't being influenced, I was like, "I'm making my own decisions, I'm learning these things and then I'm choosing, do I believe this or do I not, do I agree or not." There were all sorts of little things. For example, I remember not being able to say the word sex and beginning to think, "Why am I not able to say that word?" and then later thinking, "Me not being able to say that word is giving power to the word." I tried to explain that to my parents but they just didn't get it. And also I would go to events and be startled by what people looked like, so like girls with really short hair or guys with long hair or girls that identified as guys, just all that sort of thing that I was not used to, and the more I met new people the more I learned to accept that it was okay and it was normal. And then I was so proud of everything we were doing. I was especially proud of *Alex and Charlie*.[2] I couldn't wait to be able to say, "I'm a published author." I thought it was so cool that we'd done that and how much hard work we'd put into it and that we were helping to educate little kids.

The most important thing I've learned from all the different groups is that it's okay to think freely, that it's okay to have an opinion and that, even if people don't like your opinion, it's still okay and you shouldn't change that opinion just because you are afraid of what other people might think. YEA also taught me that I can be friends with adults. In my culture you can't be friends with them because there's a barrier of respect that you have to have for them. YEA taught me that you can respect someone and also be friends with them. None of the staff talked to us as if we were children or too stupid to understand complex things.

When I was 16 there was so much of a clash between the world that I was living in and the world my parents wanted me to live in. It got to a point where whenever I wanted to do something that I knew they wouldn't like I was too scared to talk to them about it, so I would lie and I would say that I was doing something that I wasn't just so that I could be with my friends and do normal teenager-like things. And then the more I lied, the more difficult the relationship got.

I left home and I was homeless for four months, just couch surfing, moving from house to house with my little suitcase. I finally got a place in a hostel and I lived there for nine months and it was difficult. That was the point I was quite crazy and impulsive, and I didn't care about my education at all. I stopped going to school, I stopped really caring about my future. My motivation went down and my mental health started to break down. The people who lived in the hostel they didn't care about their lives either, they didn't care about school and that was who I was surrounded by. Then eventually I got my act together towards the end of those nine months and I tried to go to school more and to prioritise what was important in my life. And then I got my own flat.

Over that time I stopped going to as many meetings with YEA because everything else was happening. It was difficult because it was just me and I didn't have parental support, but the YEA staff were amazing at helping me and making sure that I had all the support I needed to help me deal with stuff. I remember always feeling comfortable talking to them about my life and what was going on. It felt natural to talk to them because they already knew me, they knew my background and knew my story. We had a day where all of my YEA friends came round and we painted my new flat. Like everyone! People came who I hadn't seen for ages and it was a lot of fun. One of the girl's mum even came round and brought some furniture. I don't know what I would've done if I hadn't gone to that first meeting with YEA 'cos YEA is just so intertwined with a lot of things in my life.

Katherine's story

From what I remember I got involved with YEA through school. Every morning my teacher would read out things in registration class and when she read this one out she said, "This is a great opportunity, it seems like a *you* thing" and I was like, "Yes, that seems like a *me* thing!" I guess I was always a bit of a social warrior in some ways.

The first thing I did was the peer mentor training. I was a baby, a 12-year-old girl who didn't say anything and always had her hair up in a ponytail – I was so shy! Lots of shy people might have stopped going, but I kept going and I stayed silent but still took everything in. At that point I didn't know much about politics and the others would all go off on all sorts of tangents, I was learning so much about things that I'd had no idea about. It was around the time of the independence referendum and everyone was very heated in their opinions and that was really interesting; in school our teachers avoided the topic but in YEA those conversations were encouraged. And what was good about it was that it wasn't a big group, there were only about ten people, we were always sat in a circle so I never felt excluded.

Then I got involved in the gatherings and the action research groups. At first I was a bit confused about what was going on, but confused and enjoying it so it didn't matter that I was thinking, "Why am I doing this?", and then it got to the point that I was like, "Okay, I think I understand what I'm doing now" and then suddenly, "I'm also chatting loads! What? I've changed!" So you stumble slowly further and further into it and then you're like, "Okay, I'm fully in this now!"

It's like a wee community – that's important – I don't feel like we just come to do the activity, we come to see the people. It's important that there's a time in each meeting just to catch up. I feel like the staff are aware that it is a safe space for us. When people come from all over the city they want to chat and I feel like the staff are very good at respecting the fact that that needs to happen. I also feel like the open atmosphere is really important; you can say anything, there's not exactly rules but there is respect. If you disagree with someone, you can just say, "I don't agree with you because …" and then you explain why and people will respect what you say but if they disagree then they are going to tell you. You can have a debate and that's okay as long as you are respectful.

But it is also important to me to get stuff done. It's exciting seeing what you've been working on for the last six weeks come together and start to become something. When you achieve something, it makes all the bits that were confusing before tie together. We wrote a book! We created a whole new job for someone! We did important research!

I learned a lot about how research works in the real world with actual people and important social issues. The first project I did I learned everything as I was going along. It just started to make sense – it was like … "Oh okay, two weeks ago we thought of a question, and then we broke that down into five different questions and those questions have been answered by the people who filled in the survey and we've got some answers to the first question!" I learned how difficult some bits can be – like how some private schools and Catholic schools didn't want to talk about certain topics. And then I learned about how important it is to get the survey out to as many different people as possible and to highlight what didn't come up because that's still just as interesting. I learned a lot about how to analyse what we found out. Analysis is something you'd think would be really boring but we did it in really fun ways so that it was memorable, like we had the data up all over the walls or had all the things people said all cut up and put them into different piles instead of just reading through them. I also learned a lot about how to run events – I feel like I could organise a whole festival from what I've learned! And I learned to ask for the things I needed – people are usually nice and help if they can.

By the end of the sex education project, our group had spent ages talking about sex education and learning from each other, but we also knew how much we weren't taught in schools and how important it is that the education we get about sex is good. At the Conversation for Action, the adults agreed with pretty much everything we said. I feel like when we first sat down they probably thought, "This is just a thing that we have to do" but then when we started speaking they were like, "Oh they actually have real opinions that are just as good as ours." It was nice to see them scribbling down when we were saying things, it was like, "Wow! They are actually taking notes on what we're saying."

And I grew in confidence in public speaking, which is just not a thing you get to do very often at that age unless you are head boy or head girl. I was doing it all the time, whether it was in a group of ten people organising an activity or actually doing the gatherings and conferences. Who speaks at a conference when they are 15? If you said to me now, "There's a conference tomorrow could you come and speak?", I'd check my shifts at work and be like, "Yeah let's go, cool!" It's crazy, young people so rarely get to present to adults and have them properly listening and I think that's the main thing that has built my confidence a lot, that people actually listened to me.

I'm not so involved now because of work, but I know that it's there and I could be involved. I got an email from one of the staff about a meeting and when I said I couldn't go to the meeting she said, "Do you fancy catching up anyway?" and I was like, "Yes!" I always really loved those little personal emails when staff remember that we've been on holiday or remember we've had a test, it's so nice. Even some of my friends won't ask me like "How was that?" and then I get a wee email from YEA and it makes me happy.

I don't see the other people who were involved every week any more, but we have a group chat and we all look after each other. There have been people who have been through big things and it was crazy how involved we all were. Like when Myada had really difficult things in her life and people were checking in and seeing what was happening. And obviously we knew that the staff were also checking in loads and that's so nice to see. She's my friend, and to see an adult who isn't her mum or a parent taking care of her in the way I'd want her to be taken care of is so nice.

Now I'm 18 and pretty different to that shy 12-year-old. I'm confident in my actions and I've got a mind of my own – my mum might say too much of a mind of my own! I'm not smarter than other people who are 18 but I feel like I've got a better understanding of people. I know what words to use with what people and I kind of say things how they are rather than try to sugar-coat things. Now I know that my opinion is completely valid. I think that's from being involved in YEA.

Christina's story

This section of the chapter is a reflective piece based on my experiences as a participation worker. I worked at YEA from 2013 to 2019 as a participation worker and the project has a very special place in my heart. I have now moved on and work to promote young people's participation in academic settings, including the TRIUMPH project with the University of Glasgow.[3]

I have framed my account through several snapshots of memories that stand out and, I judge, are illustrative of my time with the project.

Snapshot one

It is 2014. Six young people, and nine adults are sitting at a long board meeting table in Edinburgh City Chambers for the Sex Education Action Research Group's Conversation for Action. We are surrounded by oil paintings, and the formality of the setting feels at odds with the conversation that we are having. The common theme of the meeting so far has been that young people aren't receiving the level of sex education that the policies and guidelines say they should receive. I notice that every time a young person says "sex education" one of the adults around the table makes a point of saying "RSHP"[4] in the next sentence as if to correct them. I take this to be a, probably, subconscious reminder to young people that they not using the correct language and are somehow less knowledgeable. It irritates me but I choose not to intervene and I am proud that the group don't change their language in response.

One of the young people is describing how many of the toilets in her school don't have sanitary bins. The most senior decision maker (one of only two men in the room) is visibly shocked and says, "Well, at least we can easily ensure that all girl's toilets in our schools have sanitary bins." I notice the relief on his face and the faces of others around the room, including, I imagine, my own. The issues discussed around the table have been complex and controversial; I would like an easy win, a clear outcome among other less measurable commitments. Opening up the conversation has been an achievement in itself but

I worry that the young people might not see it like that; I want them to have a hook on which to hang the success of the group.

Katherine interrupts: "Not just the girls' toilets." The director looks confused and she goes on: "Some boys have periods too – what about trans men who still have vaginas?"

My colleague and I exchange a smile. My overwhelming feeling of pride in this young woman, who has spoken up in a formal group of adults and expressed her point so clearly, is only slightly tempered by the realisation that this was no longer going to be an easy win. I am also in awe of a 14-year-old girl who confidently uses the word 'vagina' to explain a point to a middle-aged man. I often find myself explaining how young people bring different perspectives and knowledge to discussions; in that moment, this truth entered the room for all to see.

Snapshot two

It's 2017 and I'm working with a small group of young people, most of whom I know well. We are crowded into a small group-work room with glass walls and it is in the evening of what has already been a long day. I am leading a group-work activity where we brainstorm ideas and arrange them on a table-top diagram. Although the activity is finally going well, there is an edgy energy in the room. It has taken us a long time to get to the point of the activity; there was lots of chat and in-jokes from people in the room who know each other well, but I'm aware of a couple of new young people who might be intimidated by our familiarity.

Myada and Sue[5] who have both been involved in the project for a long time are, for reasons unknown, snapping at each other. At first I think it is in fun, but after a few minutes I am not so sure; they are making pointed remarks towards each other that no longer feel entirely comfortable. I know that these two young women have very different communication styles and I also know that they both have a lot going on in their lives, but I don't know how well they know each other and I wonder if there is a context of which I'm unaware.

Sue is talking a lot more than Myada and I worry that Myada is really upset. I am trying to keep the conversation light-hearted while wondering what is going on at home for her. Sue is talking loudly, repeating statements that she has been making for the past few minutes. I know – as do most of the group – that Sue is autistic. I am aware that she can get anxious in groups and that her communication style sometimes reflects this. I'm not remotely upset by either of the girls, but I am concerned about both of them and also concerned that their conversation is affecting the group dynamic. I need a bit of time to think. I want the group to refocus on the activity. And I'm tired.

I tell Sue to shut up.

I say it in a jokey way, but the moment the words have left my mouth I regret them. There is suddenly silence in the room and I feel everyone's eyes on me. My colleague says, "You can't say that!" and I'm not sure if she is shocked or amused or both. I apologise. I explain to the new group members that Sue knows me well, that she knows I don't mean it seriously. Sue says that it is fine, and laughs, but I can see that she is taken aback.

My actions have disrupted the tension; the group refocuses and the activity continues successfully. I cannot, however, stop thinking about what I've said. I know that Sue finds it difficult to read appropriate behaviour and worries that she is annoying other people. I'm furious with myself for my unprofessional and unhelpful behaviour. Mostly I'm angry that I've upset a young person I genuinely care about. The glass walls of the room simultaneously feel oppressive and make me visible to the world outside the meeting.

We finish the meeting. The activity is successful, we end up with a table-top full of post-it notes jumbled together into some semblance of organisation. I join in with the chatter of conversation and busy-ness. We all go our own ways.

Later that evening I am still thinking about my comment and I text Sue an apology from my work phone. She replies immediately saying that it is okay, I was right, she was being annoying. I reply again saying that, even if she was, it wasn't ok for me to say it. And then I return to the rest of my evening.

Snapshot three

It's 2016 and a group of young people have organised an event to ensure that young people's views are fed into a consultation about youth mental health services in the city.

The event is taking place at in a quirky venue with multiple room and activities. The whole place is decorated with fairy lights. In one room young people anonymously write their fears on balloons and let them float away to be collected and recorded later. In another room young people attend a workshop about teenage psychology. In another room young people answer survey questions as they cycle on a bike that powers a smoothie maker. Another room houses a marketplace of services that young people might like to know about.

Another room is a chill-out space with music and beanbags (the group was very specific that there needed to be beanbags). There are also multiple other rooms.

Over 120 young people pass through the event. If they take part in all of the activities (and therefore answer all the consultation questions), they get a free burrito. The event has been entirely planned, advertised and run by young people. It is the culmination of six months of weekly meetings – although we all know that there will be more work to compile and analyse all of the data that we are collecting.

My role is simply to ensure that everyone gets the burrito that they want.

Discussion

After writing and editing our stories, we (Christina, Katherine and Myada) met to discuss the similarities and differences in our stories and the most important aspects of our experiences that we wanted to highlight. In this short discussion section, we discuss two themes that feel important to us and are also reflected in the academic literature: the importance of relationships in young people's participation and the concept of 'space' in young people's participation.

Relationships

In the (not so) 'new sociology of childhood', James and Prout (1997) trace the emergence of a new paradigm of thought that moves away from a focus on childhood and young people as an apprenticeship for adulthood and children and young people as future adults ('becomings') to children as active agents in their own lives ('beings'). However, Prout (2005) subsequently points out that being/becoming is a false dichotomy since all humans (of any age) are constantly and simultaneously both being and becoming. Others have argued that the focus on being and becoming centres on the individual child or young person without taking full account of the context within which the child or young person lives and the relationships that are important in their life (Tisdall and Punch, 2012). This need to consider children's social relationships has led to some researchers moving beyond the duality of 'being' and 'becoming' to an extended typology that includes 'being', 'becoming' and 'belonging' (Haw, 2010; Sumsion and Wong, 2011).

It is clear within all three stories that a feeling of 'belonging' was important to our experiences with Young Edinburgh Action. In conversations about what 'belonging' feels like, we used the word community. Even though the young people involved might have different opinions and different ways of communicating, they all want to find a way to relate to each other because they have chosen to be there and value YEA. For Katherine and Myada, it is also important that they feel that they are part of the YEA community, even during periods of time when they are not going to meetings.

Relationships of many different variations underpin all three stories. Peer relationships were important for both Katherine and Myada, who state that they might not have stayed involved in the project in the early days of their involvement if they hadn't met other interesting young people and started to build friendships. Subsequently both of them describe how friendships forged in YEA have extended beyond the project and provide ongoing support, both practical and emotional, in other areas of their lives. However, peer relationships are not always positive. Although they chose not to include them in their stories, all three authors were able to identify challenging peer relationships that, at least for short periods of time, had a negative impact on their engagement with YEA.

It is clear from all three stories that relationships between young people and staff both are important and, at times, challenging. When discussing our stories, Myada and Katherine both said that this relationship was important because they were not used to feeling comfortable with adults who were not a part of their family. Young people appreciate the informality of their relationships with YEA staff and the genuine care and support that they receive from staff. However, as her second snapshot illustrates, Christina is constantly negotiating the boundaries of relationships with young people and sometimes not getting it right. Relationships don't happen between young people and staff but between a particular young person and a particular adult; Christina's relationship with Myada is different from her relationship with Katherine or from her relationship with a young person who has only recently become involved with the project.

Le Borgne (2017) and Le Borgne and Tisdall (2017) emphasise the important role of the participation worker in youth participation projects, but this role is often missed out of the literature, which tends to focus on the process and the outcomes of participation projects. Myada and Katherine both, however, emphasise the importance of this role. Both describe how the relationship built moves beyond the specific participation projects – Myada saying how YEA staff were the ideal people to support her through difficult times because they already knew her story, Katherine emphasising how little things such as asking how a test went are important.

In their discussion about the three stories, Katherine and Myada discussed how their relationship with Christina made it easier for them to do things that they might otherwise not be able to do, such as speaking at a conference or writing this chapter. They described how their relationships with YEA staff made it easier for them to feel comfortable with other adults in a predominantly adult setting; knowing that they are with someone they trust makes it easier to take risks. However, Myada's story illustrates that the participation worker also occupies a space in between young people and other adults in their life that might not be so positive; the personal learning and development that she believed to be a positive outcome from her time with YEA was often viewed as problematic by her parents.

In her second snapshot Christina seeks to demonstrate the thought processes that go into a group session that might appear to an onlooker as relatively fun and easy. Interestingly, when discussing the stories for this chapter, Myada could not remember the incident. Christina also asked the other young woman involved to read the snapshot and discussed whether she was happy for us to include it in the chapter. She was happy for it to be included but was sad that the incident had caused Christina to worry and gave some personal background to the situation that gave Christina more insight. The process of building relationships and of negotiating the role of the participation worker is always ongoing.

While the subject of relationships between staff was not explored in the stories, these are also important. Christina notes that, in parallel with relationships between young people that extend beyond the project, although she no longer works with YEA she is still close friends with many of the colleagues she worked with on the project.

Space

The development of the YEA model was particularly informed by an article by Barry Percy-Smith (2010), who states that 'participation is influenced by the nature of the spaces in which it happens' (Percy-Smith, 2010, p 109) and argues for a need to rethink participation in terms of creating spaces for effective youth participation. Percy-Smith also talks about participative spaces as sites of social learning and advocates for widening the focus away from decision-making structures (see also Chapter 16 in this book).

YEA indicated a move away from a more structured approach to youth participation towards an approach that prioritised creating spaces for young people to identify and explore issues that they think are important. Katherine and Myada both use the phrase "safe space" to describe their experience of YEA and credited these safe spaces with supporting their own personal journey of developing their own identify, interests and values. They emphasise how the most important things that happened in these spaces were not always the planned activities but, instead, the times when conversations went off on tangents. Myada and Katherine describe how the freedom to let the conversation stray from a set programme and be led by the interests of the young people offers opportunities for them to learn and reflect together, to strengthen their bond as a group, to develop their sense of self in the world and practice self-determination in a safe and supportive group. Myada says that "tangents are where we find our passions".

Such willingness to allow meandering tangents also challenges the power dynamic between adults and young people. In the longer version of Myada's story, before it was edited to fit this chapter, she described one action research group where young people were constantly distracted. She knew that staff were frustrated because the group wasn't making 'progress' but still let them explore their own ideas and conversations. While young people's priority is more often the relationships and the opportunities for personal learning and growth, decision makers and managers almost always see relationships as a means to achieve the desired outcome of young people influencing decisions made. The participation worker often occupies a space in between these different priorities, sometimes pushing young people to stay focused on a task at hand, sometimes persuading adults that time spent doing activities that do not directly or obviously contribute to a project's outcomes are still valuable. There is, therefore, an ongoing complex dance between tangents and structure, young people and staff, process and outcomes. While young people working with YEA often described the project as 'youth led', Christina would describe it as a partnership between young people and adults where power is openly negotiated and shared in different measures at different times.

Conclusion

In theorising about youth participation, it can be easy to forget that the people interacting with the projects are humans who affect and are affected by each other and by the work in multiple and complex ways. These three stories tell about very different and yet intertwined experiences with a youth participation project. We make no claims that our stories are representative of experiences in participation projects generally, or indeed of experiences with YEA specifically.

Rather we believe that starting with our experience can be a useful entry point to thinking about youth participation and, in particular, the importance of relationships and positive spaces that support young people in participation projects.

Notes

[1] Certain sections and details have been removed for ethical reasons.
[2] The action research group looking at gender equality published a children's storybook called *Alex and Charlie* challenging gender stereotypes. For more information, see https://www.edinburgh.gov.uk/learning-publications/alex-charlie?documentId=11922&categoryId=20264
[3] http://triumph.sphsu.gla.ac.uk/young-people
[4] An abbreviation for 'relationships, sexual health, parenting' education.
[5] The name Sue is a pseudonym and this snapshot has been discussed with both young women concerned.

References

Haw, K. (2010) 'Being, becoming and belonging: young Muslim women in contemporary Britain', *Journal of Intercultural Studies*, 31(4): 345–61.

James, A. and Prout, A. (1997) *Constructing and Reconstructing Childhood: Contemporary Issues in the Sociology of Childhood*, London: Routledge.

Le Borgne, C. (2017) *Implementing Children and Young People's Participation in Decision-Making: The Role of Non-Governmental Organisations*, Centre for Research on Children and Families Briefing 87, Edinburgh: University of Edinburgh. Available from: https://era.ed.ac.uk/handle/1842/21025

Le Borgne, C. and Tisdall, E.K.M. (2017) 'Children's participation: questioning competence and competencies?', *Social Inclusion*, 5(3): 122–30.

Percy-Smith, B. (2010) 'Councils, consultations and community: rethinking the spaces for children and young people's participation', *Children's Geographies*, 8(2): 107–22.

Prout, A. (2005) *The Future of Childhood*, Abingdon: Routledge Falmer.

Sumsion, J. and Wong, S. (2011) 'Interrogating "belonging" in belonging, being and becoming: the Early Years Learning Framework for Australia', *Contemporary Issues in Early Childhood*, 12(1): 28–45.

Tisdall, K. and Punch, S. (2012) 'Not so "new"? Looking critically at childhood studies', *Children's Geographies*, 10(3): 249–64.

4

Frontrunners Against Inequality: the stories of Darpan and Barwago

Darpan Raj Gautam and Barwago Jama Hussein

Darpan Raj Gautam and Barwago Jama Hussein participated in the project Part of the Community, organised by ActionAid Denmark, a Danish non-governmental organisation (NGO). The project began in 2014 as a collaboration between ActionAid and a youth club (Kantorparken's Youth Club) in the neighbourhood of Bispebjerg, Copenhagen. The aim was to establish a forum for young people in the club to help them gain influence and democratic experiences. Since then, working in collaboration with local agents, Action Aid has launched various kinds of youth communities in five neighbourhoods of Greater Copenhagen. The project also included a series of public events dedicated to themes of inequality and activities such as participation in the annual People's Meeting in Denmark (a four-day political event on the island of Bornholm).

Darpan and Barwago's stories are based on interviews with two researchers (Maria Bruselius-Jensen and Anne Mette W. Nielsen) centring on a journey map. As a method, journey mapping aims to create a map of the elements interview subjects find to be the most significant in a project or process they have been part of (see also Chapter 14 in this book). In this case, Darpan and Barwago chose different formats (a timeline and a sketch) for their maps, but both used their maps to connect their participation in the project with previous events and experiences in other arenas, as well as with their current lives. Through their maps and narrations, they tell us about their personal experiences and visions of being engaged in change processes and political activities.

Barwago's participatory journey

My name is Barwago and I am going to talk about my experiences of being part of Tingbjerg[1] Youth Community and what that has meant to me.

When society is organised in such a way that intangible factors like gender and cultural background limit you, that's inequality. By that I mean the fact that those who gave birth to us, where we live (suburbs or countryside), and the genes we are born with are all things outside of our control. These are choices we do not make ourselves, but they contribute to putting you at a disadvantage compared with others. It's not fair that your opportunities are limited by choices beyond your control. For me personally, my journey as a participant in Tingbjerg Youth Community has been about my hope that the next generation can live in a world where they do not suffer from inequality based on who they are, and that they will not have to face people with prejudices about them based on things beyond their control, such as their economic background, where they live, their religion, and so on. Tingbjerg Youth Community has meant a lot for this journey, so I've tried to show that.

I've drawn a suitcase that is open. The suitcase contains various things that represent what I have gained by being part of Tingbjerg Youth Community. I've included a key because it can open many doors and opportunities, which is something I think our youth community

Figure 4.1: Barwago's map of her participatory journey

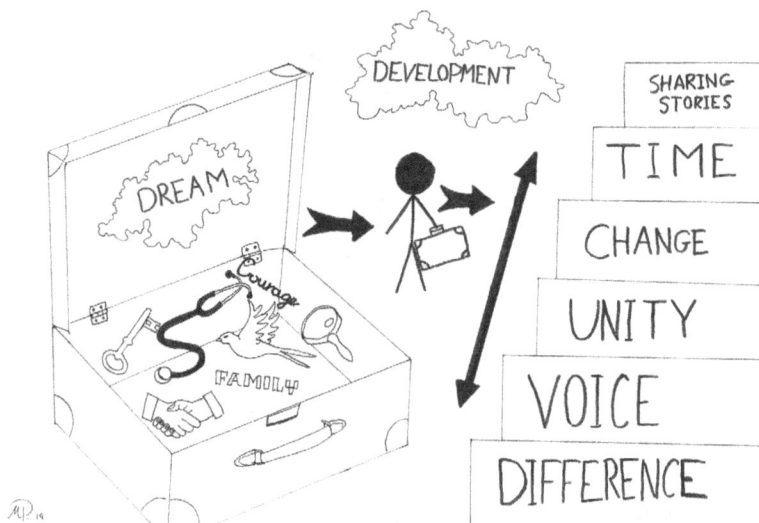

Note: Barwargo's journey map has, in agreement with Barwago, been redrawn by an artist. The colours on Barwago's map did not work well in print and when given the chance, she preferred that the drawing be made by a professional.

does. When we come together in larger groups of people, we can do more.

Sometimes I've had a feeling that I was the only one who felt like just another number in the statistics about marginalised housing areas. I used to associate Tingbjerg with something negative because Tingbjerg was labelled a ghetto, which implies a feeling of being unwanted. I feel like I've been put in the same boat as everyone else who lives here – that we are all criminals, we can't speak Danish, we're all on unemployment benefits. I have to constantly prove that I'm able and that I'm not different. That's why I didn't tell people that I lived in Tingbjerg, because they might react negatively. I discovered that we are young people with one of Denmark's most controversial addresses – and that is something beyond our control. But the community has helped give me the courage to stand up and talk about it, and it has become something that I'm proud of. We're a group of young people who have had the same problems and who actually choose to share our thoughts and experiences with the world. Because there are probably a lot of people who are also going around with the same thoughts, but they just don't know what they can do about it. So, in that sense, I think it opens a lot of doors, because now we're going out and meeting with a ton of people and talking about being a young person in Tingbjerg, and we're also inviting people to Tingbjerg.

I've also put a magnifying glass in the suitcase, because instead of just looking at people like they were statistics, we actually get close to people and see them as the people they actually are. And I've drawn a pencil because I like to write and I keep a diary. I also use my diary to write about the things I experience in the youth community. For example, when I think a meeting was interesting, I like to go home and write about it and reflect on what we've done, and what I actually think about it.

And I've included a stethoscope – the tool a doctor uses to listen to your heart. I drew that because I don't feel like we listen to what people say any more. But if we actually listen to what other young people say and to our own feelings, then we'll become more attentive to listening with our hearts – listening in a way where I'm attentive and actually try to put myself in your shoes. I've also drawn a handshake, which is just about the fact that there's always such a strong focus on viewing us as different. But I think that when we're in the youth community, we're all equal. We give each other the same handshake, or we hug each other or something like that. That's what the handshake is about. I've also written some words in the suitcase. I've written 'family', and that's because in the youth community we've grown very close to each other and we share a lot of things with each other. And I've written 'courage' because I think it can be really hard to share your stories. But it helps that there's a group of people who tell you that you can. That gives you the courage to do it. On the top of the suitcase I've written 'dream' because I also have dreams – what I want to achieve – in the suitcase. Without my dreams of making a difference for other young people, I don't think that I would have been a part of this. My hope for a better world is the essence of my dreams.

The next thing in my drawing is an arrow pointing to myself standing with the suitcase. That is to show that all of the things in the suitcase are things that I carry with me. And with the suitcase in hand, I am approaching a mountain.

The mountain is a little bit hard to explain, because it's a lot about the process of participating in the Frontrunners programme and in the youth community. Fighting for a cause and wanting to make a change. And sometimes you can make it all the way to the top. And when things are at their best you can share your stories and people listen to what you say. But you also come down again. For me, it's not just about reaching the top and doing something particularly brave and cool. You also have to remember to come down again, back to where you started – so you don't forget yourself and don't forget why you wanted to climb the mountain. When you're down at the bottom, it can also be about just feeling down and maybe doubting yourself and thinking that you're never going to succeed in making a difference. But you have to be able to manage being up at the top and down at the bottom, so that you're strong throughout the journey.

And then there are some words in the mountain. I have chosen some slightly random words, but they show some of the things that I think you get out of being part of the youth community. You know, courage, joy, being able to change something. That it's a common cause. And then the fact that it takes time. It just takes time to participate and sometimes it's hard attending a ton of meetings or doing a ton of things with school and work and so on. We organised a festival here in Tingbjerg where people could meet and people from outside Tingbjerg could come and see what it's like to live here. To see that it's not like some people might think. And 500 people came to the festival. But it was a ton of work and I spent a lot of time. But I always think about the fact that I'm actually helping to make a difference and some kind of change, or that I'm helping to bring joy to some people. So these words are the words that keep me going – even when I feel like I don't have very much time, I can find the time to do the things I want to do.

The last word I wrote was 'development'. In a way, this is a bit selfish. It's about my desire to develop as a person. After I've been a part of the youth community for a while, I want to be able to see that I've learned and evolved in some way – and perhaps that I've also gained some new skills. That I've reflected on some new things that I hadn't before. I can see that I've come a long way from where I was a year ago. I've be a part of organising Tingbjerg Festival and we actually got a lot of young people to meet each other. I want to be able to see the results of the things I've done and the changes inside me. I've actually changed a lot personally, because I had never dared stand out before. I'm a bit introverted, so I think it's hard to meet new people and then just tell them what I think and believe. If you met me two years ago, I would have been completely different. But the Frontrunner programme helped me a lot and now I have the courage to be more outgoing and the strength to share my story.

Our work on talking about things like experiencing discrimination and inequality has made me strong. It's not something you otherwise talk about. It's mostly something you hide or try to forget about – a taboo. Maybe you've experienced it on the bus or in the streets. But then you just try to forget it, because you don't think about why it happened. But we've shared those kinds of stories in the youth community and with the Frontrunners. And so, all of these experiences and stories come out, and you start to realise what a common cause we have. We all discover that we all have stories and have experienced some things that we haven't dared to talk about, but we do now.

Actually, I've also developed in the sense that, as a student at the university, I'm maintaining my focus on politics. That's because I've been captivated by the world of politics and I've realised that politics is an integrated part of our lives. I'm passionate about making a difference for children and young people, and in the future, I see myself working somewhere where I can make a difference. I want to be an inspiration for young people through my work. I don't know exactly where that will be yet, but I dream of being able to work in an NGO, the United Nations and the European Union. In any case, I will definitely continue to be politically active. Perhaps not as a candidate or giving big speeches, but I will definitely be speaking with a lot of people in any case.

Darpan's participatory journey

My name is Darpan. I am 19 years old, soon to be 20.

I have made a timeline of my life or the most important times of my life. It starts in 2009, when I moved from Nepal to Denmark and

Figure 4.2: Darpan's map of his participatory journey

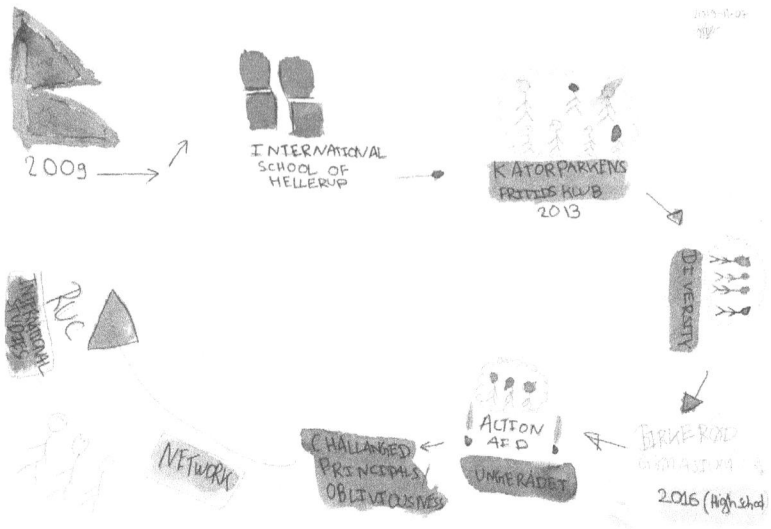

started in the International School of Hellerup. Then I have drawn the youth club that I used to go to, called Kantorparkens Fritidsklub. I started there in 2013, around seven years ago. I have drawn different colours to show the diversity that was around me at that time, which has followed me until now.

The international school was diverse, as was my youth club. In my youth club, the nationalities that surrounded me were Afghanistani, Danish, Nepalese, Indian, Thai, Iranian. So very diverse. I was surrounded by this kind of diversity. That was very new to me, as in Nepal we are only from Nepal. That was really, what can I say, not challenging but interesting because from living the same lifestyle for nine years, I came to a country where I spoke English with some people, I spoke Nepali with some people, and I spoke Danish with some people.

I went to this school for seven years and after the first year of high school, I decided that I wanted to make a change and go to a Danish school that has an international background. So I went to Birkerød Gymnasium for my second and third year of high school but in the International Baccalaureate-line. That was in 2016 and it was like the highlight of my teenage years because a lot of stuff was happening for me. At the age of 16, I was very narrow minded. My plans were to go to Copenhagen Business School (CBS), study business and make a lot of money. My thought was: "I'll be successful making money."

That was the only thing I was thinking about. That was my goal. It drove me to get good grades, a scholarship in the school I went to and generally just everything I did was to earn money.

Around the same time, I got introduced to the youth council at the youth club. I had been part of the student council of my school for six or seven years and been the student council president the last three years of my school, so I knew the system of being in a council. It was fun, but it was like … it was basically like politics, bureaucratic politics. We talked to our counsellor, who talked to our principal, who then talked to the school board, which financed the school's funds. There was a lot of bureaucracy. In our youth council at the youth club, it was easier to go directly to the board and just speak to them about the things we wanted to do.

All of this in 2016 also changed my life because our youth council in the youth club began collaborating with the Danish NGO ActionAid. In ActionAid, we talked about racism and prejudice and went to a very large People's Meeting in Bornholm with many politicians present. This project of the NGO was focused on immigrant youth in Denmark wanting to have a voice. I gave a speech about how I did not break a pattern, because I am an immigrant having good grades, going to the high school I wanted to go to. Those who are criminals are breaking the pattern. It is normal for immigrants to go to school and not be engaged in crime.

This speech changed my life entirely, as I got a lot of good feedback, which made me realise that I had moved on to challenge my principles that money equalled success. I started to think out of the box. There is so much equality in Denmark and still we have all these problems.

So the youth council in the youth club really helped make me the person I am today: I got a network, I still volunteer for ActionAid, it has been four years now. Instead of going to CBS, I go to Roskilde University (RUC) and I am studying international politics instead of studying business. I am still interested in business, but I feel like I am more interested in public work. It is amazing to study at RUC, I really like it. You get new perspectives on things. When you read a newspaper, you read news differently, you understand more things. Why a person is doing what he is doing, why a state is doing what it is doing. I am also part of the student organisation, Frit Forum (Free Forum). Right now we have RUC elections to the student council and they make a big deal out of it. They give you free coffee and "Vote for me." It is like a real election. And I feel like I am more of a social worker than a politician. I am more of a social person than I am to someone electing me. I guess it feels good to be elected, but it's not really me.

I don't see myself going into politics. Bureaucracy is a big part of it. I feel I have more influence than I think you have when you choose people through politics. I have realised that power is more valuable than money because money is too materialistic.

In the future I want to work with kids, be it here in Denmark or somewhere else. Work with kids and help them get the things that they don't have. If I decide to work in Denmark, it is about confronting a discourse that states that all immigrants do this and that. You can break that and make people believe something else. If I decide to work in Nepal, maybe it is about getting kids into education and teach them basic rights. Maybe sexual health for small girls. It depends on where you are, because every region has their own difficulties. But I do believe that children are the ones that … children are the future. I believe we should have the most focus on children because it is just more important that way. I think that Denmark doesn't have enough focus on their youth. One of the themes when I was on Bornholm was that the youth were being talked with − not talked to − which really hit me because youths want to be listened to. It is nice for the youth. They deserve attention as well.

Currently I work in my old youth club because maybe I can prevent the kids that I work with from being like some of my old friends. Give them the right guidance instead. It is really weird or nostalgic when I work there. I started four weeks ago, and it is weird because of my age. Some people are 17 and I am 19 and I am supposed to be their guidance counsellor. I feel like they know that I can still teach them something because of the things I have experienced. But the age thing is really weird in Denmark because you see age as something that determines how much you know, I guess, and not the maturity of the person. Some of the most significant people in my life have also been from the youth club because they straightened me up. They knew my potential. If I skipped school, they were like, "Come on." They push. They make you feel that you can do better than you think. They used to teach me how to be a good student and now they teach me how to be a good educator. This is the real importance of the youth club in my life.

Note

[1] Tingbjerg is a social housing area on the outskirts of Copenhagen. It is formally defined as a 'ghetto', due to low education levels among residents and high levels of residents with non-Western backgrounds. The criteria are defined by the Danish government and several social housing areas are on the so-called 'ghetto list'.

PART II

Current state and conditions for young people's participation: critiques and trends

5

Bounded agency and social participation: how socioeconomic situation and experiences influence young people's way of engaging in society

Sabine Israel, Jo Deakin, Renata Franc, Anna Markina,
Rein Murakas and Markus Quandt

This chapter presents data from the PROMISE Youth Survey gathered as part of PROMISE, a Horizon 2020 research project addressing the social participation of young people in conflict with authority. Building on the work of Evans (2002), Ekman and Amnå (2012) and Munford and Sanders (2015), we develop the concept of social participation to provide a broader, context-based definition that allows us to explore a diverse range of youth activities. Our analysis explores the diverse forms of social participation and the factors that can influence young people´s agency and ability to engage. We highlight the extent to which young people´s agency is bound by their experience and current social context, and assess under which circumstances those experiences can become an enabler of engagement.

Key findings

- Social exclusion, which is commonly expected to be a key barrier towards participation, can be a trigger for activism, everyday engagement and helping behaviours.
- The need to avoid deterministic logics in the study of youth participation emerges from the nuanced effects shown by factors often uncritically assumed as barriers and enablers of engagement.
- Factors that increase personal efficacy (education, social trust and local connections) contribute towards young people being able to enact their agency and turn negative life experiences into actions that benefit themselves and their communities.

Introduction

Young people participate in society in different ways and to different extents. Their participation (or lack of it) in collective and private settings, and in political and social activities, is influenced by multiple factors including their own life experience. This chapter explores various forms of young people's social participation, and the factors that can influence their ability to engage. We present the findings of the PROMISE survey, conducted as part of the wider PROMISE research project, Promoting Youth Involvement and Social Engagement, a research project funded by the European Union, which ran from May 2016 to April 2019.[1] Its aim was to explore young people's role in shaping society and to assess the potential, across Europe, for youth involvement in positive social action and sustainable change. The project brought together 12 collaborating centres in Croatia, Estonia, Finland, Germany, Italy, Portugal, Slovakia, Spain, the Russian Federation and the UK.

In developing the survey, we employed a broad concept of social participation, drawing on the work of Evans (2002, 2007), Ekman and Amnå (2012) and Munford and Sanders (2015). We develop the concept of social participation to provide a broader, context-based definition that allows us to explore a diverse range of youth activities. Through this broader understanding, we are able to highlight the extent to which young people's agency is bound by their experience and their current social context. The literature to support our argument is presented under three general themes: the concept of social participation; agency and personal efficacy; barriers and enablers of social participation. Our analysis contributes to discussions about the factors that influence young people's ability to engage by merging the social participation perspective with the agency perspective.

The PROMISE concept of social participation

In line with multiple scholars of youth and citizenship studies (Stolle et al, 2005; Harris et al, 2010; Bakker and de Vreese, 2011; Amnå and Ekman, 2014; Cammaerts et al, 2014), the PROMISE understanding of the concept of social participation is broad and extends beyond the political arena. We use the term social participation to refer to all kinds of social, political and environmental action that is carried out by young people in order to bring about social change. Our concept acknowledges participatory acts as a product of individual agency (Vromen, 2003, p 95), while identifying participation as activities intended to influence the social circumstances of others (Ekman and Amnå, 2012). Our concept therefore focuses on non-institutional forms of participation that can also be proximate and local. Through this, we capture the ordinary social participation of young people, which is not reflected in the often-used dichotomy between engaged versus disengaged, nor in the dichotomy between conventional and unconventional participation (Harris et al, 2010).

Our analysis encompasses three main forms: activism, everyday engagement and helping behaviour. It, thus, reflects the two extremes widely used to distinguish young people's relation to society: more risky and illegal actions on the one hand and personal forms of action on the other (Garcia-Albacete, 2014; Grasso, 2016). Activism encompasses two dimensions: forms of radical protest, and non-formal political activities (Harris et al, 2010), while everyday engagement (Vromen, 2003; Vromen and Collin, 2010) involves individualistic acts with a political or social message. The third form of participation, which we term 'helping behaviour', includes a more community-based, or neighbourhood, form of engagement, involving participation in, and attendance at, local activities. This category considers young people within the social context that describes their options and socialisation best: their local context (Harris and Wyn, 2009).

Agency and personal efficacy

While understanding participation as a product of individual agency, we conceptualise agency as young people's capacity to act in a way that would alter their (or others') situation(s). We draw on Lister's definition of agency as encompassing the legal, socio-political elements of action, participatory practice and rights as 'the object of struggle' (Lister, 2007, p 52). This struggle for agency is an undercurrent of young people's experiences, as young people's status as embodied agents is sometimes recognised and enacted, sometimes overlooked or constrained (Marsh et al, 2007). Significantly, our analysis considers young people's agency to be 'bounded' because actions are guided by past experiences and an imagined future of (limited) possibilities, as well as a subjective analysis of the obstacles and structures that constrain or support them (Evans, 2007).

> Bounded agency is socially situated agency, influenced but not determined by environments and emphasizing internalized frames of reference as well as external actions.

> By examining bounded agency, the focus moves from structured individualization onto individuals as actors, without losing the perspective of structuration. (Evans, 2007, p 93)

Young people follow very different trajectories based on their opportunities and their imagined future (Raffo and Reeves, 2000; Evans, 2002). Evans calls for an understanding of the role of inequalities and power imbalances, transmitted by social and educational policies, which constrain the actions and reactions of young people. The PROMISE data (PROMISE, 2018, 2019b) demonstrate how young people's experiences relate to their ability to enact agency. We measure agency by assessing personal political efficacy and look at the bounds, by factoring in not only the socioeconomic situation of young people, but also their personal history, such as discrimination and social exclusion – factors that can function as powerful barriers to social engagement. In the following sections, these barriers will be examined alongside enablers of social participation.

Barriers to social participation

Our analysis is based on well-known barriers to social participation identified in our qualitative case studies: low resources, social exclusion, labelling and discrimination, and conflict with authorities (PROMISE, 2018).

First, research demonstrates that young people's access to resources (material, social or cultural capital) enables their participation in society and access to political or social opportunities (Verba et al, 1995). A low level of resources such as lower education, lower income and other social disadvantages can present a barrier to participation (Schneider and Makszin, 2014).

Second, as a result of an accumulation of disadvantages (Markovic and Evrard, 2014), people become excluded 'from ordinary living patterns and activities' (Townsend, 1979), including economic, social, cultural and political life. Reactions towards social exclusion include feelings of powerlessness and anxiety (Hagquist and Starrin, 1996; Creed and Reynolds, 2001) that link with reduced agency. For young people, social exclusion can result from not being able to realise one's potential and not feeling recognised by society for one's contribution and effort (Eurofound, 2015).

Third, the labelling of young people as abject groups, or as powerless in society, heightens exclusion and, in many cases, reduces young people's agency and perceived self-efficacy (Walker, 2014). Their labelling and discrimination, by people or institutional policies, are closely linked to unequal power relations (Link and Phelan, 2001; Lister, 2015) that feed into a cycle of stigma (Deakin et al, 2020; see also Chapter 11 in this book).

Finally, we argue that conflict with authorities (in particular the police) feeds into labelling and social exclusion that in turn reduces levels of participation. Kennelly (2011) found that young people are expected to conform to the normative behaviour of legitimate citizens-to-be. When they do not comply with the norms (such as congregating in 'appropriate' spaces), they may become labelled as permanent suspects (McAra and McVie, 2005) and experience recurrent conflict-ridden encounters with the police. These encounters reduce trust in authorities, amplify social disadvantage and serve to embed social divisions (Kennelly, 2011).

Enablers of social participation

Addressing the enablers of social participation, our analysis focuses on education, social trust and a sense of belonging, since these factors showed most importance on the qualitative side of the PROMISE study (PROMISE, 2018). However, we also control for other standard enablers of participation, such as income, activity status and degree of independence from parental household.

While low resources generally reduce participation, one of the resources most necessary for engagement seems to be education. This can be attributed to an effect of being familiar with (or learning about) the political system, political information being spread more easily within educational institutions, and those with higher levels of education growing higher levels of internal efficacy. Henn and Foard (2014) note, for example, that: 'Those in possession of higher educational qualifications are significantly more confident in their own knowledge and understanding of politics … whilst they too hold an antipathy towards the political parties and the professional politicians, they are noticeably less sceptical than are their contemporaries' (Henn and Foard, 2014, p 374).

Social trust and, specifically, enabling relationships are linked to higher engagement. Following Putnam's (1993) social capital model, trust developed during interactions on a personal level can translate into social engagement. Our qualitative case studies highlighted the impact of trustworthy relationships and mentors on the agency of young people (PROMISE, 2018).

Previous studies point towards the importance of feeling part of the (local) community (belonging) as a positive correlate of different types of participation (Chavis and Wandersman, 1990; Talò, 2018). Within the PROMISE survey, we explore the respondents' feelings of ties or 'closeness to' the local community.

Data and methods

The data stem from the PROMISE online survey conducted between December 2018 and March 2019 in the ten PROMISE countries: Croatia, Estonia, Finland, Germany, Italy, Portugal, Russia, Slovakia, Spain and the UK. The online questionnaire contained a set of relevant measures from the European Social Survey (2018) and the European Values Survey (2016), and further questions were formulated based on the preceding qualitative part of the PROMISE research involving 22 case studies. The master questionnaire was developed in English with translation into nine languages by the project partners using a team approach.[2] A quota sampling, typical of web surveys, was used to collect data. The target population of the survey was permanent residents of the country (regardless of citizenship) between the ages of 16 years and 74 years (inclusive). The targeted size of an effective (interviewed) sample in each country was at least 1,200 respondents of whom at least 600 respondents were aged 16–29 and 600 respondents were over 30. Each subsample was representative of the respective population as regards their main socio-demographic features. The sample was intentionally non-proportional due to the need to compare young people with adults. The final dataset includes information on 12,666 respondents in total, 6,288 from young respondents aged 15–29 and 6,378 from older respondents aged 30–74. For each country, data were weighted using population data about gender, age group and education (higher versus other). Detailed information on population, sample and weighting statistics is available from the PROMISE report *Barriers and Enablers of Social Participation of Young People* (PROMISE, 2019b).

Concerning the limitations of the current data collection approach, the following aspect should be taken into account. The quota sampling approach used by web panels results in a non-probability sample of respondents (as opposed to probability samples, for which the selection of respondents is strictly random, thus excluding the possibility of systematic biases coming from the respondent sample composition). So, in principle there could be biasing effects of the self-selection of respondents into the web panel. However, web panels have been used successfully in survey research (Hays et al, 2015), and we have no indication of such biases in our survey.

The data were analysed using a latent class analysis (LCA) to identify typical patterns of participation in terms of activism and everyday engagement. The analysis was conducted with Latent Gold 5.1 (Vermunt and Magidson, 2016). LCA (Magidson and Vermunt, 2004) is a statistical procedure used to allocate respondents into several distinct classes or clusters, where those respondents with high similarity to each other on a whole set of characteristics (such as, for example, their responses to a list of survey questions) are allocated to the same class. We provide descriptive and bivariate analysis for forms of youth social participation, and finally present the results of a multi-level regression analysis (Snijders and Bosker, 1999; Hox, 2002). The multi-level analysis was used to identify which explanatory factors are statistically associated with the participation behaviour patterns. The models for activism and engagement were estimated as multinomial models within Stata15 using generalised structural equation models ('gsem'), and the linear models for efficacy and helping were estimated using the procedure 'mixed'. Even though presented separately for easier interpretation, the multi-level regression analyses always included all control variables, listed in Annex 1 (of the online report PROMISE, 2019b). Further information on the applied methods and results is available online (PROMISE, 2019a, 2019b).

Forms of youth social participation

Activism

For the analysis of the activism classes, four questions were considered: signing petitions, taking part in legal demonstrations, taking part in illegal demonstrations and strikes, and squatting in buildings. Possible responses to each question are '1: Would never do', '2: Would do', '3: Have done'. The LCA identified a distinction of the respondents into four different classes of reported behaviours as the optimal solution (see PROMISE, 2019b for response profiles of each class).

Using the response profiles, which depict the average response score for an item on the 1/2/3 scale per class, we characterise the four classes as follows. One class is engaged in 'only petitions', consisting of a quarter of the young population. In fact, even for petitions the average response is hardly beyond '2', indicating that the respondents tend to *consider* using petitions as a viable instrument, but many have not actually *done* so yet. Therefore, this is a low–activity class characterised by its members' rejection of effortful and illegal forms of activism.

The second class ('Only Legal') is, on average, manifestly engaged in petitions, somewhat less in legal demonstrations, but clearly shies away from any illegal activities. It comprises 27% of the young population.

The third class ('All Activism, Moderate') comprises people ready to carry out most of our activities to a moderate extent, but they have not necessarily done so yet, and are somewhat reluctant about occupying property. This class forms the largest group, at 38%.

Finally, respondents in the smallest class ('All Activism, High') often report actually having used most activism forms, except for occupying buildings (9% of the young population). That this class of 'real' activists is so small is in line with expectations. Since we asked for any behaviours ever displayed, the probability of being in the more radically active classes increases with age. This is to be expected at least as an effect of 'cumulated opportunity' over the years of the respondents' politically active life, but it may also show a greater resourcefulness for political activities that comes with increasing age.

Everyday engagement

For the analysis of the everyday engagement classes, five variables were considered: donating money; boycotting products; making a statement in writing, art or music; participating in political online activities; and other. Again, all response options '1: Would never do', '2: Would do', '3: Have done' were considered here. Three classes emerge from the LCA: low engagement, consisting of 13% of the young population; a moderate engagement class, consisting of 69% of the young population; and a high engagement class, consisting of 18% of the young population. The response profiles (see PROMISE, 2019b for response profiles of each class) show a clustering that follows a simple ordering by the intensity of engagement. Those respondents who have a high preference for, for example, everyday engagement through making public statements, also tend to make donations, boycott products and so on. In the high engagement class, using the internet for political self-expression is the most prevalent activity, but, somewhat surprisingly, donating money is almost as important.

Helping others in a local context

Our concept of helping behaviour measures how often young people 'get involved with (or work for) voluntary or charitable organisations', 'actively provide help for other people outside family, work or voluntary organisations' and 'help with, or attend, activities organized in the local area' (every day, several times a week, once a week, several times a month, once a month, less often, never). For this analysis, we constructed an index of the three items, as they tap into the same participation dimension (alpha reliability score of 0.84); no LCA was used. We note that a cumulative 55% engage once a month or more often in charitable ways privately outside their family, and a cumulative 33% in voluntary organisations. Only around a third of young people never become involved in voluntary organisations, while 15% never provide help to others outside of the family. In local activities, around 35% engage once a month or more, while 30% never become involved. A display of the frequency of activities can be found in PROMISE (2019b).

The role of personal efficacy for social participation of youth

Determinants of young people's feeling of efficacy

Before analysing the importance of personal (political) efficacy for social participation, we consider the determinants of personal efficacy. We isolate this aspect of efficacy here for bivariate analyses because personal efficacy is related to the concept of personal agency, which has been identified as an important mediator variable in the qualitative strands of the PROMISE project. Personal efficacy was assessed by the question 'How much would you say that the political system in [country] allows people like you to have a say in what the government does?'

The determinants of personal efficacy are shown in Figures 5.1 and 5.2. Three factors – not currently being in education, having a low perceived income, living with parents – are associated with lower personal political efficacy. The activity status (being unemployed, working, caring or other) does not register any significant effect.

Social exclusion has a mixed impact. While young people agreeing to the statement 'Life has become too complicated, I can barely find my way' show a lower efficacy, those who agree to feeling left out, or to feeling looked down upon, do not report lower, but rather higher, efficacy. Discrimination does not show an effect on efficacy, while police contact does generally not reduce efficacy, except for those who were suspected, profiled, or protested and reported negative treatment by the police. On the other hand, social trust and local connections increase personal political efficacy.

Figure 5.1: Social position effect on efficacy

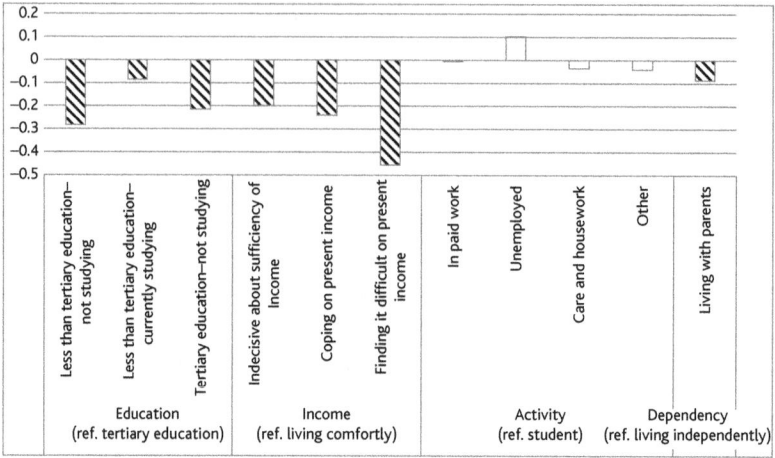

Note: Regression coefficients of a linear multi-level model for efficacy, coded 1 (low) to 5 (high). White bars represent insignificant values that cannot be interpreted. Reading example: young people finding it difficult on present income have a much lower probability to report high personal efficacy than those living comfortably on their income.

Figure 5.2: Social experiences effect on efficacy

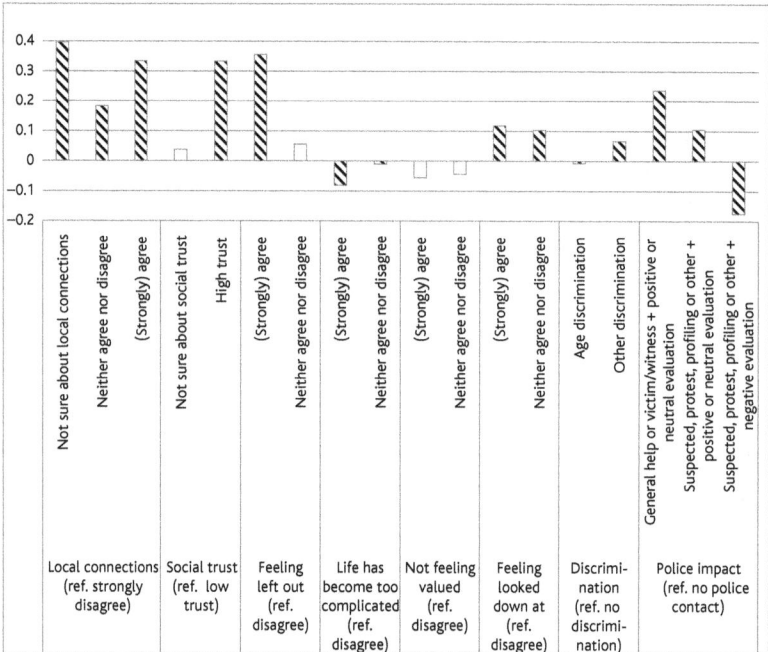

Note: Regression coefficients of a linear multi-level model for efficacy, coded 1 (low) to 5 (high). Non-filled bars represent insignificant values that cannot be interpreted.

Figure 5.3: Personal efficacy effect on activism, everyday engagement and helping

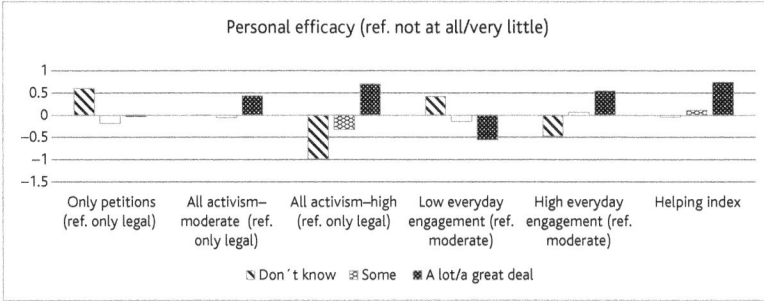

Note: Non-filled bars reflect non-significant values.

Political efficacy as a determinant of youth social participation

In the following analysis, we assessed the effect of efficacy and other predictors on our dependent variables. In Figures 5.3–5.11, the bars for the models of activism and everyday engagement represent so called relative risk ratios derived from a multi-nominal, multi-level model. They show the probability of choosing one outcome category over the probability of choosing the base category (Agresti, 2007). For activism, the base category is 'only legal activism', and for everyday engagement it is 'moderate everyday engagement'. For helping, the bars show the coefficients of a linear regression, where positive values refer to stronger helping behaviour. The bars left non-filled show non-significant values, meaning that for this specific set of variables, the results cannot be interpreted as the data are inconclusive.

Overall, we see (in Figure 5.3) that a low level of personal efficacy is associated with stronger forms of activism. Those reporting 'don't know' or 'some' personal efficacy do not seem to be necessarily more involved than those lacking it. However, young people reporting high personal efficacy do show significantly higher levels of 'all activism', together with a high everyday engagement and a strong tendency for helping.

To assess this very hard-to-grasp effect of efficacy better, we also evaluated the effect of 'group efficacy'. Group efficacy is a predictor of people's perceived ability to influence the government when organised in groups. We find that people with high group-efficacy beliefs are significantly less likely to only exercise petition rights, but statistically not significantly more present in all forms of activism. For everyday engagement, group efficacy seems as important as, or even more important than, personal efficacy. It is strongly negatively related to low engagement profiles and also strongly positively related to high engagement profiles. By contrast, for helping only, a very small effect is found. This corresponds to the expressed 'political' nature of group efficacy. To consult the regression coefficients, please refer to PROMISE (2019b).

Barriers and enablers of youth social participation

Barriers

Our data identified low resources as a barrier to social participation. The highest perceived income group displays higher shares in the most radical forms of activism and in high everyday engagement. However, this high–income group is also somewhat more represented in the low–activist group (see Figure 5.4).

This latter effect could be due first to the young age group examined here, for whom household income might be difficult to assess. Young people do not necessarily have knowledge of the household's resources, nor do they (at least for the youngest age groups) largely participate in achieving them.

Social exclusion, which we expected to be a key barrier towards social participation, and especially the stronger forms of participation, does not show the expected negative effects (see Figure 5.5). The separate analysis of the social exclusion factors confirms that there is no consistent effect of social exclusion on low engagement and activism. Of the four social exclusion factors, only 'feeling looked down upon' is associated with lower engagement. In contrast, a strong tendency towards all forms of activism, high everyday engagement, and helping, is shown for the overall index. Therefore, from young

Figure 5.4: Perceived income effect on activism, everyday engagement and helping

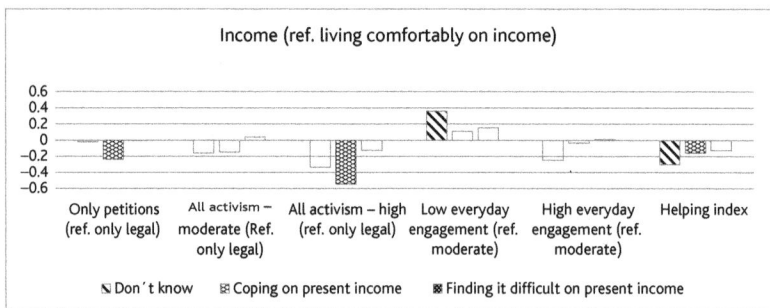

Note: Non-filled bars reflect non-significant values.

Figure 5.5: Social exclusion effect on activism, everyday engagement and helping

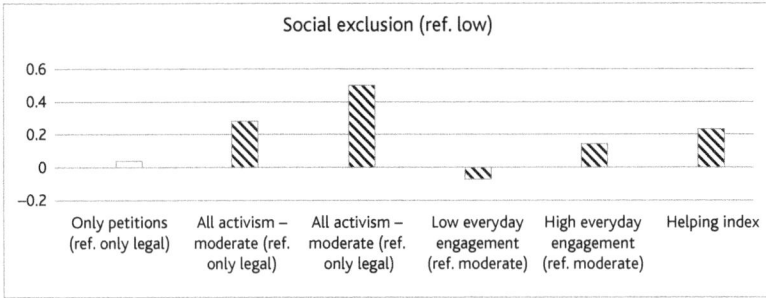

Note: Non-filled bars reflect non-significant values.

Figure 5.6: Discrimination effect on activism, everyday engagement and helping

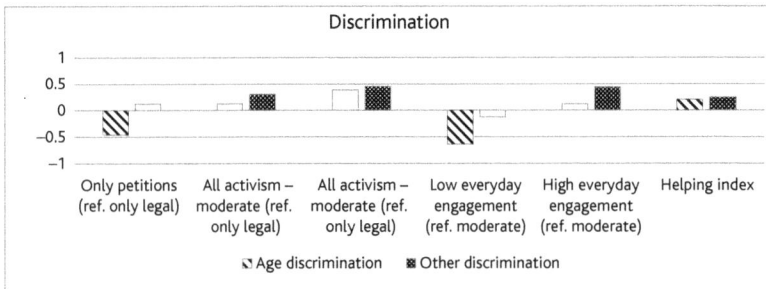

Note: Non-filled bars reflect non-significant values.

people's self-perceived social exclusion, protest rather than resignation seems to arise.

For discrimination (see Figure 5.6), we distinguished between age discrimination, which can potentially occur to all young people as such and may in some part be a matter of sensibility and perception, and other forms of discrimination that occur among more marginalised groups of young people. Age discrimination is related to a low withdrawal rate from activism and engagement and to a stronger likelihood of helping. Those people reporting other forms of discrimination (including, for example, race, ethnic group, religion or gender) are more often found in the illegal activism profiles. But they are also more likely to be everyday engaged and to be helping other people. For both social exclusion and discrimination, young people therefore seem to see the reasons in structural disadvantages rather than in their own behaviours, leading them not to withdrawal but rather towards protest activities.

Figure 5.7: Education effect on activism, everyday engagement and helping

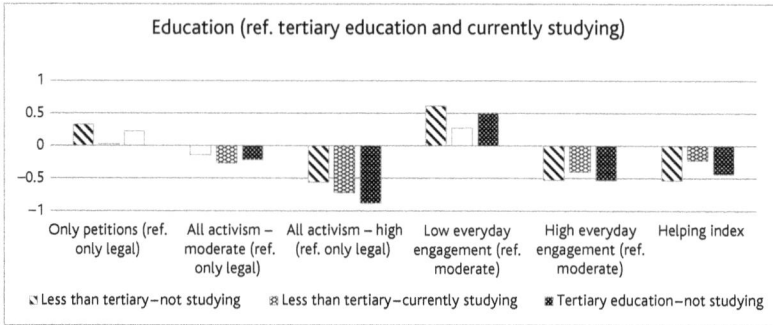

Note: Non-filled bars reflect non-significant values.

Figure 5.8: Activity status effect on activism, everyday engagement and helping

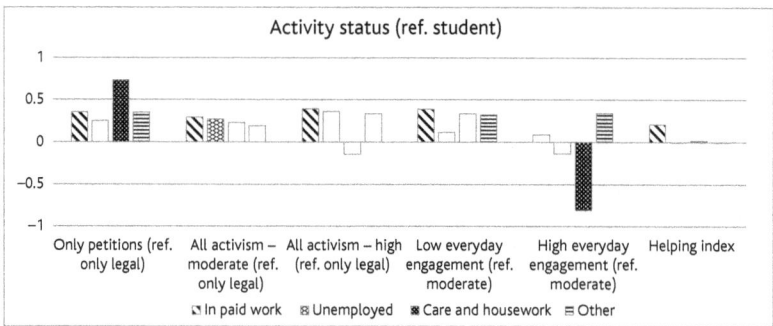

Note: Non-filled bars reflect non-significant values.

Enablers

In line with previous studies, education is confirmed to be one of the key determinants of participation (see Figure 5.7). This is shown not only for activism and everyday engagement, but also for helping. Compared with those who are currently enrolled in tertiary education, those in nearly all other education categories and activity status categories show lesser social participation. The only exception holds for helping behaviours, where working young people demonstrate slightly more helping activity than students. But the working young also appear more frequently in the low everyday engagement class than students (see Figure 5.8). This is likely due to those in paid work already having arrived in a life phase with higher personal commitments in families and personal networks. Plausibly, both the availability of resources (cognitive and physical capacity, and time) as well as mobilisation networks would make students more susceptible to becoming involved in activism.

Figure 5.9: Local connection effect on activism, everyday engagement and helping

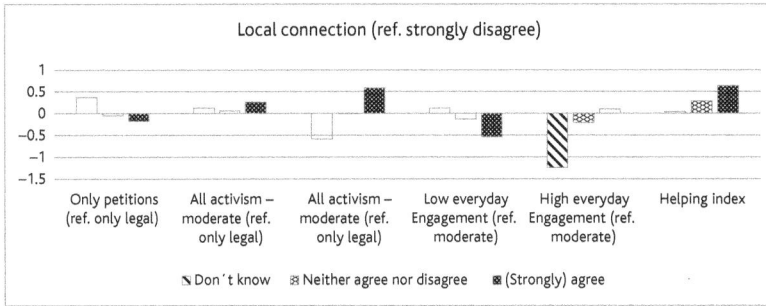

Note: Non-filled bars reflect non-significant values.

Figure 5.10: Social trust effect on activism, everyday engagement and helping

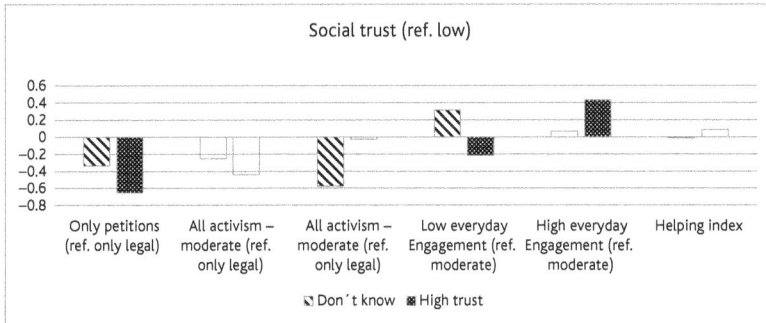

Note: Non-filled bars reflect non-significant values.

Local connections, which were assessed by asking to what extent people agreed to the statement 'I feel close to people in the area where I live', reveal an impact on all three forms of social participation (see Figure 5.9). They reduce weaker forms of activism and engagement and increase the forms that involve high engagement and illegal activism activities. For helping, a strong impact is shown, as was already expected due to the strong 'local' dimension of both questions.

Interestingly, general social trust is strongly associated with activism and engagement, but not with everyday helping activities (see Figure 5.10). The lack of the importance of general trust for helping, however, could indicate that this general form of trust is less relevant when the engagement concerns local and personal relationships, where familiarity with the other person (or people) may reduce the role of general trust.

Figure 5.11: Police contact effect on activism, everyday engagement and helping

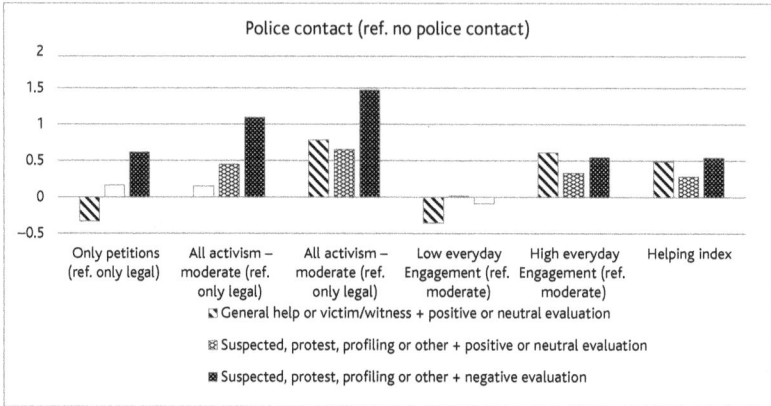

Note: Non-filled bars reflect non-significant values.

Conflict

Within our survey most police contact was conflict-based (profiling; being a victim of, or a witness to, an offence; being a suspect of an offence or crime; participation in a demonstration or protest), but the absolute number of conflict-based actions against offenders was small and can therefore not be considered in detail. Therefore, we collated various types of policing experiences into larger groups, with the main intention of distinguishing positive or neutral situations from conflict-based ones (see Figure 5.11).

Policing experiences without conflict, and positive or neutral treatment, were linked to increased protest activism – which was not expected – but also to higher everyday engagement and more helping behaviours. The most interesting cases are those where a conflict-based policing experience went hand-in-hand with negative treatment by police officers. For these cases, protest activism increases strongly. It must be noted that our police contact experience measure does include contact at demonstrations, which overlaps with attending demonstrations in the dependent variable, especially illegal ones, and thus naturally increases the association for the 'high activism' class. But the same measure of police contact is also linked to a higher withdrawal from legal activism, towards only petitions. Thus, we suppose that these data are valid, and indicate on the one hand an active response in reaction to negative policing, that is, the attempted sanction provokes more activism; on the other hand, however, attempted sanctions can also have a repression effect.

Comparing the effects of social position and life circumstances on agency

A comparison of the effects of social position and life experiences on activism, engagement and helping shows that education and personal efficacy, but also social exclusion, have a significant positive effect on all or most forms of agency (see Table 5.1). Also, group efficacy shows importance, and is only negative for 'all activism – high' – a plausible effect, because these young people believe that already legally organised action can lead to change. Moreover, local connections and social trust have a positive effect on agency. Likewise, however, age discrimination leads to a reaction that is related to reduced withdrawal (in other words, 'Yes, we do care!') and other forms of discrimination are linked to a change in the form of agency from legal/moderate to stronger/illegal forms.

This list combines more or less established enablers of participation with negative life experiences. The effect of social exclusion is particularly interesting, as it does not act as the barrier towards efficacy and engagement we expected, but is rather associated with stronger (also illegal) forms of activism and helping. This fits with our results from the qualitative studies (PROMISE, 2018), that young people's reactions to stigma occur along a continuum (Deakin et al, 2020). Reactions can include 'fighting back' linked to increased agency on the one hand, or withdrawal and passivity on the other (Lalonde and Cameron, 1994). In the case of social exclusion, the injustice implied in the situation seems to act rather as a motivator for political and social action.

Other negative life experiences show a mixed result. Negative police contact is positively related to withdrawal but might also incite young people to more illegal forms of action. Perceiving life as too complicated is linked to lower engagement but also to increased activism.

A mixed effect can be established for social position, a factor we would normally have thought to have a positive effect on agency. Activity status (with the exception of care work), perceived income and independence from parents reduce engagement and activism in some instances and encourage it in others. A high social position is therefore not necessarily linked with engagement; it can also lead to a perceived lack for a need of action.

Our analysis therefore revealed that negative experiences that are linked to a decrease in agency can sometimes also increase demonstrations of agency and engagement in generative activities (for example, to help other people from experiencing similar situations)

Table 5.1: Overview of the positive and negative effect of social position and life experiences on agency

Social position/life experiences		'Legal action' versus 'Only petitions'	'All activism moderate' versus 'legal action'	'All activism high' versus 'legal action'	'Moderate everyday engagement' versus 'low engagement'	'High everyday engagement' versus 'moderate engagement'	Increasing 'helping'
Tertiary education		+	+	++	++	++	++
High perceived income		–	/	+	/	/	++
Activity status (ref. student)		Unemployed: / Working: – Care work: – Other: –	Unemployed: + Working: + Care work: / Other: /	Unemployed: + Working: / Care work: / Other: /	Unemployed: / Working: – Care work: / Other: –	Unemployed: / Working: / Care work: – Other: +	Unemployed: / Working: + Care work: / Other: /
Dependency		/	/	/	+	–	–
Personal efficacy		/	+	+	+	+	++
Group efficacy		+	/	–	++	+	+
Local connections		+	+	+	+	–	++
Social trust		++	/	/	+	+	/
Social exclusion	Feeling left out	/	++	++	/	+	++
	Life too complicated	/	++	++	/	–	/
	Not feeling valued	/	++	++	+	+	++
	Feeling looked down upon	/	++	+	+	+	++

(continued)

Table 5.1: Continued

Social position/life experiences		'Legal action' versus 'Only petitions'	'All activism moderate' versus 'legal action'	'All activism high' versus 'legal action'	'Moderate everyday engagement' versus 'low engagement'	'High everyday engagement' versus 'moderate engagement'	Increasing 'helping'
Discrimination	Age discrimination	+	/	/	+	/	+
	Other discrimination	/	+	+	/	+	+
Police contact	Positive police contact	+	/	+	+	+	+
	Neutral police contact	/	+	+	/	+	+
	Negative police contact	–	+	+	/	+	+

Note: + positive effect in variable or at least observable in one response category; ++ positive effect observable in two or more response categories; – negative effect in variable or at least one response category; / no significant effect on a 10% significance level.

(see also Chapter 12 in this book). Certain life experiences, thus, can provide a trigger for action, especially where treatment by others is considered unjust or experienced because of belonging to a certain, stigmatised, group.

Conclusion

The PROMISE survey combined information on different forms of social participation with an assessment of life experiences and the social situation of young people to analyse the way in which their agency is 'bounded'. We included local and personal forms of engagement to extend the, often very political, understanding of participation that is employed in most surveys. Our survey used online panels, and is therefore different in approach and sampling to established European surveys, yet, it did manage to collect answers from a wide range of young people across ten European countries and provides a sound basis for analysis of social behaviour.

We started from the question, in what way Evans' (2007) concept of bounded agency shows its influence in the social world of young people. Are inequalities in participation influenced by negative experiences in a young person's life? Do negative experiences act as barriers and prevent participation in collective and private, political and social settings? Our survey indicates that life experiences do indeed influence the actions of young people, at least to the same extent, and sometimes more than the effect of their social situation.

The agency perspective teaches us that there are multiple response options to problematic life experiences of young people, ranging from resignation over small personal changes to active political responses (Lister, 2004). Our survey demonstrates the extent of young people's responses across the spectrum, and it confirms that young people, largely, do not resign themselves to their situations but, instead, engage in activism, everyday engagement and helping behaviour to change them. Significantly, young people in our survey opt for forms of activism even when they report negative life experiences such as social exclusion and discrimination. Young people who report negative life experiences may locate the underlying 'causes' in structural disadvantages rather than in their own behaviour, leading them not to withdraw but rather to become involved in protest activities.

The nuances of the data gathered in the PROMISE survey lead us to conclude that there is no deterministic logic that can be applied towards the barriers and enablers of social participation. However, what is clear is that factors that increase personal efficacy, such as education, social trust and local connections, can play a role in enabling young people to enact their agency and turn their life experience into action that benefits themselves and their communities.

Disclaimer

This publication reflects only the views of the author(s); the European Commission and the Research Executive Agency are not responsible for any information it contains.

Notes

[1] PROMISE (GA693221) received funding from the European Union Horizon 2020 research and innovation programme under grant agreement 693221. See www.PROMISE.manchester.ac.uk/en/home-page

[2] Two translators translated the questions independently from each other and then, at a joint meeting with a third person, that is, the reviewer, the translations were reviewed and reconciled. Still, in cross-national studies the meanings of some questions may be culture-specific, despite the efforts in question translation.

References

Agresti, A. (2007) *An Introduction to Categorical Data Analysis*, London: John Wiley & Sons.

Amnå, E. and Ekman, J. (2014) 'Standby citizens: diverse faces of political passivity', *European Political Science Review*, 6(2): 261–81.

Bakker, T.P. and de Vreese, C.H. (2011) 'Good news for the future? Young people, internet use, and political participation', *Communication Research*, 38(4): 451–70.

Cammaerts, B., Bruter, M., Banaji, S., Harrison, S. and Anstead, N. (2014) 'The myth of youth apathy: young Europeans' critical attitudes toward democratic life', *American Behavioral Scientist*, 58(5): 645–64.

Chavis, D.M. and Wandersman, A. (1990) 'Sense of community in the urban environment: a catalyst for participation and community development', *American Journal of Community Psychology*, 18: 55–82.

Creed, P.A. and Reynolds, J. (2001) 'Economic deprivation, experiential deprivation and social loneliness in unemployed and employed youth', *Journal of Community & Applied Social Psychology*, 11(3): 167–78.

Deakin, J., Fox, C. and Matos, R. (2020) 'Labelled as "risky" in an era of control: how young people experience and respond to the stigma of criminalized identities', *European Journal of Criminology*, Online first 20 April, doi: 10.1177/1477370820916728

Ekman, J. and Amnå, E. (2012) 'Political participation and civic engagement: towards a new typology', *Human Affairs*, 22(3): 283–300.

Eurofound (2015) *Social Inclusion of Young People*, Luxembourg: Publications Office of the European Union.

European Social Survey (2018) *ESS Round 9 Source Questionnaire*, London: ESS ERIC Headquarters c/o City, University of London.

European Values Survey (2016) *European Values Study 2008: Integrated Dataset (EVS 2008)*, ZA4800 Datenfile Version 4.0.0, Cologne: GESIS Datenarchiv, https://doi.org/10.4232/1.12458

Evans, K. (2002) 'Taking control of their lives? Agency in young adult transitions in England and the new Germany', *Journal of Youth Studies*, 5(3): 245–69.

Evans, K. (2007) 'Concepts of bounded agency in education, work, and the personal lives of young adults', *International Journal of Psychology*, 42(2): 85–93.

Garcia-Albacete, G. (2014) *Young People's Political Participation in Western Europe: Continuity or Generational Change?*, Basingstoke: Palgrave Macmillan.

Grasso, M.T. (2016) *Generations, Political Participation and Social Change in Western Europe*, London/New York, NY: Routledge.

Hagquist, C. and Starrin, B. (1996) 'Youth unemployment and mental health: gender differences and economic stress', *Scandinavian Journal of Social Welfare*, 5(4): 215–28.

Harris, A. and Wyn, J. (2009) 'Young people's politics and the micro-territories of the local', *Australian Journal of Political Science*, 44(2): 327–44.

Harris, A., Wyn, J. and Younes, S. (2010) 'Beyond apathetic or activist youth: "ordinary" young people and contemporary forms of participation', *YOUNG*, 18(1): 9–32.

Hays, R.D., Liu, H. and Kapteyn, A. (2015) 'Use of internet panels to conduct surveys', *Behavior Research Methods*, 47(3): 685–90.

Henn, M. and Foard, N. (2014) 'Social differentiation in young people's political participation: the impact of social and educational factors on youth political engagement in Britain', *Journal of Youth Studies*, 17(3): 360–80.

Hox, J.J. (2002) *Multilevel Analysis: Techniques and Applications*, Mahwah, NJ: Lawrence Erlbaum Associates.

Kennelly, J. (2011) 'Policing young people as citizens-in-waiting: legitimacy, spatiality and governance', *The British Journal of Criminology*, 51(2): 336–54.

Lalonde, R.N. and Cameron, J.E. (1994) 'Behavioral responses to discrimination: a focus on action', in M.P. Zanna and J.M. Olson (eds) *The Psychology of Prejudice: The Ontario symposium, Volume 7*, Mahwah, NJ: Lawrence Erlbaum Associates, pp 257–88.

Link, B.G. and Phelan, J.C. (2001) 'Conceptualizing stigma', *Annual Review of Sociology*, 27(1): 363–85.

Lister, R. (2004) 'A politics of recognition and respect: Involving people with experience of poverty in decision-making that affects their lives', in *The Politics of Inclusion and Empowerment*, London: Palgrave Macmillan, pp 116–38.

Lister, R. (2007) 'Inclusive citizenship: realizing the potential', *Citizenship Studies*, 11(1): 49–61.

Lister, R. (2015) '"To count for nothing": poverty beyond the statistics', *Journal of the British Academy*, 3: 139–65.

Magidson, J. and Vermunt, J.K. (2004) 'Latent class models', in D. Kaplan (ed) *The Sage Handbook of Quantitative Methodology for the Social Sciences*, London: Sage Publications, pp 175–98.

Markovic, D. and Evrard, G. (2014) *EVS Competences for Employability: Project Narrative Report, November 2012 – August 2014*, EVS Competences for Employability Project.

Marsh, D., O'Toole, T. and Jones, S. (2007) 'The study of political participation', in D. Marsh, T. O'Toole and S. Jones (eds) *Young People and Politics in the UK: Apathy or Alienation*, London: Palgrave Macmillan, pp 9–30. Available from: http://link.springer.com/ 10.1057/9780230625631_2 [Accessed 16 June 2016].

McAra, L. and McVie, S. (2005) 'The usual suspects? Street-life, young people and the police', *Criminal Justice*, 5(1): 5–36.

Munford, R. and Sanders, J. (2015) 'Young people's search for agency: making sense of their experiences and taking control', *Qualitative Social Work*, 14(5): 616–33. Available from: http://journals. sagepub.com/doi/pdf/10.1177/1473325014565149 [Accessed 23 May 2018].

PROMISE (2018) *Collated Case-Study Reports*, PROMISE, [online]. Available from: www.PROMISE.manchester.ac.uk/wp-content/ uploads/2019/03/Collated-case-studies-public-website-Feb-2019. pdf

PROMISE (2019a) *Report on Value Gaps*, PROMISE, [online]. Available from: www.promise.manchester.ac.uk/wp-content/uploads/2019/02/Report-on-Value-Gaps-revised-Feb-2019-2.pdf

PROMISE (2019b) *Barriers and Enablers of Social Participation of Young People*, PROMISE, [online]. Available from: www.promise. manchester.ac.uk/wp-content/uploads/2019/09/promise-barriers-and-enablers-of-social-participation-of-young-people-2019.pdf

Putnam, R. (1993) 'The prosperous community: social capital and public life', *The American Prospect*, 13(4): 35–42.

Raffo, C. and Reeves, M. (2000) 'Youth transitions and social exclusion: developments in social capital theory', *Journal of Youth Studies*, 3(2): 147–66.

Schneider, C.Q. and Makszin, K. (2014) 'Forms of welfare capitalism and education-based participatory inequality', *Socio-Economic Review*, 12(2): 437–62.

Snijders, T.A. and Bosker, R.J. (1999) *Multilevel Analysis: An Introduction to Basic and Advanced Multilevel Modeling*, London: Sage Publications.

Stolle, D., Hooghe, M. and Micheletti, M. (2005) 'Politics in the supermarket: political consumerism as a form of political participation', *International Political Science Review*, 26(3): 245–69.

Talò, C. (2018) 'Community-based determinants of community engagement: a meta-analysis research', *Social Indicators Research*, 140(2): 571–96.

Townsend, P. (1979) *Poverty in the United Kingdom*, London: Allen Lane and Penguin.

Verba, S., Schlozman, K.L. and Brady, H.E. (1995) *Voice and Equality: Civic Voluntarism in American Politics*, Cambridge, MA: Harvard University Press.

Vermunt, J.K. and Magidson, J. (2016) *Upgrade Manual for Latent GOLD 5.1*, Belmont, MA: Statistical Innovations Inc.

Vromen, A. (2003) '"People try to put us down …": participatory citizenship of "Generation X"', *Australian Journal of Political Science*, 38(1): 79–99.

Vromen, A. and Collin, P. (2010) 'Everyday youth participation? Contrasting views from Australian policymakers and young people', *YOUNG*, 18(1): 97–112.

Walker, R. (2014) *The Shame of Poverty*, Oxford: Oxford University Press.

6

From ideology
to strategic engagement

Jonas Lieberkind

Based on a secondary analysis of the International Civic and Citizenship Education Study (ICCS) – a comparative, quantitative study involving grade 8 students in 24 countries – and a qualitative study of more than 50 Danish grade 9 students, this chapter explores young people's attitudes toward political engagement and participation. The chapter aims to study drivers for and barriers to civic engagement, but also to challenge conventional understandings of political participation. Many studies have shown that inequality has a significant impact on young people's political participation. However, this chapter argues that young people's engagement is a consequence of current discourses of post-politics rather than conventional ideological conflicts, distribution of material goods and values, and societal inequalities. The thesis in this chapter is that young people's engagement in society is changing from ideological engagement to strategic engagement.

Key findings

- Young people's engagement in democracy is increasing.
- Young people have a conventional rather than an unconventional attitude to society.
- Young people's political engagement is changing from ideological to strategic engagement.
- The future generation is beyond left-wing and right-wing ideologies.
- Today we see new forms of inequality with respect to political participation.

Introduction

This chapter explores and discusses young people's attitudes toward political engagement and participation. It studies new and changing forms of political engagement and aims to challenge what can be defined as conventional understandings of youth, inequality and political participation.

The ICCS reveals that, in terms of knowledge, interest and engagement, the level of young people's engagement in society is increasing, but it also shows that the form of their commitment is changing (Schulz et al, 2018a). These findings are particularly significant in Denmark (Bruun et al, 2018; Schulz et al, 2018a) and, therefore, this chapter focuses on Danish youth and aspects of their political education. In this context, Danish students and the Danish educational system are not unique but exemplary. By investigating Danish students, it becomes possible to examine new and particular features of young people's political engagement more generally. The ICCS shows that significant tendencies among Danish young people are indicative of a general and prevailing trend occurring across Europe.

In order to understand young people's current political engagement as well as how the form and content of their engagement are changing, this chapter compares the attitudes of young people today with the counter-cultural commitment and rebellion of young people in the 1960s and '70s. The chapter draws on theoretical, historical and empirical studies to sketch some of the crucial aspects of the youth of the 1960s and '70s. The comparison between the youth of today and those of the 1960s and '70s makes it possible to focus and expand on an arguably exemplary characteristic of the political participation of the youth today.

The point of departure in this chapter is that, in the 1960s and '70s, young people's political engagement and ideological beliefs were generally based on an ambition to transcend conventional structures and power relations in order to foster a 'counter-culture' (Wallerstein and Zukin, 1989) and a break with the conventional system (Daniels, 1989). The data used in this chapter indicate that young people no longer exhibit such a rebellious and counter-cultural attitude. The main thesis is that young people's engagement is changing from ideological to strategic engagement. What is meant by these concepts and how this change is manifesting itself among young people is explored and discussed throughout the chapter.

Ideological engagement

In the 1960s and '70s, young people across Western Europe and around the world began to protest against existing societal conditions. New ways of living and political ideas motivated them. Theirs was not simply a rebellion against the dominant class, exploitation and the distribution of material goods and values (on which the increasingly organised labour strikes of the latter part of the 19th century and onwards were based (Mikkelsen, 1986, p 6; Wallerstein and Zukin, 1989)) nor was it simply a continuation of the spirit of the Civil Rights Movement of the mid-1950s (Harrison, 1992, p 29). Instead, it was primarily a youth rebellion that could be defined as young people breaking with a previous system and generations. It was a struggle against traditional forms of authority, family structures, the authoritarian teacher, the capitalist economy and Western imperialism. This struggle was typically reflected in the large demonstrations against the Vietnam War and nuclear weapons, political action for the environment, unconventional art and the many alternative 'happenings' (Daniels, 1989; Wallerstein and Zukin, 1989; Horn, 2008). For the first time, the young generation became a political force in society (Grasso, 2014).

The youth movements were motivated by profound criticism of contemporary socialisation and the ideology that legitimised people's acceptance of Western capitalism (Schmidt, 1978). The older generations naturalised a conventional culture through their lifestyle, gender roles and over-consumption. Consequently, the conventional culture and system had to be transformed by new lifestyles, protests and unconventional political activities (Inglehart, 1997; Putnam, 2001; Nielsen, 2015). Based on the idea that capitalist ideology could be replaced by new and alternative ideas, young people necessarily embraced political activity.

Young people of the 1960s and '70s maintained that they had political choices, and many of them claimed that they struggled to choose between different ideological directions. Most of the young people, even those who were not politically active, grounded their values and attitudes to society in one of the many left-wing ideologies (Inglehart, 1971; Nielsen, 2015, p 19) or what has been described as 'the new left' (Horn, 2008). Their political choices were not based on single concerns or issues, such as climate change, global economics, humanitarianism or gender (even though these issues were crucial). The large majority of young people were oriented to the political left and they all seemed to agree that large parts of, or even the whole of, the conventional system – from education and housing policy, to the environment and the economy, to warfare and the distribution of symbolic capital – should be revitalised. As the historian Robert Vincent Daniels concludes: 'They were, more than ever before in history, generational revolutions of youth' (Daniels, 1989, p 10).

In short, their political engagement was bolstered by their belief in alternative social orders.

During the same period, the intellectual world was characterised by the thesis of *The End of Ideology* (Bell, 1988), or 'the end of the grand narratives' (Lyotard, 1987). It was no longer as simple as it had been to maintain the notion of a coherent set of political ideas (Daniels, 1989; Jost, 2006). In particular, during the 1950s, '60s and '70s, the ideologies were challenged by the expansion of educational systems, technological advances, the baby boom following the Second World War, and the improved economic situation. Young people dissociated themselves from 'the old left' (Horn, 2008), the labour movements and particularly from the worker as the privileged subject of the revolution and the future. The young people, even the intellectual neo-Marxists, found it increasingly difficult to relate to the workers' values and ways of living (Inglehart, 1971). They believed in a more profound and privileged subject position, but this subject position was not the conventional left-wing worker: '1968 was the ideological tomb of the concept of the "leading role" of the industrial proletariat' (Wallerstein and Zukin, 1989, p 437).

Ronald Inglehart (1971) argues that a consequence of the period of post-war prosperity in the Western world was that the political focus on material values and economic uncertainty was replaced by 'a set of "post-bourgeois" values' (Inglehart, 1971, p 991). In this way, the counter-cultural youth transformed the ideological struggle against material inequalities and capitalism into a counter-cultural revolt based on post-material values. This generational perspective and, consequently, the emergence of a new generation of what Inglehart calls 'post-bourgeois' leftists, emphasises how young people addressed new types of political issues in alternative ways throughout the 1960s and '70s, issues that the conventional system – from the Social Democratic Party (worker) to the right-wing parties (bourgeois) – was unable to address or even articulate. In fact, there was a clear link between the young people's alternative political values, the rise of new social movements, and the countless number of unconventional activities. The young people's political engagement began to develop into new forms of ideological narratives based on post-material values and a new kind of privileged subject position that reflected the notion of a more authentic human being that transcends artificial living and the conventional system. For this generation, ideological engagement was associated with involvement and unconventional participation, as their values and attitudes were barely represented by the politicians and the established democratic system (Daniels, 1989; Inglehart, 1997; Levinsen, 2003; Horn, 2008; Grasso, 2014).

Towards new forms of political engagement

This section analyses and discusses young people's political engagement today and how this engagement has changed since the proud days of youth rebellion in the 1960s and '70s. The analysis draws on two empirical studies of grade 8 and 9 students (14–16-year-olds) in lower secondary school:

- The ICCS 2016 (and 2009). ICCS is a comparative international study of grade 8 students' knowledge, attitudes to society, and the ways in which they are prepared to undertake their roles as citizens in a democracy (Bruun et al, 2018; ICCS, 2018; Schulz et al, 2018a). In 2016, the ICCS gathered data from over 94,000 students in 24 countries.
- A qualitative study of 51 grade 9 students' political education and engagement. The interviews were carried out in 2017, and the students who participated were part of the sample from ICCS 2016.

One year after ICCS 2016 was completed, 51 Danish students were interviewed in order to gain a deeper insight into their individual motives, drivers and barriers related to political engagement. The interviews were based on a semi-structured model so that it was possible to explore the students' new and altered understanding of engagement while also ensuring comparability across students and schools. Furthermore, the model ensured that the interviews systematically covered the process of subjectification, that is, the process through which one becomes a political subject and politically engaged (Butler, 1997; Rancière, 1999; Biesta, 2011). The 51 students were recruited from ten private and state schools across various types of residential locations (for example, urban, rural, expensive residential and high-density housing areas) in the eastern part of Denmark (Zealand) and, furthermore, from different student types within residential locations (academically strong, academically weak, socially strong and socially weak). Based on a post-structuralist approach, the qualitative research was designed to focus on how students articulated themselves in relation to societal engagement, and, furthermore, how they established storylines and subject positions throughout the processes of subjectification (Søndergaard, 2002; Corbin and Morse, 2003; Butler, 2005; Davies, 2006).

The principle of free and informed consent has been at the core of these studies. Although the test, questionnaire and interviews do not intend to touch on sensitive topics, the focus on personal development, biography and political attitudes may inadvertently result in ethical challenges. To address such issues, the recruitment, test situation, interview guide, interview situation and use of data were meticulously planned and potential ethical challenges considered from the preliminary to the final phase.

In the interviews, it soon became clear that the students were not generally critical of the previous generations, the political system or the ideology of their time. Such issues gave rise to important political questions that the students believed should be handled differently, since the students sometimes experienced what they considered unreasonable demands made by the system. But, in general, the students had no objection to the system. Throughout the interviews, the Danish grade 9 students revealed that they had no alternative set of values or counter-cultural expectations. In this respect, there is a striking contrast between the youth of the 1960s and '70s and their children and grandchildren born between 1995 and 2002 (the target group).

Behind the scenes of the media coverage of environmental activist Greta Thunberg, the climate strikes and the rising interest in global warming, young people today seem to be cautious and reserved politically. As demonstrated in this chapter, Danish youth of today do not face ideological choices in the same way as the youth of the 1960s and '70s did; instead, they seem to devote themselves to navigating wisely in a complex society and coordinating their life within existing structures. In the interviews, the students appear to be strategic citizens rather than ideological activists.

In this context, the term 'strategic' must be understood as an analytical concept that captures the interviewed students' different articulations of how they navigate *within the system* and sometimes even stretch the limits of the system itself. Unlike the ideological activist, the strategic citizen essentially accepts the system as it is. This term is based on empirical findings and is elaborated further in the following analysis. Through this conceptualisation, it becomes possible to analyse and understand young people's changing political engagement. With reference to Max Weber's concept of the 'ideal type' (Weber, 1988, p 190), this chapter describes a shift from ideological to strategic engagement, and, in this way, outlines some of the key ways in which young people participate politically today.

Knowledge, deliberation and involvement

The first and perhaps most interesting result of the ICCS is that there is a clear trend among most of the students in all countries to show an increased interest in, and engagement with, social, political, and democratic issues. This trend becomes significant when the results from ICCS 2009 and 2016 are compared. In Denmark, the students follow this same trend. Nevertheless, the Danish students differ significantly in some specific areas. The chapter concentrates on these areas.

One of these areas is the ICCS cognitive test, which measures the grade 8 students' knowledge of economic, social, political and democratic issues as well as their ability to analyse, understand and explain critical perspectives in this context. The 2016 test consists of 87 items, which include multiple-choice and constructed-response items; the results are reported as scale scores. The final scales have a mean of 500 and a standard deviation of 100; the scales are based on the Rach model (Schulz et al, 2018a, 2018b). In 2009 and 2016, the Danish students were among the best-performing students.

The ICCS test reveals that Danish students have extensive political knowledge and the ability to consider complicated societal scenarios critically. It also suggests that they have a distinct capacity to reflect strategically (see Table 6.1).

Another part of the ICCS focuses on the students' perceptions of and attitudes towards school and political issues. This part is based on questionnaires that measure the students' self-efficacy, values and engagement. To facilitate comparison, each country's results are reported as scale scores. Each scale is set to a metric with a mean of 50 and a standard deviation of 10 for the equally weighted national samples. Two of these instruments reveal some remarkable findings: the students are asked to what extent they deliberate political and social issues with parents and friends, and to what extent they think their classroom environment is open to and stimulates debate. On both instruments, the Danish students achieve the highest scores in the international comparison.

In contrast to the three areas of knowledge, deliberation and classroom environment, the average score of the Danish students drops dramatically when they are asked how much they identify with citizens who regard being involved in social-movement-related activities (such as peaceful protests and activities to promote human rights and protect the environment) as an important obligation; on this measure, they have the lowest scores in the study (Bruun et al, 2018; Schulz et al, 2018a).

Table 6.1: ICCS test, European average scores for civic knowledge

Country	Average scale score 2016	Average scale score 2009
Denmark	586	576
Sweden	579	537
Finland	577	576
Norway	564	538
Estonia	546	525
Russian Federation	545	506
Belgium (Flemish)	537	514
Slovenia	532	516
Croatia	531	–
Italy	524	531
Netherlands	523	–
Germany (Nordrhein–Westfalen)	519	–
Lithuania	518	505
Latvia	492	482
Malta	491	490
Bulgaria	485	466
ICCS average	**521**	**505**

Source: Schulz et al (2018a).

Although the Danish students are increasingly interested and engaged in social, political and democratic issues, it is remarkable to discover the discrepancy between their knowledge, willingness to deliberate and their perception of the classroom on the one hand and their attitudes to social-movement-related activities on the other hand.

Political trust and reflexivity

Before discussing the studies' findings, it is important to consider the notion of political trust, since an essential condition of political participation is the citizen's confidence and trust in other people, societal institutions and the future. In order to engage politically, one requires courage and a surplus of mental resources. In the international literature, these are often described as 'self-efficacy' and 'social trust'. In this context, these categories are kept broad in order to capture what is described as young people's political reflexivity. Reflexivity is a self-awareness of one's own actions and social positioning that affects your confidence in society (Giddens, 1992; Beck et al, 1994; Ziehe, 1995). The young people's political trust is not simply a matter of trust in institutions and self-efficacy (that is, their ability to generate an intended result) but also of the capacity to reflect on and orientate themselves in existing structures and to take an interest in and have confidence in the future. Hence, this chapter focuses on five elements: the students' interest in social and political issues; trust in government, parliament and the court of justice; trust in other people; sense of political self-efficacy; and perceptions of globalisation and the world's future (Bruun et al, 2018; Schulz et al, 2018a). The students' political trust and reflexivity become important in this context, because the concepts offer crucial insights into the young people's preconditions for entering into, committing to, participating in, and, hence, engaging with, the political community.

Figure 6.1 depicts the five elements in a pentagon. This pentagon is based on the percentage of students who responded positively to items in the instruments. The larger the area of the pentagon, the greater the students' political trust and reflexivity.

The pentagon very clearly shows that, compared with students from other European countries, the average scores of Danish students indicate abundant political trust and reflexivity.

Danish students are among the most interested in social and political issues. The pentagon also reveals that students generally have a great

Figure 6.1: Political trust and reflexivity

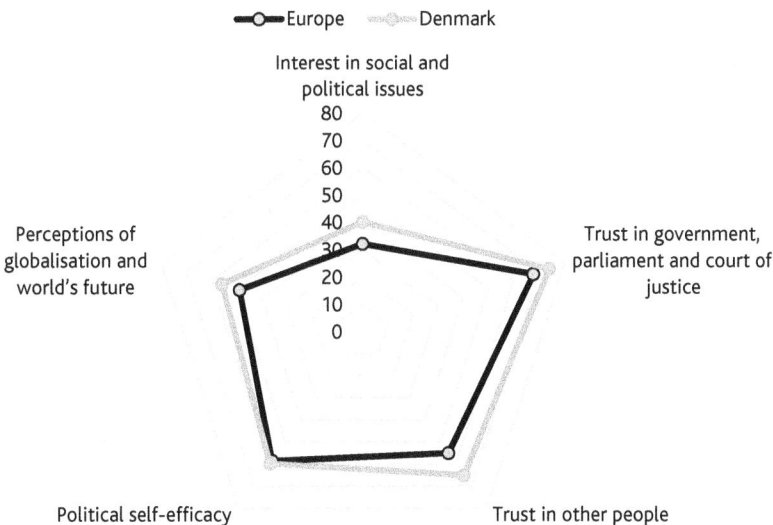

deal of trust in their democratic institutions. The Nordic countries, including Denmark, are among those with the largest percentages of students. Likewise, the Nordic countries and the Netherlands have the largest percentage of students with a positive perception of globalisation and the future of the world. The two lower corners of the pentagon in Figure 6.1 suggest that Danish students have slightly higher self-efficacy than the average European student, and, in general, a remarkably high degree of trust in other people.

The pentagon portrays a generation with some unique preconditions for being and forming themselves as politically involved and active citizens. Compared with other European students who participated in the ICCS, the Danish students demonstrate a high level of self-confidence with regard to their political reflexivity and ability to produce an intended political result, to take an interest in social and political issues, and to reflect on and orientate themselves in a local, national and global world. However, it is difficult to identify general issues that irritate or challenge the Danish students or that motivate them to call for political alternatives or engage in activate participation. Their relatively trusting and unconcerned attitudes towards the leading institutions and the future contrasts with the rebellious and counter-cultural attitudes of the youth in the 1960s and '70s.

Conventional and unconventional political participation

International research distinguishes between different types of political participation (Whiteley, 2012; Lindekilde and Olesen, 2015, p 29). The most common distinction is between conventional and unconventional participation (Ekman and Amnå, 2012; Pachi and Barrett, 2012; Husted, 2015).

Conventional political participation is directed at the formalised democratic system. Voting is the exemplary form of conventional participation. Such participation also involves keeping up with the news, joining a political party or standing for election, seeking information about and supporting a candidate, showing respect for authorities and respecting the rights of others to have their own opinions. A classic description of conventional political participation is:

> By political participation we refer to those legal acts by private citizens that are more or less directly aimed at influencing the selection of governmental personnel and/or the actions that they take .... participation that

involves attempts (successful or otherwise) to influence the government. (Verba et al, 1978, p 1)

Hence, conventional participation is associated with the notion that political change is best achieved through patient political work in which individual participation is indirect. It also requires the participant, at least to a certain extent, to support and accept the prevailing political logic and the conventional system.

Unconventional forms of political participation are based on social movements and initiatives in civil society. Here, the ambition is not to be a part of the formalised and conventional processes but to act promptly and without adherence to formalities. Such participation encompasses a range of activities such as fundraising, volunteering, protesting, supporting vulnerable groups, organising groups for or against a given cause, struggling for a single issue, and engaging in political consumerism (Barnes, 1979; Pitti, 2018). The strong commitment of those who engage in this form of participation is based on the claim that direct and active participation is key for political change. In the literature, the social movements of the 1960s and '70s are often associated with unconventional activities (Inglehart, 1997; Putnam, 2001; Grasso, 2014; Nielsen, 2015).

ICCS 2016 investigates the students' conventional and unconventional political activities on the basis of 49 items. The items are divided into five subgroups of conventional and unconventional activities respectively (see Table 6.2).

Figure 6.2 displays the average percentages of responses in Denmark and ICCS for these items, distributed between five subgroups of conventional participation (ICCS, 2018).

Danish students' attitudes towards these two forms of participation clearly demonstrate that they primarily identify with conventional political participation. However, the students do not identify equally with all elements of conventional participation. Once the participation relates to aspects that are more active and involve a more public appearance (joining a political party, individual action), the Danish students in particular become reserved (also compared with ICCS average).

There is a radical difference in the students' attitudes when their perception of unconventional political participation is measured. The Danish results are remarkably low. For about one third of all 28 items concerning unconventional participation, the Danish students have the lowest average percentages of all participating countries.

Table 6.2: ICCS items, conventional and unconventional political participation

Conventional political participation (see Figure 6.2)	Unconventional political participation (see Figure 6.3)
Voting (parliamentary elections, municipal elections, European Union parliamentary elections, student council elections)	Participation at school (promoting a political/social/environmental cause, writing articles or on websites)
Respecting authorities and other citizens (the authorities, the law, other people)	Participation in society (political associations, voluntary groups or organisations regarding environment, human rights, specific causes, charities, animal welfare, fundraising)
Seeking knowledge and information (in newspapers, radio and TV, on the internet, about nominated candidates)	Expected participation (peaceful demonstrations, social media, political consumption, petitions)
Joining a political party (and a trade union)	Identification with the good adult citizen (peaceful protests, for groups in society, human rights, the environment and nature, make a personal effort)
Individual action (stand for student councils and municipal elections, in a youth political association, contact and help a politician/party)	Expected illegal activities (graffiti, demonstrate and block traffic, occupy public buildings)

Figure 6.2: Conventional and unconventional political participation

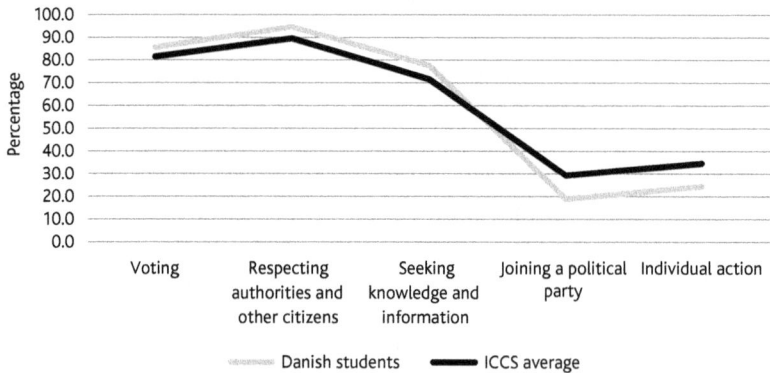

Figure 6.3 compares the percentages of Danish students and ICCS averages for five subgroups (ICCS, 2018). Comparing the average percentages for all 28 issues, there are approximately 10% fewer Danish students than students internationally who consider these forms of participation important. The vast majority of students find it extremely difficult to recognise the value of illegal political activities.

Figure 6.3: Unconventional political participation

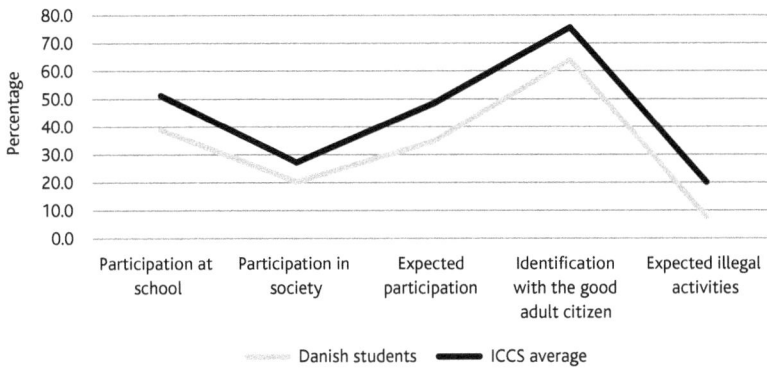

The next section discusses these remarkable findings based on an analytical and comparative framing of young people of the 1960s and '70s. It also considers the insights of the qualitative study to better understand the individual motives, drivers and barriers that form and encourage the Danish students' attitude towards political engagement.

The reserved and strategic citizen

Unlike the young people of the 1960s and '70s, for whom the conventional political system was the problem rather than the solution, the contemporary generation seems pragmatic and much more aligned with the system. As we have seen, they have great confidence in the political system, the authorities and the law, and they envisage a bright future within the structure of the current society.

An instrument in ICCS that investigates students' identification with conventional citizens supports the conclusion that the vast majority of students in all countries are becoming increasingly conventional. In Denmark, this trend is among the largest (Schulz et al, 2018a). This shows that students are embracing conventional democratic values and gradually feeling more committed to supporting democratic institutions and processes. Again, Danish students' support for unconventional political activities, and even for conventional processes that call for their active and public participation, is remarkably low. This precise combination of their attention to social and political issues and their ability to understand and orientate themselves in the existing structures demonstrates a reflective and contemplative, but also reserved, political temperament.

In summary, Danish students are politically involved with regard to knowing about, having an interest in, deliberating on and supporting the formalised and conventional system. They are thus *active* insofar as one considers this engagement the students' active choice and involvement (from knowledge, interest and deliberation to respecting others, voting and obeying the law). At the same time, they appear contemplative and *passive* compared with students in other countries, particularly with regard to direct, active and unconventional political participation (such as social-movement-related activities, including participating in peaceful protests and activities that promote human rights and protect the environment). It is due to this duality – active/ passive – that this chapter describes the Danish students' political engagement as 'reserved'.

In the interviews, there were several examples of this remarkable combination of engagement and an inactive attitude. A female student from a private school engaged in music and politics describes her political participation: "I try to engage in discussions, but I do nothing [political] directly."

Another female student from an expensive residential area, who is very interested in social science, answers to the same question on being politically active: "I don't think ... I think I rather would be a bystander to be completely honest." A male student explains why he will not take a political stand: "I don't feel I'm ready. Because I think, I want to live like this ... I will collect knowledge so I can commit myself the right way." Throughout the interviews, the students did not draw on a particular set of political interests (right- or left-wing) or express a general criticism of the previous generations, the political system, or current ideologies: "I want to live like this." A politically self-confident female student from the private school began to have doubts when asked if she knew which party she would vote for:

> 'So if I say I would vote left wing, and then suddenly the right wings comes up with a proposal that I really think is pretty cool, and the left wings are against. Then it would be hard to choose a side.'

When pushed to say something critical, many students spontaneously revealed their satisfaction with the Danish system by saying: "We live in Denmark!" However, it was remarkable that they did not appear politically indifferent or unengaged; on the contrary, they seemed extremely interested and highly articulate, and they reflected on their own position and opportunities as well as the positions of their friends, school, and community stakeholders in society. They hardly ever translated their arguments, reflections or even criticism into alternative political visions or expressed a counter-culture attitude. Instead, their discourse was often supportive, pragmatic and aligned with what a female student from a wealthy residential area called the "mainstream" culture. This student described herself as a person who read many of the national newspapers on the internet, which is definitely not mainstream. Another female student from a rural area claims: "Also because I think that Denmark is a mega-good society and stuff like that, so there is nothing that I believe, okay, this we must change."

The Danish students did not express critical ideas of a manipulative system that prevents them from acting freely. It was impossible to capture something that might remind them of the notion of a privileged or more authentic subject position from which society could be analysed and that they might strive to realise.[1] On the contrary, they repeatedly demonstrated that there are many subject positions, even for themselves, and many acceptable sets of values – values that combine, and even go beyond, the right and left. The general attitude among young people today, and perhaps their most crucial political value (which the ICCS also reveals), is that it is important to respect others' rights to their opinions.

The interviews show that education, formation and the realisation of their individual capacities are among Danish students' greatest concerns. These students occasionally found it difficult to navigate their own development and between accessible (though, for many, inaccessible) opportunities and subject positions: the high-performing school student or the dropout, the cool kid or the good friend, or the stable or the rebellious child. Yet, although they find this navigation challenging and perhaps even stressful, they all seem aware that such navigation is their responsibility and that this responsibility calls for strategic engagement rather than an ideological struggle. A female student from an average residential area was finding it difficult to decide who she wants to be. Throughout her subjectification, she changes her mind:

Student:	'I had a period of two years in which I photo-shopped all my pictures on Facebook, because I didn't dare to post anything that did not look perfect. And then I realised, that's not me. So who the hell am I looking at?'
Interviewer:	'Okay, so you realised that you were constructing a person?'
Student:	'Yes, yes, a new person that I would like to be.'

The students' concerns were related to questions of how to navigate, organise and coordinate their lives, and, importantly to them, questions about personal and social development in a complex society that requires a lot of them but of which they also have high expectations.

Danish students' strategic engagement becomes even more evident in their strong willingness and need to deliberate and talk to their friends, parents and even teachers. In particular, their parents and teachers play a new and different role in their many conversations on life, becoming subjects, and political issues. The students often describe parents and teachers as friends or as legitimate stakeholders, and, when they conflict with them, they have no difficulty understanding the older generations' interest and strategic assumptions. For them, deliberation is a strategic exercise and not a motivation for political interaction. A male student outlines the focus he has on how to talk and how he translates this focus into strategic consideration:

> 'They are different ages, you know, but it teaches you to handle how you talk differently to people of any age. Um, because they are different people, you have to navigate like this, in a social network of people, you know … I don't know if I'm the only one analysing these kinds of ways people talk and how to talk to them. But at least I have always, always noticed.'

He was definitely not the only student in the interviews who analysed other people's behaviour.

Strategic participation, post-politics and inequality

The Danish students' political beliefs seem to point in a post-political direction, whereby the aim is no longer to choose among conflicting sets of political ideas and to struggle to transcend the structures of society (Mouffe, 2005). The students do not see anything wrong with their parents, their teachers or the system; it is as though they have no alternative perspectives on the roles of the conventional authorities, the capitalist economy, Western values, or modern liberal democracy. They seem to view institutions as unquestionable and necessary. They believe that there are errors made by politicians and the civil service to correct – for example, with regard to climate change and meeting the aims of the 2015 Paris Agreement to reduce carbon emissions – but they do not see this process as a political choice or a struggle between different ideologies. These young people have moved far beyond 'left' and 'right' ideologies, as already noted by Anthony Giddens (1994).

Danish students' political beliefs are associated with necessary calculations, scientific evidence, knowledge and strategic choices. Single concerns, such as climate change, particular humanitarian issues, and ethical challenges characterise their political attention. These very distinct issues are often defined as abstract and distant from themselves, which is perhaps why, for Danish students, they appear as unquestionable and necessary rather than as a choice between different political beliefs. There is therefore no coherent set of political ideas or an ideology worth fighting for. In contrast, their engagement is characterised by more or less systematic planning, tactics, and the desire to navigate wisely in a complex society. The good life is based on a good strategy rather than on counter-culture and a good ideology. Although they work hard within the system or stretch the limits of the system to find a path for themselves, their friends, their families, and the local and global community, they essentially accept the system as it is.

In conclusion, for the young generation today, political participation is related to strategic engagement. A wise strategy makes it possible to establish and create a good life for oneself and others within the contemporary culture and system.

Those who devise unwise strategies, for whom navigation and coordination are complicated, will become the (new) unsuccessful. Hence, there are groups of young people who engage in ideological struggles and groups that are excluded from political engagement. The capacity to develop one's own personal strategy and a type of common, socially strategic engagement is becoming a parameter of the future generation's inequality. In the interviews, there were many students who did not possess the strategic ability across the social/geographical distribution. This transverse or socially diagonal division of inequality in strategic ability and engagement challenges the conventional sociological categories used in analysing young people's political participation.

In light of Max Weber's notion of the ideal type (Weber, 1988) – yet in full knowledge that, from a nuanced sociological perspective, his idea may seem somewhat general – this chapter concludes that, today, we are witnessing a new political attitude based on strategic participation. The most important findings of this chapter are outlined in Table 6.3.

Table 6.3: An outline of empirical findings

	Ideological participation	Strategic participation
Goal	Realisation of a collective programme based on a (new) set of coherent ideas and beliefs	Realisation of a wise strategy, so that living a good life becomes achievable for oneself and others locally and even globally
Challenge	The traditional structures, the conventional system, the wrong ideology, and alienation	The complex society, countless opportunities and single issues
Solution	The political choice	Rational decisions, evidence-based
Method	To identify alternative lifestyles and engage in protests in order to transcend existing structures	To navigate, organise and coordinate a life within the existing structures
Participation	Direct, reaction and unconventional political participation	Indirect, reserved action and conventional political participation
Youth	Opposition and new lifestyles – mistrust and action	Education, skills and individual development – trust and reflexivity
Inequality	Alienated and subject to material and post-material constraints and deprivation	Lack of ability to develop one's own personal strategy and share a common strategy
Political subject	A privileged and more authentic subject	Many subject positions

Note

[1] Based on the early left-wing and Marxian notion of the working class as the subject of the revolution, the rebellious young people in the 1960s and 70s developed new forms of ideological narratives based on post-material values and a new kind of privileged subject position that reflected a more authentic human being that transcended artificial living and the conventional system. Although they abandoned the working class as the privileged subject, they retained the notion of a more authentic and privileged subject, which they were to realize through their rebellion against the system. These notions of a more authentic or privileged subject position, which transcends the system and the current social order, were absent among the Danish students. On the contrary, they were realistic, accepting, and pragmatic in their reflections on themselves and the system.

References

Barnes, S.H. (1979) *Political Action: Mass Participation in Five Western Democracies*, Beverly Hills, CA: Sage Publications.

Beck, U., Giddens, A. and Lash, S. (eds) (1994) *Reflexive Modernization: Politics, Tradition and Aesthetics in the Modern Social Order*, Cambridge: Polity Press.

Bell, D. (1988) *The End of Ideology: On the Exhaustion of Political Ideas in the Fifties*, Cambridge, MA: Harvard University Press.

Biesta, G. (2011) *Learning Democracy in School and Society: Education, Lifelong Learning, and the Politics of Citizenship*, Rotterdam: Sense Publishers.

Bruun, J., Lieberkind, J. and Schunck, H.B. (2018) *Unge, Skole og Demokrati* [Youth, School and Democracy], Aarhus: Aarhus Universitetsforlag.

Butler, J. (1997) *The Psychic Life of Power: Theories in Subjection*, Stanford, CA: Stanford University Press.

Butler, J. (2005) *Giving an Account of Oneself*, New York, NY: Fordham University Press.

Corbin, J. and Morse, J.M. (2003) 'The unstructured interactive interview: issues of reciprocity and risks when dealing with sensitive topics', *Qualitative Inquiry*, 9(3): 335–54.

Daniels, R.V. (1989) *Year of the Heroic Guerrilla: World Revolution and Counterrevolution in 1968*, Cambridge, MA: Harvard University Press.

Davies, B. (2006) 'Subjectification: the relevance of Butler's analysis for education', *British Journal of Sociology of Education*, 27(4): 425–38.

Ekman, J. and Amnå, E. (2012) 'Political participation and civic engagement: towards a new typology', *Human Affairs*, 22(3): 283–300.

Giddens, A. (1992) *Modernity and Self-Identity: Self and Society in the Late Modern Age*, Cambridge: Polity Press.

Giddens, A. (1994) *Beyond Left and Right: The Future of Radical Politics*, Cambridge: Polity Press.

Grasso, M.T. (2014) 'Age, period and cohort analysis in a comparative context: political generations and political participation repertoires in Western Europe', *Electoral Studies*, 33: 63–76.

Harrison, B.T. (1992) 'Roots of the American protest of the 60's', *Peace Research*, 24(3): 19–31.

Horn, G.-R. (2008) *The Spirit of '68 rebellion in Western Europe and North America, 1956–1976*, Oxford: Oxford University Press.

Husted, E. (2015) 'Organiseringen af alternativ politisk deltagelse: udkast til en typologi' [The organization of alternative political participation: a draft to a typology], *Politik*, 18(2): 13–23.

ICCS (2018) 'International Civic and Citizenship Education Study 2016', International Association for the Evaluation of Educational Achievement, [online]. Available from: www.iea.nl/data-tools/repository/iccs

Inglehart, R. (1971) 'The silent revolution in Europe: intergenerational change in post-industrial societies', *The American Political Science Review*, 65(4): 991–1017.

Inglehart, R. (1997) *Modernization and Postmodernization: Cultural, Economic, and Political Change in 43 Societies*, Princeton, NJ: Princeton University Press.

Jost, J.T. (2006) 'The end of the end of ideology', *American Psychologist*, 61(7): 651–70.

Levinsen, K. (2003) *Unges Politiske Værdier – i et Generationsperspektiv* [Political Values of Young People - in a Generational Perspective], Odense: Syddansk Universitetsforlag.

Lindekilde, L. and Olesen, T. (2015) *Politisk Protest, Aktivisme og Sociale Bevægelser* [Political Protest, Activism and Social Movements], Copenhagen: Hans Reitzel.

Lyotard, J.-F. (1987) *The Postmodern Condition: A Report on Knowledge*, Manchester: Manchester University Press.

Mikkelsen, F. (1986) 'Indledning' [Introduction], in F. Mikkelsen (ed) *Protest og Oprør: Kollektive Aktioner i Danmark 1700–1985* [Protest and Rebellion: Collective Actions in Denmark 1700–1985], Aarhus: Modtryk, pp 3–8.

Mouffe, C. (2005*) On the Political*, Abingdon: Routledge.

Nielsen, K.H. (2015) *Elevoprør og Studenteroprør i Danmark: Protestaktiviteter Blandt Lærlinge, Elever og Studerende 1960–2014* [Student Uprising in Denmark: Protest Activities among Apprentices, Pupils and Students 1960–2014], Copenhagen: KULT.

Pachi, D. and Barrett, M. (2012) 'Perceived effectiveness of conventional, non-conventional and civic forms of participation among minority and majority youth', *Postdisciplinary Humanities and Social Sciences Quarterly*, 22(3): 345–59.

Pitti, I. (2018) *Youth and Unconventional Political Engagement*, Cham: Springer.

Putnam, D.R. (2001) *Bowling Alone: The Collapse and Revival of American Community*, London: Simon & Schuster.

Rancière, J. (1999) *Disagreement: Politics and Philosophy*, Minneapolis, MN: University of Minnesota Press.

Schmidt, L.-H. (1978) *Socialisationskritik og Politisk Praksis: Indførende Eksperimenter* [Critique of Socialization and Political Practice: Introductory Experiments], Copenhagen: Rhodos.

Schulz, W., Ainley, J., Fraillon, J., Losito, B., Agrusti, G. and Friedman, T. (2018a) *Becoming Citizens in a Changing World: IEA International Civic and Citizenship Education Study 2016 International Report*, Amsterdam: Springer.

Schulz, W., Carstens, R., Losito, B. and Fraillon, J. (2018b) *ICCS 2016 Technical Report*, Amsterdam: International Association for the Evaluation of Educational Achievement.

Søndergaard, D.M. (2002) 'Poststructuralist approaches to empirical analysis', *International Journal of Qualitative Studies in Education*, 15(2): 187–204.

Verba, S., Nie, N.H. and Kim, J.-O. (1978) *Participation and Political Equality: A Seven-Nation Comparison*, Cambridge: Cambridge University Press.

Wallerstein, I. and Zukin, S. (1989) '1968, revolution in the world-system: theses and queries', *Theory and Society*, 18(4): 431–49.

Weber, M. (1988) 'Die "Objektivität" socialwissenschaftlicher und sozialpolitischer Erkenntnis', in M. Weber (ed) *Gesammelte Aufsätze zur Wissenschaftslehre*, Tybingen: Mohr, pp 146–214.

Whiteley, P. (2012) *Political Participation in Britain: The Decline and Revival of Civic Culture*, New York, NY: Palgrave Macmillan.

Ziehe, T. (1995) *Ambivalenser og Mangfoldighed: En Artikelsamling om Ungdom, Skole, Œstetik og Kultur*, Copenhagen: Politisk Revy.

7

Digital participation and digital divides in a former socialist country

Airi-Alina Allaste and David Cairns

This chapter discusses the issue of youth digital participation. Social media in particular is thought to be able to open up new means of being political, albeit with strong criticism of participation via this means also noted. The chapter focuses on this theme of digital participation in Estonia, a country labelled as the 'first digital nation' that also has the legacy of being a former socialist country with limited levels of civic engagement and variable levels of participation between different groups of young people. The chapter hence analyses how young people politically engage through the internet, and how differences persist between those who use the internet for politics and those who do not. Empirical evidence is taken from a large-scale European project, MYPLACE (Memory, Youth, Political Legacy and Civic Engagement), which gathered data from two contrasting sites within Estonia, thus enabling contrasts to be made between different youth digital participation experiences.

Key findings

- Participation via social media can have democratic value because young people tend to use the internet to engage in politics.
- Social media opportunities are especially important in countries without a history of strong civic engagement as they allow young people to get involved in a less public and more individualised manner.
- Internet access and the availability of services offering easy access to engagement with political issues means differential access to these opportunities.
- The gap between those who use the internet for politics and those who do not may persist regardless of equal access and skills.

Introduction

Young people's limited trust in political systems has been frequently noted and discussed, particularly the assumption that this leads to a lack of political participation. However, there is growing evidence to support the idea that in the digital age, conventional participation is being replaced by new, more individualised forms of political awareness that may provide a youth-centric means of participating. Young people, it has been argued, are more likely to devote time to social activities outwith traditional political institutions, with the meaning of participation undergoing profound change (Stolle and Hooghe, 2011). A variety of concepts have been introduced to encapsulate these changes; for example, Bakardjieva's subactivism (2009) and Amnå and Ekman's (2013) standby citizen. Social media in particular is thought to be able to open up these new and exciting means of being political, with Isin and Ruppert (2015) stressing the importance of investigating how new forms of political subjectivity are made online, in a range of different contexts (Isin and Ruppert, 2015).

Estonia presents an excellent case study in which to explore the digital participation of young people. On the one hand, it is the country that has been described as the 'first digital nation' and a 'European Silicon Valley' that launched the world's first e-residency programme. On the other, it is a former socialist country characterised by a traditionally low level of political trust and limited levels of civic engagement, with discrepancies in participation rates between different groups of young people. In explaining why, the chapter considers the fact that unlike many other Western European societies, democratic society was interrupted in Estonia by authoritarian rule, until the return of independence again in 1991, several years after the collapse of the Soviet Union. However, youth participation over the past 30 years has remained affected by the past and is still different from much of Western Europe, suggesting that temporal and spatial contexts, and the historical and political background, remain of crucial importance, as may current inequalities in the socio-political context of Estonia.

This chapter looks at how young people in Estonia participate online, taking into account that there may be differentials between groups. First, the chapter presents a brief overview of theoretical approaches to digital participation and sketches the debate on participation via social media more specifically. After introducing data and methods, the chapter provides an overview of the regional context and the Estonian locations where the study was conducted, adding some quantitative data to contextualise the qualitative analysis. The aim of the micro-level qualitative analysis is to elaborate on the following issues: how young people become informed and involved in political discussions via social media; how internet opportunities help young people to take a stand and feel engaged; and, finally, how digital participation is influenced by offline participation and the attitudes and norms surrounding it. In the final section, youth digital participation in Estonia is discussed in the light of previous theoretical approaches.

Young people's digital participation

Widespread use of the internet is believed to have the potential to facilitate social inclusion. The claim is that access to and use of the internet for obtaining and sharing information, and participating in society's services online (Mossberger et al, 2008), promotes democracy in the same way as the spread of literacy once did. However, an additional question asked in more recent studies concerns the ways in which technological devices are used. For example, Banaji and Bhat (2018) have pointed out that widespread use of new technology does not necessarily contribute to a more democratic society, using the examples of WhatsApp and the spread of mob violence and lynching (Banaji and Bhat, 2018). In encapsulating this position, Min (2010) has distinguished a first- and second-level digital divide: the first refers to differences between those who do and do not have access, and the second, the gap between those who use the internet for politics and those who do not.

Some authors have stressed that social media supports political engagement, especially among young people as 'networked young citizens' (Loader et al, 2014), and that 'social media is used for sharing information and discussing points of view by activists as much as they are employed by politicians' (Allen et al, 2014, p 1134). It is even claimed that as a result of networked technologies, young people can create new forms of citizenship: 'actualising' versus old-type 'dutiful'. While the dutiful citizen model emphasises obligations to participate in government-centred activities and the expression of interests through political parties, the actualising citizen model implies a higher sense of individual purpose as the main role in citizenship. Young people in particular are believed to favour loose networks of community action, and harbour mistrust towards the media and politicians (Bennett, 2008, pp 13–14). Developing the same idea, Bennett and Segerberg (2012) have argued that digital communication technologies not only constitute a new set of tools for politics, but also provide a new, connective logic to political identity and group formation. Bennett and Segerberg use the term 'connective action' (instead of collective action) to approach and define the logic of political activities that rely on the self-motivated sharing of personalised ideas, resources, images and plans on social networks (for example Facebook, Twitter and online forums). They claim that in 'connective logic', taking public action or contributing to a cause is an act of personal expression and recognition of self-validation, achieved by sharing ideas and actions within an online community rather than being an expression of pre-existing collective political identities (Bernnett and Segerberg, pp 752–3; see also Allaste and Saari, 2020).

There are nevertheless different views about social media and whether or not the internet encourages participation or actually endangers it, and increases or reduces inequalities between different groups. In political engagement, social media is seen as an opportunity that otherwise would not have existed, and as something that might contribute to a feeling of being more engaged (Dimitrova et al, 2011, p 97). Social media is also seen as providing a space for democratic discussion and for facilitating new forms of civic learning via digital media (for example, Hobbs et al, 2013). Theocharis and Quintelier (2016, p 4) claim that posting, commenting, tweeting and joining groups has 'democratic value, since they have the potential to involve people in forms of engagement that conform to classic definitions of participation'. Schlozman et al (2010, p 501) stress the importance of social media affordances, especially for younger people, while it allows them to overcome the historical under-representation of younger citizens with respect to political activity. Consuming political information online raises the likelihood of participating in politics offline (Yamamoto et al, 2015), and that social media can be viewed as an important gateway to other forms of political participation that take place in the public sphere (Östman, 2013), constituting a connection to formal politics.

On the other hand, there is strong criticism of participation via social media. Certain authors imply that such forms of participation lack gravitas, employing pejorative terms such as 'slacktivism' (Morozov, 2012) and 'clickism' (Amin, 2010). These concepts are used to convey the impression that online participation makes individuals feel good about themselves, but constitutes a poor replacement for traditional offline participation. Ekström and colleagues (2014) add that frequent engagement on Facebook does not necessarily lead to the development of public orientation; it is also argued that the use of internet platforms fosters a logic of self-centred participation, something that might even pose a threat to collective action (Fenton and Barassi, 2011). These pessimistic views regarding social media extend to the potential for overcoming inequalities. Cantijoch and colleagues (2008) have found that social media use leads to a widening of the knowledge gap between the politically interested and those who actively screen out political information. Elsewhere, it has been stated that the internet will not help the sharing of information between different groups because it creates 'filter bubbles', wherein citizens hear the same narrow band of opinions (for example, Pariser 2011), increasing the likelihood of polarisation (Stroud, 2010). It has also been pointed out that using social media alone does not mobilise previously inactive people (Gustafsson, 2012) and that social media platforms do not re-engage young people who have already lost interest in politics (Keating and Melis, 2017).

Context and data

Methodological approach of MYPLACE

This chapter draws on data gathered during the course of the European Commission Framework 7 project, Memory, Youth, Political Legacy and Civic Engagement (MYPLACE). This study was carried out between 2011 and 2015 by a consortium of researchers from 14 different European countries.[1] The project integrated a number of different methodological elements. Alongside ethnographic case studies and contextual analysis of political legacy issues affecting youth politicisation in each region, a large-scale quantitative survey was conducted. This involved an extensive questionnaire on the theme of political activism and civic engagement among 1,200 young people aged between 16 and 25 living in the participating regions, with the respondent body constructed following a random-sampling approach. Concurrently with these surveys, a total of 60 interviews were completed in each region, split between two contrasting research sites.

In each of the regions, two sites were selected by country teams to illustrate diversity within their respective countries. The rationale was one of demonstrating contrasting socioeconomic or ethno-cultural characteristics within a national territory or region, typically one area that epitomised mainstream youth and the other characterised by socio-demographic marginality (Pilkington and Pollock, 2015). In Estonia the survey was conducted in Tartu County (n=634) and Ida-Viru County (n=616), followed by face-to-face, open-ended interviews with 29 people from Tartu County, all of them ethnic Estonians, and 31 in Ida-Viru County, all but one of them Russian-speakers (Allaste et al, 2014). The MYPLACE survey data are not statistically representative at a national level; nevertheless, qualitative data from contrasting sites should give diversified explanations of how young people participate.

This chapter is primarily based on Estonian qualitative data. The interview material has been transcribed and analysed using NVivo 9.2, with open coding and axial coding. The MYPLACE qualitative data analysis strategy is based on an inductive approach (inductive coding in the early stages of analysis), with a conscious process of 'theoretical matching' in the later stage of analysis (Allaste and Saari, 2020). Although interviews covered a wide range of topics (political heritage; participation and understanding of 'the political'; culture and lifestyles and so on), for the purposes of this chapter, material coded under 'social media and participation' is mostly used in qualitative analyses. All statements are based on an analysis of all materials, and quotations are used to illustrate the arguments.

The case of Estonia

The regional context of this study is rooted in the participatory practices of a former socialist country. Although most of the previously 'real socialist' countries have been integrated into Western Europe, some important differences have remained. Levels of trust in other people, institutions and the media are generally lower in the East than in the 'old democracies' of the West (Kalmus et al, 2018), and civic society in general is relatively weak (Howard, 2002). Moreover, young people in former socialist countries tend to have a lower level of engagement compared with their Western counterparts, and have inherited passive attitudes from the former socialist regime due to the negative effects (for example, poverty and corruption) of the post-socialist transformation (Vukelic and Stanojevic, 2012).

Among the former republics of the Soviet Union, Estonia (with a population of 1.3 million) is known for its radical reforms and fast transformation to liberal capitalism (Norkus, 2007). This process has also had an ethnic dimension. The Russian-speaking minority lost the status it enjoyed in Soviet times, as Estonian national sentiments were the basis of the restoration of independence in 1991. This minority became disadvantaged in several ways compared with ethnic Estonians: they had difficulties obtaining Estonian citizenship, and faced relative economic deprivation, a spatial segregation of the population and a weaker position in the labour market. The opinions and dispositions of the ethno-linguistic groups differ; for example, while ethnic Estonians follow Estonian media, Russian-speakers tend to use Russian media channels (see also Allaste and Cairns, 2016).

Estonia chose a path of radical, neoliberal economic and political reforms after regaining independence, which led to the popularisation of a success-oriented, materialistic and individualistic public discourse. Hence, young people have mostly focused on individualistic and materialistic goals, rather than caring about social issues and becoming activists (Allaste and Cairns, 2016). At the same time, technological development has been a crucial component of the Estonian transition. 'Internetisation' became one of the central symbols of a rapidly changing society, leading to a widely held perception of Estonia as a leading e-state (Runnel et al, 2009), an image further entrenched with the advent of electronic voting from 2005, and the launching of e-Residency[2] in Estonia in 2014. The share of internet users has grown speedily in the 2000s, reaching 100% among younger age groups in 2014 (Kõuts-Klemm et al, 2017). Internet voting is claimed to have the potential to help ease people into political participation. However, according to a study from 2005 to 2015, its effects do not surface immediately in the electorate, but need time until usage has diffused to a wider public (Vassil et al, 2016).

Young people in Estonia tend to be more open to online participation than to other forms of participation. While different studies show lower civic engagement levels or less belief in influencing society among Estonian young people than their Western counterparts (for example, Allaste and Cairns, 2016; Kalmus et al, 2018), differences tend to be smaller in regard to participation related to the internet. For example, only 34% of Estonian young people, in contrast to 51% on average in European countries, considered voting in European elections the best way to participate in public life, but 51% of Estonian youth (on average 46%) had the belief that social networks represent progress for democracy, allowing everyone to take part in public debate (Myllyniemi, 2016). Existing studies in Estonia also point out that youth online and offline participation can be interrelated, and new modes of participation tend to be employed more by active youths to reinforce their existing forms and levels of engagement (Kalmus et al, 2018).

Youth participation in Tartu County and Ida-Viru County

As mentioned earlier, two localities, Tartu County and Ida-Viru County, which differ in terms of socioeconomic and ethno-cultural characteristics, were included in the analysis. In socioeconomic terms, Tartu is the second largest town of Estonia and the cultural, economic and entrepreneurship centre of southern Estonia, where ethnic Estonians constitute the majority of inhabitants (75% in 2010 and 78%

in 2019). In this region (Tartu and surroundings) the unemployment level has been relatively low and prospects for socioeconomic development have been good in recent decades. Several universities are located in the town, which make it a youthful location. In contrast, Ida-Viru County is a region that lost its industrial importance and economic prosperity after the collapse of the Soviet Union and has been characterised by high unemployment, an ageing population and a mostly Russian-speaking population (the percentage of ethnic Estonians is less than 20%).

There were major differences between the two sites reflected in the survey. Young people in Ida-Viru County had lower participation rates. However, a lower rate in voting is partly explained by a higher number of respondents without the right to vote.

The most pertinent survey questions for this chapter concerned uploading political material to the internet and signing petitions. These activities were also less prevalent in Ida-Viru County than Tartu County (Allaste et al, 2014). Even though petitions do not necessarily refer to the online environment, qualitative interviews showed that in most cases signing was done via the internet or other e-petitions.

Table 7.1: Dimensions of participation in Estonia in the MYPLACE study

| | | Participation (%) | |
| | | ESTONIA (n =1250) | |
		Tartu County (n=634)	Ida-Viru County (n=616)
Type of participation activity Formal political participation		38	24
Protest/non-institutionalised actions (including: signed a petition)		36 (20)	17 (8)
Expressive activities (including: uploaded political material to the internet)		35 (10)	15 (2)
Political consumption		16	4
Voting	Abstention	21	22
	No right to vote	32	50
	Voted	47	28

Source: Allaste et al (2014).

The difference in percentages is influenced by the fact that the online environment is only in Estonian, which means that without language proficiency, people have no realistic access to it (and in the Ida-Viru County the majority of people are Russian speakers). The different results between location for uploading political material in internet can be interpreted as lack of motivation, which is further explained in the next section.

Digital participation, social media opportunities and digital divides

Becoming informed and involved in political discussion

On the basis of open-ended interviews, it is possible to isolate various instances of young people becoming informed and involved in political discussion via the internet. In illustrating how this process works, the chapter draws on material from both of the research localities that demonstrates the role of social media, and in particular the process of politicisation. Interviewees were active social media users, although often only to the extent of 'liking', commenting on, or sharing stories online. How this happens is illustrated by Liisa, a 17-year-old from Tartu County: "I read comments of all kinds in YouTube, Facebook and then I share these ... When I think that others should also know."

This position illustrates that while social media is popular it is not commonly used for explicitly political aims. Although this outwardly suggests that such activity is not meant to have a great deal of political importance, sharing the news or 'liking' Facebook postings still has the potential to lead young people towards a less shallow interest in politics. This may entail engagement with networks that distribute more in-depth information about a specific issue, and by this means, there may be an impact on understandings of the issue and the process of opinion making. How this happens is explained by a number of interviewees from Tartu County. For example, Gerli, aged 18, demonstrates how awareness is raised:

> I remember I started looking at these videos on YouTube which were made by the Anonymous or this Legion, so to say ... And after that, all kinds of information came from there. Then I looked around on the internet, did some more research.'

Gerli is suggesting that a cumulative process is taking place, initiated by joining groups, giving 'likes' and even commenting on YouTube videos. What is significant is that as well as being a form of entertainment, this process can be interpreted as a part of staying alert through finding a position for oneself in a topical debate or situating one's own opinions within a broader public discourse.

Young people often preferred to observe comments and forums, without adding to them, as a strategy for keeping well informed, or keeping an eye on things, thus being a good 'standby citizen' (Amnå and Ekman, 2013). Not commenting was, in these cases, framed as a rational choice, as stated by Tarmo, aged 21, in Tartu County:

> 'In general, I just go on forums to read, to keep informed. Well … by and large I think that there are so many others, who share my opinion and they've already been very vocal about it, so I don't think it's necessary for me to do it.'

The main claim here is that the internet offers participation opportunities to young people who do not necessarily consider themselves to be 'politically active'. Through everyday activities of monitoring, 'liking' and 'sharing' in internet debates, even those who are not interested in politics can get involved in political discussions, often through what seem on the surface to be less serious actions. In many cases, young people were comfortable with sharing political content on social media if it were packaged as humour, as was stated by Andrus, 21, from Tartu County: "Yes, I do 'share', 'like' and 'comment'! Only if it is political, absurd and humorous! Most definitely absurd political stuff." In such a case, the political content was expressed in a more hidden, implicit or interpretative form. While parody is a legitimate form of political critique, the argument here is that humour neutralises political content and makes it more palatable for young people who prefer to stay away from mainstream politics. Nevertheless, using humour could also be interpreted as an 'expression of disillusionment on the part of individuals who feel that they cannot make a difference to wider society' (Sinanan and Hosein, 2017).

What matters is that there is a range of social media platforms to support such debate, and possibly reflection, creating a point of entry to the political sphere. While the same process can be initiated via other means, with social media there is an opportunity to directly engage with the outside world and to become informed about political issues in a very easy and convenient way. This is an important distinction, as explained by Kristel, 25, from Tartu County:

'When there is a topic that like, interests me, for example, on Facebook somebody has posted on the wall then I will, for example, read this article, right? Basically, it works! If the article hadn't been put on the wall, then I would not have read it. But I am not myself, like, active in this sense.'

The data allow us to infer that participating via social media has democratic value, with the potential of involving people (Theocharis and Quintelier, 2016). As Estonian young people have inherited passivity, and a tradition of civic engagement is missing, involvement through social media can have greater importance than in older democracies. It could be said that social media provides new forms of civic learning (Hobbs et al, 2013), as people become informed and accustomed to thinking about political topics.

Taking a stand and feeling engaged

Young people can form an opinion or take a stand through participation in online petitions, especially if the topic is connected to matters of everyday life. For example Lembit, aged 17 from Tartu County, has used such a platform to influence decision making about housing development in his own community:

'We have this Raja park and now they plan to build apartment houses there. I like sports, I am used to running there in summer, and when they opened the petition in the internet, I signed that I am against this construction plan.'

Young people seek to generate small changes through their interactions, but see these interactions as acting personally. Lembit's signature was an individual decision 'submerged in the flow of everyday life' (Bakardjieva, 2009) but, independently of the result (whether or not the park would be saved), he has taken a stand. The suggestion here is that young people learn to take a stand or form an opinion regarding a political topic with the aid of the internet. Although information may be available offline, online environments for petitions make it more widespread and easier to engage.

Taking a stand towards political action and making the effort to belong to a particular interest group could be interpreted as, potentially, a stronger statement of political intent. As Ly, 23, the only Estonian-speaking interviewee from Ida-Viru County, noted: "When this Charter 12 started, it was very interesting. We immediately joined the petition or I am not sure how to say it. When they set something up on the internet, on Petitsioon.ee, then we joined."[3]

This quotation exemplifies the fact that it is possible to feel part of a protest movement through the online petition environment, with Ly and several others using social network sites and 'feeling more engaged' (Dimitrova et al, 2011), becoming part of a greater body of opinion.

Choosing to be part of a digital network can also be a conscious choice and provide alternative environments for people who are interested. For someone who does not find discussions on Estonian social media interesting, an option could be to turn to international forums, as in the case of Oskar, 25, Tartu County: "On these foreign forums I discuss but I say that internet discussions in Estonia are so small and if there is anything then these are not serious issues."

On the other hand, there was also self-censorship evident in interviewees' explanations of their preference for taking a stand, connected to fears that the traces of their activities via the internet could disadvantage them. Ida-Viru respondents especially felt apprehensive about leaving digital tracks that could be traced back to them.

Georg, 16, Ida-Viru County, explained:

> 'I'd rather say what I think without it being written down somewhere, it's possible that it will get warped later on … that can't be good for me. So I try to not write comments … because what if someone reads these comments later, and they don't like what I have said – maybe an employer … so who knows what it could lead to.'

Insecure feelings could be related to the wider context of young people's position in society and inequalities between different groups of young people.

Digital divides and the relation between online and offline participation

As explained earlier and illustrated in the survey results, the research sites differed in their socioeconomic contexts as well as in terms of youth participation in general. In Ida-Viru County, there was also less online participation, and more scepticism about internet-based engagement, implying that this process may differ among different groups of young people.

Although monitoring rather than taking a stand on social media platforms was quite common among all interviewees, keeping one's opinions neutral was more frequent among Russian-speakers from Ida-Viru County. As Alek, 24 years old, said: "I think … there are other people who love commenting. I keep to being neutral, I think it's better to stay away." In some cases, young people from Ida-Viru County did not see social media platforms as a good space for discussion, perceiving them as authoritarian or even rather depressing. For example, Edik, 24 years old, says: "No, I do not like Facebook, I think it can be too controlled." Several interviewees in Ida-Viru County in fact considered the internet to be politically quite useless or mere escapism. This position is illustrated by Alexander, 25, from Ida-Viru County: "To me, it seems that only people who have nothing to do get involved in it … they are some kind of obscure activists. It would be better for them to do some work instead."

This position can be connected, at least partially, to the attitudes of Russian-speaking young people from socially marginalised areas, and Ida-Viru County in general: they tend to have less involvement in and be less informed about different opportunities for participation, and be more pessimistic about the possibility of influencing Estonian society (Allaste et al, 2014). As Dimitri, 22, from Ida-Viru County puts it: "Nobody's going to suddenly take you somewhere where you can change something."

Such circumstances are not simply dictated by the young people themselves but are partly a consequence of the availability of opportunities for participation. With regard to online affordances, Petitsioon.ee was not established by young people but by an organisation, and as mentioned, there is no equivalent online space in the Russian language. It might be interpreted as the responsible organisations believing that organising something like this in Russian would be ineffective because they do not believe that petitions in Russian would be popular among potential users, or that claims in Russian would be heard in Estonian society. It can be said therefore that opportunities on the internet do not necessarily bridge the two language-based communities, while sites differ according to language and people tend mostly to follow social media in their own language. Most probably, a separate space could be also intensified by filter bubbles (Pariser, 2011).

Conclusion

In Estonia, the internet is, in theory, accessible to all citizens, including young people, who not only have online access but also access to services provided by the state that exceed the level of opportunities available in most other countries in the world. Young people in Estonia are constantly online and previous studies show that while, generally, youth political participation is lower in Estonia than in Europe, digital participation is more appreciated.

Asking the question about the formation of new political subjectivities (Isin and Ruppert, 2015), it is possible to see how the internet facilitates the politicisation of young people in Estonia, with interviewees confirming that political dialogue is being initiated, or at least sustained, via social media. Although it cannot be concluded that this activity will be sustained or lead to other types of participation, a reflexive process of opinion making is taking place, mediated by online peers and implicating a connective logic of group formation (Bennett and Segerberg, 2012) as well as a constitution of a kind of democratisation of participation (Theocharis and Quintelier, 2016). For this reason, it can be argued that social media can act as a point of entry to the political world for young people.

Online expressive practices can be seen as participatory acts in their own right, even if they do not lead to further action. We can illustrate how young people participate in public life, talk with others about politics via social media, take a stand and feel a sense of belonging to a group of people sharing similar understandings. What is important here in the Estonian case is that online participation might not be recognised as 'political' by young people themselves. Even though a group of multi-active young people exists in Estonia (Allaste et al, 2014), young people tend to distance themselves from politics and might need a more individualistic point of entry to the political sphere to make participation palatable. Rather than replacing one model with another in Bennett's (2008) terms, changing from a dutiful citizen model to an actualising one, it is possible to discuss emerging micro-level 'connective action' (Bennett and Segerberg, 2012) in Estonia that might (or might not) replace the passivity prevalent among many young people (see also Allaste and Saari, 2020).

Not conforming to the 'slacktivist' (Morozov, 2012) or 'clickist' (Amin, 2010) archetypes cited earlier, social media does not definitively draw young people away from more serious activism in the Estonian case. On the contrary, social media has an important role in moving young people towards political activity. In practice, this involves getting informed about and becoming involved in discussion, with information circulated through expressive communicative activities that help users to think more concretely about political issues and to relate politics to their own lives, sharing material or highlighting political topics of particular relevance to youth life (see also Yamamoto et al, 2015).

However, access to, or the availability of, services and possibilities for engaging with political issues in an easy and distant way does not mean that all young people use this opportunity. Besides technological skills, participating in society online also requires certain norms to support this behaviour. Although social media can encourage participation, there is no reason to believe that simply having access to the internet solves the problems of participation for different groups of young people. The case of Estonia shows that even though young people can become more easily involved through social media, participation partly reflects predispositions towards offline participation. As found in the Estonian study of electronic voting, different groups in society adopt and use new technologies differently (Vassil et al, 2016), and this basic premise can be extended to other forms of online participation. Differences in political participation in Estonia have an ethnic dimension and Russian-speaking young people from Ida-Viru County investigated for this study are in a doubly disadvantaged position, living in a regionally marginalised community.

Furthermore, as noted in previous studies, social media platforms do not tend to re-engage those who have already lost interest in politics (Keating and Melis, 2017), or at least it takes more time for habits in participation via social media to develop and diffuse. The Estonian case adds that young people in a marginalised position in society tend to lack the self-confidence necessary for involvement in both offline and online activities (that is, in contrast to the findings in Chapter 6 of this book, which report a tendency among marginalised young people to be more politically involved). While the question of access to information technology, the so-called first-level digital divide, is not relevant for Estonia, there may be a second-level digital divide that constitutes a barrier to participation in democracy (Min, 2010); that is, there is a gap between those who use the internet for politics and those who do not, exemplified by the dichotomy between the opinions found in the two research sites. Among the interviewees, therefore, Russian-speakers with passive attitudes in society due to their relatively marginalised position also tend to be also less politically active within social media environments.

Notes

[1] Croatia, Denmark, Estonia, Finland, Georgia, Germany, Greece, Hungary, Latvia, Portugal, Russia, Slovakia, Spain and the UK. Two teams from Germany were included, making a total of 15 partner regions in 14 countries.

[2] For more information, see https://e-resident.gov.ee

[3] Charter 12 was an open letter from intellectuals that inspired public meetings initiated by activists.

References

Allaste, A.-A. and Cairns, D. (2016) 'Youth political participation in a transition society', *Studies of Transition States and Societies*, 8(2): 3–8.

Allaste, A.-A. and Saari, K. (2020) 'Social media and participation in different socio-political contexts: cases of Estonia and Finland', *YOUNG*, 28(2): 138–56.

Allaste, A.-A., Pirk, R. and Taru, M. (2014) *Mapping and Typologising Youth Activism (Tartumaa and Ida-Virumaa)*, MYPLACE Research Report.

Allen, D., Bailey, M., Carpentier, N., Fenton N., Jenkins, H., Lothian, A., Linchuan Qiu, J., Schäfer, M.T. and Srinivasan, R. (2014) 'Participations: dialogues on the participatory promise of contemporary culture and politics', *International Journal of Communication*, 8: 1129–51.

Amin, R. (2010) 'The Empire strikes back: social media uprisings and the future of cyber activism', *Kennedy School Review*, 10(1): 64–6.

Amnå, E. and Ekman, J. (2013) 'Standby citizens: diverse faces of political passivity', *European Political Science Review*, 6(2): 261–81.

Bakardjieva, M. (2009) 'Subactivism: lifeworld and politics in the age of the Internet', *The Information Society*, 25: 91–104.

Banaji, S. and Bhat, R. (2018) *WhatsApp Vigilantes: An Exploration of Citizen Reception and Circulation of WhatsApp Misinformation Linked to Mob Violence in India*, London: London School of Economics and Political Science. Available from: www.lse.ac.uk/media-and-communications/assets/documents/research/projects/WhatsApp-Misinformation-Report.pdf

Bennett W.L. (2008) *Civic Life Online: Learning How Digital Media Can Engage Youth*, Cambridge, MA: The MIT Press.

Bennett, W.L. and Segerberg, A. (2012) 'The logic of connective action: the personalization of contentious politics', *Information, Communication & Society*, 15(5): 739–68.

Cantijoch, M., Jorba, L. and San Martin, L. (2008) 'Exposure to political information in new and old media: which impact on political participation?', Paper presented at the 2008 annual meeting of the American Political Science Association, 28–31 August, Boston.

Dimitrova, D.V., Shehata, A., Stromback, J. and Nord, L.W. (2011) 'The effects of digital media on political knowledge and participation in election campaigns: evidence from panel data', *Communication Research*, 41(1): 95–118.

Ekström, M., Olsson, T. and Shehata, A. (2014) 'Spaces for public orientation? Longitudinal effects of internet use in adolescence', *Information, Communication & Society*, 17(2): 168–83.

Fenton, N. and Barassi, V. (2011) 'Alternative media and social networking sites: the politics of individuation and political participation', *The Communication Review*, 14: 179–96.

Gustafsson, N. (2012) 'The subtle nature of Facebook politics: Swedish social network site users and political participation', *New Media & Society*, 14(7): 1111–27.

Hobbs, R., Donnelly, K., Friesem, J. and Moen, M. (2013) 'Learning to engage: how positive attitudes about the news, media literacy, and video production contribute to adolescent civic engagement', *Educational Media International*, 50(4): 231–46.

Howard, M.M. (2002) 'The weakness of postcommunist civil society', *Journal of Democracy*, 13(1): 157–69.

Isin, E. and Ruppert, E. (2015) *Being Digital Citizens*, London: Rowman & Littlefield.

Kalmus, V., Kõuts-Klemm, R., Beilmann, M., Rämmer, A. and Opermann, S. (2018) 'Long-lasting shadows of (post)communism? Generational and ethnic divides in political and civic participation in Estonia', in J. Wimmer, C. Wallner, R. Winter and K. Oelsner (eds) *(Mis)Understanding Political Participation: Digital Practices, New Forms of Participation and the Renewal of Democracy*, Abingdon: Routledge, pp 35–56.

Keating, A. and Melis, G. (2017) 'Social media and youth political engagement: preaching to the converted or providing a new voice for youth?', *The British Journal of Politics and International Relations*, 19(4): 877–94.

Kõuts-Klemm, R., Pruulmann-Vengerfeldt, P., Siibak, A. and Lauristin, M. (2017) 'Internetikasutus ja sotsiaalmeedia kasutus [The use of the internet and social media]', in P. Vihalemm, M. Lauristin, V. Kalmus and T. Vihalemm (eds) *Eesti Ühiskond Kiirenevas Ajas: Uuringu Mina. Maailm. Meedia 2002–2014 Tulemused [Estonian Society in the Accelerating Time: Results of the Survey Me. The World. The Media 2002–2014]*, Tartu: Tartu University Press, pp 279–98.

Loader, B.D., Vromen, A. and Xenos, M.A. (2014) 'The networked young citizen: social media, political participation and civic engagement', *Information, Communication & Society*, 17(2): 143–50.

Min, S.-J. (2010) 'From the digital divide to the democratic divide: internet skills, political interest, and the second-level digital divide in political internet use', *Journal of Information Technology & Politics*, (7)1: 22–35.

Morozov, E. (2012) *The Net Delusion: The Dark Side of Internet Freedom*, New York, NY: Public Affairs.

Mossberger, K., Tolbert, C.J. and McNeal, R.S. (2008) *Digital Citizenship: The Internet, Society, and Participation*, Cambridge, MA: The MIT Press.

Myllyniemi, S. (ed.) (2016) *Youth Barometer 2015*. Helsinki: Ministry of Education and Culture.

Norkus, Z. (2007) 'Why did Estonia perform best? The North-South gap in the post-socialist economic transitions of the Baltic states', *Journal of Baltic Studies*, 38(1): 21–42.

Östman, J. (2013) 'When private talk becomes public political expression: examining a practice- field hypothesis of youth political development', *Political Communication*, 30(4): 602–19.

Pariser, E. (2011) *The Filter Bubble*, London: Penguin.

Pilkington, H. and Pollock, G. (2015) ' "Politics are bollocks": youth, politics and activism in contemporary Europe', *The Sociological Review*, 63(S2): 1–35.

Runnel, P., Pruulmann-Vengerfeldt, P. and Reinsalu, K. (2009) 'The Estonian tiger leap from post-communism to the information society: from policy to practice', *Journal of Baltic Studies*, 40(1): 29–51.

Schlozman, K.L., Verba, S. and Brady, H. (2010) 'Weapon of the strong? Participatory inequality and the internet', *Perspectives on Politics*, 8: 487–510.

Sinanan, J. and Hosein, G.-J. (2017) 'Non-activism: Political engagement and Facebook through ethnography in Trinidad', *Social Media + Society*, July–September: 1–10.

Stolle, D. and Hooghe, M. (2011) 'Shifting inequalities: Patterns of exclusion and inclusion in emerging forms of political participation', *European Societies*, 13: 119–42.

Stroud, N. (2010) 'Polarization and partisan selective exposure', *Journal of Communication*, 60(3): 556–76.

Theocharis, Y. and Quintelier, E. (2016) 'Stimulating citizenship or expanding entertainment? The effect of Facebook on adolescent participation', *New Media & Society*, 6: 1–20.

Vassil, K., Solvak, M., Vinkel, P., Trerchel, A.H. and Alvarez, M.R. (2016) 'The diffusion of internet voting. Usage patterns of internet voting in Estonia between 2005 and 2015', *Government Information Quarterly*, 33(3): 453–59.

Vukelic, J. and Stanojevic, D. (2012) 'Environmental activism as a new form of political participation of the youth in Serbia', *Sociologija*, 54(2): 387–99.

Yamamoto, M., Kushin, M.J. and Dalisay, F. (2015) 'Social media and mobiles as political mobilization forces for young adults: examining the moderating role of online political expression in political participation', *New Media & Society*, 17(6): 880–98.

8

The participation project: how projects shape young people's participation

Maria Bruselius-Jensen and Anne Mette W. Nielsen

This chapter focuses on professionally facilitated efforts to promote young people's participation through project-based activities located within young people's everyday spaces. Inspired by theories of the emergence of a 'project society' (Jensen, 2012) and 'projective regimes' (Boltanski and Chiapello, 2005), the chapter discusses the implications of a regime driven by social mobility, fast and continuous innovation and managerial logics with the aim to promote societal activity through projects. Drawing on case studies of young people's experiences while taking part in two project-based initiatives that aim to promote young people's participation in school and in the psychiatric system respectively, the chapter demonstrates how this project regime greatly affects who, how and to what aims young people are able to participate in change and decision making.

Key findings

- Professionally facilitated projects are a core contemporary feature of young people's participation and generate both new opportunities and new barriers for their participation.
- These facilitated participatory spaces allow for less hierarchical relations between young people and professionals, but tend to have difficulties in addressing more permanent concerns in the arenas or institutions that accommodate the activities.
- Projects often follow predefined programmes. This allows for many organisations to apply the programmes, but limits the room for young people's own priorities.
- Projects often produce and reproduce inequalities because they tend to have a core group of highly engaged young participants, while the vast majority become mere recipients.

Introduction

Pupil 1:   'On this school, like, suddenly, then we are a Rights Respecting School [RRS]. Yes, and then we are some kind of food school, and then we are suddenly another school.'
Pupil 2:   'And physical activity school.'
Pupil 1:   'Yes, and physical activity school.' (Pupils from the Rights Council in an RRS)

RRSs are developed by UNICEF with the aim of implementing a rights-based teaching programme. The introduction of the programme into the Danish public school context is one of the cases followed in this study. In the opening quotes, young people who are members of the Rights Council in an RRS explain that being named as a 'something'-school is a routine part of everyday school life. These pupils relish being council members, but becoming an RRS is one more additional activity that comes and goes in a long line of projects introduced into the schools. Curriculum teaching is the permanent core activity, but projects continually pop up with other activities alongside the curriculum (Bentsen et al, 2020), sometimes providing additional spaces for young people's participation. Our goal in this chapter is to question the propensity of young people's participation being framed as project-based activities. Further, the chapter encourages consideration of how features such as short-term activities, externally defined programmes, predefined aims, and fast-paced and innovative methodologies frame participatory spaces in certain ways and might at times overrule others agendas, such as making room for young people's own priorities and creating sustainable change.

In their much-cited work, James and colleagues (1998) underline how childhood, youth and young people's position as social actors are continually shaped by contemporary discourse and social orders. During the past three decades, young people's position as competent agents with both the rights and the ability to take part in decision making has been cemented (Baraldi and Cockburn, 2018). Underlined by the near-universal adoption of the United Nations Convention on the Rights of the Child, this position has resulted in numerous processes of consultation and collaboration with young people in change making and decision making in their everyday arenas. Walsh and Black (2018) argue that we have entered 'an age of entitlement' where young people are viewed as entitled to be consulted and engaged on matters that concern them. While much of this change in the position of young people has been ascribed to a general change in discourse and a wish to realise young people's rights to have their views considered, there are also other strong agendas behind this change, and young people's participation is negotiated and locked in to the face of broader social tendencies and priorities (Holloway et al, 2018).

Youth participation in change and decision making takes multiple forms, for example, youth activism (Loncle et al, 2012) as described in Chapter 9 in this book; participation in formal democratic mechanisms such as hearings and councils (Percy-Smith, 2010), discussed in Chapter 13 in this book; through formal institutional programmes as discussed in Chapter 11 in this book; or simply embedded within young people's everyday life routines in what Warming and Fahnøe (2017) define as lived citizenship. In our work we have become increasingly aware of numerous examples of an additional framing of youth participation: namely project-based initiatives defined and driven by third parties aiming to facilitate youth participation through a variety of new programmes implemented into young people's everyday arenas. The aims and methods of these projects have many resemblances to other forms of participation, but they all have the common denominator of being time-limited activities that are additional to permanent core activities and initiated by external organisations. While a project is not an aim in and of itself, a certain set of logics and orders in projects produces specific framings of the participatory processes. Thus, when we want to understand the contemporary conditions for young people's participation, it is vital to look at the characteristics of projects. Based on the study of two project-based initiatives, this chapter demonstrates how the dynamics of a project produces orders and logics that become decisive for whom, how and to what purposes young people can take part in decision and change processes on matters that concern them.

Facilitating young people's participation through projects

The inclusion of young people in change and decision making is still developing (Walther et al, 2020) and participatory activities for young people are often organised as projects for testing ways to include young people in new arenas of youth life (Tsekoura, 2016). Thus projects are a basic organisational framework for short-term activities that are loosely tied to the more permanent core activities of organisations (Grabher, 2002). Projects are used to test something, to develop new approaches or to make room for activities that are additional to standard practices.

However, projects are not just for breaking new ground. Recent works in sociology argue that projects have increasingly become an inherent societal dynamic to the extent that projects have become an omnipresent human condition that penetrates all spheres of life: a 'project society' (Jensen, 2012, p 2).

Boltanski and Chiapello (2005) demonstrate the manifestation of a new regime, the 'projective regime', that contemporary society values as a desirable quality in organising social activity. The identification of the projective regime is based on studies of managerial logics in large enterprises and it is also defined by logics such as timelines and resource management. More generally, the projective regime is driven by a belief that promoting activity is always a gain and that social mobility and change-readiness must always be maintained by forming new networks and supporting creativity and innovation. These activities converge into projects that emerge, dissolve and reappear continually. According to Boltanski and Chiapello (2005), the projective regime is so strong that it has constructed a 'new spirit of capitalism', where the commodity is *activity*: the fast and continuous innovation, change and social mobility generated through projects. This is a rejuvenation of capitalism that meets contemporary ideals of individual freedom and silences the critique of the immanent inequalities in the distribution of power and resources. This desirability of promoting activity likewise shapes policies and discourses on youth participation. Walther (2012) argues that there is presently a strong connection between the discourse of youth participation and that of activation. Young people's active participation in democratic activities is associated with their employability and general ability to contribute to society. Therefore the promotion of young people's participation has a tendency to become a push to ' "get involved" – in activities that have been predefined or held as relevant for society' (Pohl et al, 2020, p 2), with little attention to the form of participation and the concerns of young people.

This grammar of projects has dispersed into the work of civil society organisations (CSOs) (Andersen, 2018), resulting in CSOs being driven by goals to strengthen the rights and living conditions for vulnerable social groups, while simultaneously being guided by managerial logics. CSOs generate a substantial share of initiatives to promote young people's participation within civic and institutional contexts. So, when CSOs introduce funded projects to promote young people's participation they also introduce the logic of projects. Within this logic, the promotion of young people's participation is translated into continually facilitating new activities, ideas, programmes and learning processes. This is the focus in the analysis of the two case studies.

Methodology

The findings as well as the analytical focus in this chapter stem from a research study (Bruselius-Jensen and Nielsen, 2020) aiming to analyse when and how participation in change and decision processes makes a difference to young people. The research followed the development and implementation of six quite different projects that all aimed to facilitate space for young people's participation within a range of arenas. These initiatives were all funded from the same call by a private foundation and aimed to support the participation of young people in vulnerable situations. The analytical focus in this chapter appeared as a cross-cutting theme across all six projects. Even with quite diverse aims, methods and settings, all six projects shared common features such as: being organised by agents outside of the organisation; having predefined goals; being an addition to core organisational activities; and having as a long-term goal the spreading of activities to new settings. These are features that all appeared to be constitutive for the form of youth participation rendered possible within the projects. Subsequently, literature on the organisational trends and social orders embedded in project organisation was studied, and the case study data were revisited with a specific focus on how the order and logic of projects affect young people's participation, first across all the six projects. Second, a detailed analysis was performed on the two cases that highlighted the six themes presented in the chapter. In the presentation we use quotes that are representative of findings across the whole dataset.

The two cases

In this chapter we draw on the analysis of two selected cases. The six cases are very different in their aims, settings and participants, and so a focus on two cases allows for a more detailed analysis and demonstration of the main points. The two cases were selected to represent diversity. Both are set within an institutional arena, but still represent a variety because the arenas are very different: a public school and a regional psychiatric care unit. They also differ in size, one being a large long-term project with many young participants and the other a small short-term project with few young participants.

The project Knowledge Leads the Way (KLW) was an 18-month-long development project initiated by a regional administrative unit for the psychiatric care system and administered by the project development unit, CoLab. CoLab does not carry out treatment or have daily contact with the psychiatric care units. The general aim of KLW is to strengthen young people's access to participation in decision making within psychiatric care, but also more specifically to strengthen the communication between the young people in care and the health professionals. Within this project, we followed a small group of young people who were involved in the development of a digital application (app) that aims to create new communicative structures around the recovery process of young people in psychiatric care. We interviewed four young people aged 19–23 who had finished their treatment at the care unit. These four were the most involved in the development process. Two were interviewed separately as they lived very far apart and two were interviewed together. A few others who were more sporadically involved in the project did not wish to be interviewed. Thus, we only have data for the young people who were most involved and are likely to have experienced the strongest involvement. All interviews were structured as journey maps as described on the following page. We also conducted a group interview with three young people, who were not a part of the development process, but whose treatment programme was chosen by the project leaders to test the application as part of their ongoing treatment for depression. Only three out of six young testers agreed to take part in the group interview. The interview was quite short and focused on concrete experiences with the app, out of respect for the mental health of the young participants. We interviewed the project leaders in CoLab as well as three psychiatric nurses who were part of developing and testing the application. All participation in the study was voluntary and all participants gave written, informed consent for their data to be used in the research study, and were promised confidentiality, as well as the option to withdraw from study at a later stage. All participants were informed that they were participating in a study about young people's experiences with being involved in change and decision making and several expressed appreciation of our endeavours and their opportunity to contribute.

The RSS project was initiated by UNICEF Denmark. The project aims to introduce the concept of RRSs from a British into a Danish context and to develop 35 RRSs over a three-year period. The general aim is to strengthen pupils' knowledge about their rights, as defined in the UN Convention on the Rights of the Child, as well as their ability to practise these rights. Within each RRS a small group of pupils forms a Rights Council dedicated to dealing with rights and educational activities following a framework defined by UNICEF, and the whole school undertakes yearly activities concerned with mostly learning about and practising rights (for example, through 'feature weeks', school weeks devoted to a special topic). Within this project we interviewed young people from three schools. They were chosen to represent diversity: a small village school, a medium-sized city school located in a deprived area and a large city school in an affluent part of town. The study focused on the oldest pupils aged 12–15 and included group interviews with pupils from the Rights Council (13 participants in total) and group interviews with pupils who were not involved in organising RRS activities (13 participants in total). In the Rights Council we interviewed the oldest members, all of whom volunteered to participate. The other pupils were selected by teachers who would ask for volunteers in the most senior classes and aim to have both genders represented. Thus, it is likely that we talked with young people who were most involved in issues related to being in an RRS. We interviewed the groups twice over a year in order to study how perception and engagement in the RRS would change over the year. Additionally, we interviewed both a group of teachers organising the RRS (six teachers in total) and a group of teachers who were not involved (two teachers in total) as well as interviews with the project leaders in UNICEF Denmark.

All group interviews with respondents from both projects were conducted as journey mapping (Hall, 2005; see also Chapter 14 in this volume). Through 'journey maps', the young people worked on individual illustrations of their 'journey' as participants in the projects. In the interviews they started by talking about their individual journey and subsequently discussed their experiences in groups, facilitated by the researcher. This enabled both individual and group perspectives. All interviews were recorded and transcribed, and illustrations were photographed.

Disembedded bubbles of participatory activities

One of Boltanski and Chiapello's (2005) main points in their identification of a projective regime is that the aim is not permanence, but constant change-readiness, mobility and promotion of activity. This dynamic is present in our study, demonstrated by the fact that all projects were initiated by agents who were not involved in the core activities in the institutions where the projects were implemented, and moreover the projects aimed to create additional new spaces and new methods to promote young people's active participation. This is evident in the two selected case studies: UNICEF does not teach at the schools, but offers a predefined programme that schools can subscribe to, with predeveloped activities and guidelines applicable in schools. CoLab is not involved in psychiatric treatment programmes, but facilitates a participatory process to develop an app for young patients, which it hopes will be integrated into the general treatment programmes for young people in mental health care in the region. In that sense, both projects introduce new activities and new spaces for participation that are additional to, and somewhat disembedded from, the core activities in the school and psychiatric unit. In the following sections this disembedding will be explored, considering how it considerably defined the participatory processes experienced by and available to the young participants within these projects.

Project bubbles as meaningful participatory spaces

According to the young participants, the projects created spaces for profoundly meaningful experiences of taking part in decision making and having their views and experiences recognised. While the conditions and the agendas were effectively defined by the professionals, the projects still positioned young people as competent core participants in development processes and decision making. In KLW, the young people were invited to be co-developers and were positioned as having valuable knowledge and experiences from their own treatment processes, as well as being possible future users of the app. They took part in the initial development workshops and some of them became part of the planning committee. They all found the participatory experience immensely meaningful, as stressed in the following quote:

> 'So, I have written "It makes sense to have been ill." I have a thing about finding meaning in things and it becomes meaningful for me to have been through all the things that I have been through, when I can share my experiences afterwards and someone actually finds it useful.' (KSW, Young co-developer 1, on notes written on journey map)

The young co-developer finds that her whole history of being ill becomes meaningful, when her participation makes it possible for her to share her story and help other young people by co-developing the app. Her reflections are in line with the findings of McMahon and colleagues (2018) that young people's sense of meaningful participation is often tied to solidarity with other people and with a wish to share their stories. This experience was rendered possible through her participation in KLW. Such meaningfulness is likewise underlined by the young participants perceiving the KWL 'project space' as vastly different from their experiences of trying to influence their own treatment plans within the mental health care system:

> 'When you are used to being in the health system and everything is just one-way communication or force. Then being in this is like … Wow … they actually want to know my opinion.' (Young co-developer 2, KWL)

As expressed in the quote, the young people were positively surprised that they could feel appreciated and encouraged to voice their opinions, in order to help others. This practice was far from the usual relationship between young patients and health professionals, in that participation in the KLW project was experienced as an exception to the health system's very restricted access for young people to take part in decision making regarding their own treatment plans. KLW became a space where young people and professionals could meet under different presumptions and share experiences. However, this was possible because the focus was on developing a new tool and not on changing the treatment system.

The participants in the RRS project reported similar experiences. The young people in the Rights Council were invited to participate in workshops outside the schools in the UN City in Copenhagen where UNICEF Denmark is based. Here they met young people from a number of schools, in workshop activities related to rights. Taking part in these workshops was generally experienced by the young people as being given access to arenas that they did not usually perceive as accessible:

Pupil 1: 'Well, we become a part of "How do we do this?" and we are included in something that adults usually do.'
Pupil 2: 'It makes you feel like you are part of something.' (Pupils in the Rights Council)

The pupils emphasised how they felt extremely privileged to be invited into these decision-making processes. They had an experience of their views being taken seriously and of participating on a more equal level with adults. Being selected and taking part in the local Rights Council likewise formed a space within the school that was perceived as one with a different logic to regular school activities, as members and teachers would discuss school-related issues on a more equal footing. Young participants expressed their sense of being part of something meaningful and how having a common aim produces different and more equal relations between young people and teachers.

By coining the term 'generagency', Leonard (2015) stresses that the relationship between grownups, professionals and young people is a core point of attention for research within inequalities in participation. In both cases, the project-generated spaces allowed for a different relationship between professionals and young people, as they focus on developing the projects together. In both cases, the projects created new participatory spaces that facilitated access for selected young people to participate in decision making in ways that provided a strong sense of recognition and meaningfulness.

Fun respites from everyday routines

Much in line with Boltanski and Chiapello's (2005) projective regime, Thévenot (2013) identifies an explorative form of engagement in society, driven by breaking routines, trying something new and being innovative, creative and embracing change. The young people in the two projects highly valued the fast-paced innovative processes, trips to new places and other fun activities offered to them. In the RRS project, both the visits to UNICEF's headquarters and the activities in the local Rights Council were described by young participants as fun and engaging breaks from the everyday school routines. Likewise, the yearly feature weeks, with a rights-related theme for the whole school, were experienced as a respite. Young people had the opportunity to socialise across different grades, try out new activities, and gain some respite from thinking about exams, as feature weeks were outside the normal curriculum. In this sense, being in an RRS was not only associated with learning about and performing rights inside and outside school, but also a chance to interact and have fun, free from the performance pressure that weighs heavily on many older pupils (Sørensen and Nielsen, 2014).

Even though KWL dealt with a serious topic, the young participants likewise highlighted what they experienced as fun elements. As one of the participants stated:

> 'The first part was really the best. We would just throw ideas around. It was a lot of fun.' (Young co-developer 2, KWL)

The young co-developer mentioned this experience early on in the interview, emphasising how much she liked the playful atmosphere even though they were dealing with mental illness. Therefore, the findings indicate that the playful, dynamic and creative logic of projects can encourage young people's enjoyment and motivation to engage.

The detached quality of participatory bubbles

As illustrated in the previous section, projects constructed new spaces and practices that allowed for new forms of participation. However, the activities also tended to be bubbles of participatory activities that floated on the periphery of the core institutional activities. While it is in the nature of projects to create spaces where new ideas can be developed and non-regular activities can be practised, it is also an inherent aim in most projects to affect or become a permanent part of the core organisational features in order to make sustained change (Grabher, 2002; Bentsen et al, 2020). Both projects aimed for sustainable change but our findings indicate that it was not easy for projects to be integrated permanently.

The development processes of KLW was completely detached from the psychiatric care unit and, thus, could only affect the treatment processes by way of implementing the application. The RRS processes aimed to become more embedded in the core school activities. The aim was to change the school ethos into on that had a rights-based approach that was integrated into curriculum teaching. However, the pupils in the Rights Council felt that their new positions as council members, and their changed relationships with teachers, did not have a place outside the council activities.

> 'Well, not that many in our class are actually interested in the work we do – not even the teachers. They never want to give us time during class.' (Pupil from the Rights Council)

The pupil explains how the feeling of recognition experienced in the council was not maintained when council members returned to class. Their fellow students were disinterested and teachers gave their RRS work lower priority than teaching the formal curriculum. This indicates that the participatory space of the RRS was in danger of becoming a space to learn about rights and how to make decisions for a small group of pupils, rather than a way to make changes in the ethos of the school at large. This was echoed by the RRS teachers, who generally found it very difficult to include rights aspects meaningfully into their curriculum teaching. The main activity for pupils outside the local Rights Councils became the annual feature week and thereby the work with rights continued only in occasional bubbles of alternative activities. We interviewed a group of pupils who participated in a feature week workshop named 'the school parliament'. They were very engaged and had lots of fun with the process of campaigning. But in the subsequent interview, when asked what they expected afterwards, a pupil said:

> 'Okay, so what I expect is that these ideas will be thrown directly in the bin, like they always do. Because, I don't think that they, like, listen to what we say.' (Pupil at RRS, on drawing a garbage bin on his journey map)

The pupils in this group had had bad experiences with participatory processes in their school that did not actually lead to change, and they did not expect the outcome of the rights feature week to be any different. Thus, the rights feature week was fun, but awakened pupils' former experiences of generally not having their ideas considered in school rather than underlining their access to change and decision making.

The detached quality of the two projects did not support the young people to engage with questions that they perceived as pertinent, a key consideration when promoting young people's access to decision making (Percy-Smith, 2010). In KLW, the young participants found it immensely meaningful to take part in developing the app, but in the interviews they all mentioned that their priority was to make changes in the mental health treatment system itself in order to increase young patients' access to co-decision making. This was not within the reach of KWL, where the aim was merely to strengthen communication with the system and not to address treatment practices. Neither the development process nor the use of the app facilitated access to how treatment programmes were applied.

Coming back to how projects shaped young people's participation, the projects tended to create new participatory spaces that were disembedded from the everyday core activities of young people. In line with project logic, young people's participation was temporary, intense and sometimes fun, but had no impact on their everyday core conditions.

Unequal access to participate

Even though the two projects created new possibilities for young people's participation, they were only accessible to a very few

130

participants, leaving the majority excluded from taking part in core project activities.

In KWL, a central aim was creating new ways to include young patients in the development processes. However, it turned out to be very difficult for young people who were still in treatment to participate in the development processes. They were too sick to travel to the meeting venues and they found the workshops too overwhelming to participate in. After trying several different approaches to include these patients in the core decision-making group, the project leaders in CoLab decided to only include three young people who had a long history of dealing with mental health problems, but who were all presently in good health. Thus, even though KWL facilitated new opportunities for young people with mental health issues to be included in development processes, this space was only accessible to very few young people. The remaining group of young people in treatment were merely the recipients of the developed app. The app did not offer decision-making powers, even if, as Cockburn (2013) argues, it could be an improved tool due to its co-development with young people.

In the RRS project, only a few pupils were selected to be in the local Rights Council. In contrast to the Students' Council for which members were elected by the pupils and who represented pupils' general interests in school matters, Rights Council members were not elected and thus did not formally represent their class. They were generally selected by RRS teachers and headmasters, and the selection criteria varied greatly. At some schools, pupils' interest in being on the council was very low and RRS teachers sought out members to join. At other schools, the pupils wrote applications. Across the schools, a common selection criterion seemed to be pupils whom the RRS teachers considered would benefit from being council members, including those who were lonely or bullied, had difficulties speaking in front of others and were generally considered as outsiders. Thus, access was not equal for all and few young people overall could be members of the core groups. Other scholars within youth research (Lundy, 2018) have made claims that not all young people have the same access to taking part in decision making and this study calls attention to the fact that project-based participatory activities are only accessible to very few selected young people. This leaves the majority of young people in the institutions as peripheral participants or merely as recipients of the programmes and activities co-developed by the core participants.

Project-based participatory spaces and beyond

This chapter answers the core questions of how, under what conditions, and for what purposes young people participate in making decisions and fostering changes, by focusing on how and to what effect the logic and orders of project organisation frame youth participation. Structural tendencies such as economic austerity, new patterns of migration, and youth unemployment visibly affect young people's participation. More subtly, how we organise social work and change processes also has considerable influence on young people's participation, as demonstrated in this chapter. At a time when promoting activity though fast change and innovation is imperative in social development, projects become a way to promote young people's participation in change processes. This became increasingly obvious across the cases in this study, leading to the writing of this chapter.

Our study identifies both positive and negative effects of project-based participatory initiatives. Most importantly, the findings indicate that the types of third-party-initiated project highlighted in this chapter produce new opportunities for young people to engage meaningfully in change and decision making. In both projects, the young people had prior experiences of not being listened to or taken seriously in the institution; being participants in these processes provided them with confidence and recognition of their agency, a key point in citizen education (Walsh and Black, 2018). Furthermore, the fast-paced, innovative and fun nature of the project activities strongly appealed to the young people and stimulated their engagement. The fact that the projects were externally organised, somewhat detached from the core institutional activities and focused on a concrete goal, helped to create a playful atmosphere and provided the core participants with a sense of cross-generation equality in the projects and a sense of the possibility of making positive impacts.

However, participation within project spaces seem to be two-sided and, while the disembeddedness of the projects from the core institutions is their strength, it is also a weakness. The two cases demonstrate how the projects produced spaces for participatory activities that tended to close in on themselves. First, the activities were only accessible to a very limited group of core participants, and the majority of the young people would be mere recipients or participate on the periphery of the projects while being either unaware, indifferent or feeling left out of the projects. Therefore, projects might allow more young people to take part in change and decision making and to be in a more equal relationship with adults and professionals, but they do not give equal access to all young people. To prevent inequality, projects need to aim for a broad range of participants in order to give access to all groups of young people, not only the most privileged or disadvantaged, or 'achievers' and 'troublemakers', as pinpointed by Nairn and colleagues (2006). Second, the projects' disembeddedness prevented the core participants from affecting institutional practices. The projects were pre-established with aims and methods that did not allow much room for young people's own interests. Moreover, the unique atmosphere experienced by the young core participants within the projects could not be transferred readily into the everyday practices within the school and the psychiatric system.

Much of this critique has also been voiced in relation to children's participation in institutions by Moss and Petrie (2005), who find that children's participation within early years institutions is often merely about adjusting services. This chapter highlights the need to prevent young people's participation being treated as only a way to promote *activity*. A core discourse in Boltanski and Chiapello's (2005) definition of the projective regime is that being active is imperative, and, in line with Walther's (2012) claim that participation and activation are strongly associated in neoliberal policies, our cases indicate not only that project-based participation aims to meet young people's rights to participation, but also that activation became an aim in and of itself. Thus, in some ways, participation merely becomes a matter of taking part in activities without the possibility of affecting everyday conditions. In his much-cited work, Hart (1992) stresses that youth participation is often in danger of being tokenistic or only aiming to be citizen education without actual influence (Walsh and Black, 2018). It can be argued that for the core participants in the two studied projects there was experience of genuine participation and activities that go beyond being merely education or service adjustments. But when studied more carefully what is apparent is that neither of the two projects actually supports young people to affect their core living conditions and therefore the power relationships between young people and adults are unchanged. Adults facilitate the frameworks for participatory activities and decide which subjects are included. Thus, the projectification of participation is in danger of producing multiple initiatives that appear as genuine participation but become mostly a few selected young people's superficial experiences with being included in decision making on superficial subjects.

References

Andersen, L.L. (2018) 'Neoliberal drivers in hybrid civil society organisations: critical readings of civicness and social entrepreneurism', in M. Kamali and J. Jönsson (eds) *Neoliberalism, Nordic Welfare States and Social Work*, Abingdon: Routledge, pp 43–52.

Baraldi, C. and Cockburn, T. (2018) *Theorising Childhood: Citizenship, Rights and Participation*, London: Palgrave Macmillan.

Bentsen, P., Bonde, A.H., Schneller, M.B., Danielsen, D., Bruselius-Jensen, M. and Aagaard-Hansen, J. (2020) 'Danish "add-in" school-based health promotion: integrating health in curriculum time', *Health Promotion International*, 35(1): 70–7.

Boltanski, L. and Chiapello, E. (2005) *The New Spirit of Capitalism*, London: Verso.

Bruselius-Jensen, M. and Nielsen A.M.W. (2020) *Veje til Deltagelse: Nye forståelser og tilgange til facilitering af børn og unges deltagelse*, Aalborg: Aalborg University Publishing.

Cockburn, T. (2013) *Rethinking Children's Citizenship*, Basingstoke: Palgrave Macmillan.

Grabher, G. (2002) 'Cool projects, boring institutions: temporary collaboration in social context', *Regional Studies*, 36(3): 205–14.

Hall, R. (2005) *The Value of Visual Exploration: Understanding Cultural Activities with Young People*, West Bromwich: The Public.

Hart, R.A. (1992) *Children's Participation: From Tokenism to Citizenship*, Innocenti Essay No. 4, Florence: UNICEF Office of Research.

Holloway, S.L., Holt, L. and Mills, S. (2018) 'Questions of agency: capacity, subjectivity, spatiality and temporality', *Progress in Human Geography*.

James, A., Jenks, C. and Prout, A. (1998) *Theorizing Childhood*, New York, NY: Teachers College Press.

Jensen, A.F. (2012) *The Project Society*, Aarhus: Unipress.

Leonard, M. (2015) *The Sociology of Children, Childhood and Generation*, London: Sage Publications.

Loncle, P., Jackson, G. and Muniglia, V. (2012) 'Youth participation in Europe: Beyond discourses, practices and realities', *Policy Press Scholarship Online Youth*.

Lundy, L. (2018) 'In defence of tokenism? Implementing children's right to participate in collective decision-making', *Childhood*, 25(3): 340–54.

McMahon, G., Percy-Smith, B., Thomas, N., Becevic, Z., Liljeholm Hansson, S. and Forkby, T. (2018) *WP5 – Young People's Participation: Learning from Action Research in Eight European Cities*, Huddersfield and Gothenburg: University of Huddersfield and University of Gothenburg.

Moss, P. and Petrie, P. (2005) *From Children's Services to Children's spaces: Public Policy, Children and Childhood*, Abingdon: Routledge.

Nairn, K., Sligo, J. and Freeman, C. (2006) 'Polarizing participation in local government: which young people are included and excluded?', *Children Youth and Environments*, 16(2): 248–71.

Percy-Smith, B. (2010) 'Councils, consultations and community: rethinking the spaces for children and young people's participation 1', *Children's Geographies*, 8(2): 107–22.

Pohl, A., Batsleer, J., Loncle, P. and Walther, A (2020) 'Contested practices, power and pedagogies of young people in public spaces: an introduction', in A. Walther, J. Batsleer, P. Loncle and A. Pohl (eds) (2020) *Young People and the Struggle for Participation: Contested Practices, Power and Pedagogies in Public Space*, Abingdon: Routledge, pp 3–13.

Sørensen, N.U. and Nielsen, J.C. (2014) 'Et helt normalt perfekt selv: konstruktioner af selvet i unges beretninger om mistrivsel', *Dansk Sociologi*, 25(1): 33–54.

Thévenot, L. (2013) 'The human being invested in social forms: four extensions of the notion of engagement', in M. Archer and A. Maccarini (eds) *Engaging with the World: Agency, Institutions, Historical Formations*, Abingdon: Routledge, pp 168–186.

Tsekoura, M. (2016) 'Spaces for youth participation and youth empowerment: case studies from the UK and Greece', *YOUNG*, 24(4): 326–41.

Walsh, L. and Black, R. (2018) *Rethinking Youth Citizenship after the Age of Entitlement*, London: Bloomsbury Publishing.

Walther, A. (2012) 'Learning to participate or participating to learn?' in P. Loncle, G. Jackson and V. Muniglia (eds), *Youth Participation in Europe: Beyond Discourses, Practices and Realities*. Bristol: Policy Press, pp 189–207.

Walther, A., Pohl, A., Loncle, P. and Thomas, N.P. (2020) 'Researching youth participation – theoretical and methodological limitations of existing research and innovative perspectives', in A. Walther, J. Batsleer, P. Loncle and A. Pohl (eds) (2020) *Young People and the Struggle for Participation: Contested Practices, Power and Pedagogies in Public Space*, Abingdon: Routledge, pp 14–35.

Warming, H. and Fahnøe, K. (eds) (2017) *Lived Citizenship on the Edge of Society: Rights, Belonging, Intimate Life and Spatiality*, Cham: Springer.

PART III

Broadening participation: young people's own approaches to participation

9

Young Italians and the crisis: emerging trends in activism and self-organisation

Ilaria Pitti and Nicola De Luigi

This chapter discusses young Italians' political activation against the exacerbation of socioeconomic and intergenerational inequalities fostered by the 2008 economic crisis and the austerity measures. The study contributes to the book and to the broader scholarship in youth studies and social movement studies by providing an in-depth analysis of young people's collective reaction to inequalities through self-organisation and mutualism. The chapter is based on qualitative materials (interviews, focus groups and participant observations) collected on five experiences of youth activism in political squats (*centri sociali*). These materials are analysed in relation to three main research questions: how did the crisis transform activists' practices of participation? How has this transformation changed the relationships between activists and the surrounding communities? And what about young activists' relationships with institutions?

Key findings

- Practices of self-organisation let young people experiment with alternative solutions to their own problems, limiting young people's risk of disengaging with their communities because of experiences of inequalities.
- Practices of self-organisation, working at a small scale and focusing locally, foster interactions between young people and other local community members.
- Young people's interest and involvement in political issues are reinvigorated by the combination of small-scale actions with long-term political goals, even though young people may remain sceptical of institutional politics.

Introduction

This chapter presents emerging similarities in the reasons, aims and modes of political activation of young Italians against the growth of socioeconomic and intergenerational inequalities occurring in Italy following the 2008 economic downturn and the adoption of austerity measures by the national and European governments. The chapter considers a specific form of youth participation – namely self-organisation through squatting of public buildings (Mudu, 2012; Genova, 2018; Piazza, 2018) and contributes to the book by analysing young people's collective reaction to inequalities created or harshened by the austerity.

The chapter conceptualises 'inequality' in terms of uneven distribution of social resources and opportunities between generations, which has severely hindered young Italians' possibilities of achieving economic independence and social integration (Chevalier, 2018) during the years of the crisis. The 2008 economic downturn, known as the Great Recession, and subsequent austerity measures have certainly led to a hostile landscape for Italian society as a whole. However, different groups have been affected in different ways. In the aftermath of the Great Recession, unresolved long-term problems affecting young Italians have been exacerbated, leading many scholars to warn that new generations will likely experience a decline in opportunities in comparison with those of their parents for the first time since the Second World War (Bello and Cuzzocrea, 2018). Along with immigrants and low-skilled workers, young people have been particularly hard hit by the crisis: their unemployment rates rose, and they also struggled with earning a decent wage in a more and more insecure labour market. Moreover, the adoption of austerity policies has negatively affected the already weak capacities of the Italian welfare state to alleviate social risks related to young people's instable position in the labour market (De Luigi et al, 2018). Young people's dependency on their socioeconomic background has consequently increased, as well as their sense of social insecurity and cognitive uncertainty toward the future.

The chapter analyses how young Italians have reacted to this scenario through participation. The practices of participation considered in this chapter can be understood as forms of 'unconventional political participation'. According to the classic definition of Barnes and Kaase, this concept refers to any 'non-institutionalised direct political action that does not aim to disrupt or threaten the stability of liberal democracies' (Barnes and Kaase, 1979, p 27) such as blocking traffic, participating in (lawful) demonstrations and (un)official strikes, boycotting products, using physical force, damaging property, and occupying buildings. In line with this definition, the practices we observe develop outside institutionalised settings and entail elements of protest towards institutions whose solutions to the crisis benefit, according to the young activists, the interests of the adult generation. These practices do not intend to threaten democracy, but young people work to improve it. However, by showing the limits of existing policies, elaborating alternative solutions and asking for a radical change of approach, young activists involved in this study do not simply 'protest' towards institutions, but also engage in a sort of competition with them (Pitti, 2018). As we argue in the chapter's conclusion, this change of approach questions existing understandings of unconventional forms of political participation. Like Sand's contribution within this book (see Chapter 10), this chapter deals with self-organised forms of engagement. However, in comparison with the cases analysed by Sand, this chapter's examples acquire an explicit political nature because they are realised with a political motivation, the character of the addressed issues is collective and young people's actions target political authorities (Van Deth, 2014).

The examples on which this chapter is based are all experiences of political activism developed in the so-called 'years of the crisis', which will be analysed to 'disentangle' the complex changes that the crisis has produced on young people's participation. In particular, the examples considered in this chapter show how the economic crisis has fostered the adoption of new strategies and forms of involvement, the development of a different representation of the role of young people's activism in society and a change in young activists' understanding of the role of institutions. Three main research questions have guided our analysis: how has the crisis transformed activists' practices of participation? How has this transformation changed the relationships between activists and surrounding communities? And what about young activists' relationship with institutions?

After presenting the case studies and the methodology, the chapter answers the research questions by combining findings with discussion of relevant literature. Findings are divided into three themes. The first theme considers how youth practices of activation have changed during the crisis. While providing general information about the economic crisis' impacts in Italy, the section considers why self-organisation became the preferred means of action for the activists. The second theme looks at changes that these forms of participation have fostered in the relationships of the young activists, other citizens and their surrounding communities. Presenting radical activism's evolution within political squats from the 1970s to today, the second theme pays attention to the latest changes in young people's perspectives on radical activists' role in society. Lastly, the third theme discusses how young people's relationships with institutions evolve when young activists start to supply autonomously a series of services traditionally offered by institutions. In the concluding section, the findings serve as a basis for a reflection on the relationships between young people, inequality and political participation.

Methodology and presentation of the experiences

Casa Bettola, Làbas, Casa dei Beni Comuni, Ex-OPG 'Je so pazzo' and Baobab Experience are the five examples of youth participation on which this chapter is focused. These experiences of engagement have several commonalities that allow for their collective analysis. First, in all these experiences of participation, young people have a prominent role in both quantitative and qualitative terms. Not only are most of the people involved in the cases aged between 18 and 30, but young people have also assumed leading roles in developing these initiatives. Challenging existing understandings of young people as passive political actors, all these experiences can be considered examples of youth empowerment through participation. On a second level, the young people involved in all these experiences were largely already engaged in radical[1] social movement organisations (SMOs) at the local level. Hence, the young people involved in them had a previous and substantial expertise in activism. This allows us to consider if and how the crisis changed this kind of activism, its practices and its motives.

In 2009, following the occupation of a dismissed former roadmen's house in the medium-sized city of Reggio nell'Emilia, a group of young activists opened Casa Bettola creating "a pocket-sized common" (interview with S., activist, April 2016). The group started a series of campaigns and initiatives aimed at defending and promoting rights to housing, public education and work, as well as migrants' rights. The space has progressively become a reference point for the local inhabitants and the home of various social projects such as a school of Italian for migrants, a help-desk that provides legal advice on job-related matters, and a free afterschool for children. In 2012, during a day of strike against crisis and youth unemployment, a group of young activists squatted a former barrack located in Bologna's city centre. During the following five years, young people turned the building into Làbas: a social centre where different projects were developed for and with the local inhabitants. Làbas grew to include a self-managed shelter for migrants, a weekly farmers' market, a micro-brewery, an organic garden, a pizzeria, a library and a study room, a bike-repair shop, and a kindergarten, as well as hosting daily seminars, workshops, self-training activities and cultural events. In 2013, a group of young people who were previously involved in a local SMO started the renovation of a former barrack of 35,000 square metres located in the outskirts of Belluno, a city in north-eastern Italy. The renovation was carried out in collaboration with other local political groups and associations and led to the creation of the Casa dei Beni Comuni, a social space for social, political and cultural initiatives, mostly related to protecting local environmental resources. In 2015, a group of young activists from Naples occupied an abandoned psychiatric hospital to create the social centre Ex-OPG 'Je so pazzo'. Its name – 'Je so pazzo' – literally means 'I am a fool'. Located in a central area of the city mostly inhabited by disadvantaged families, Ex-OPG 'Je so pazzo' offers an array of free services. These include: a medical unit for gynaecological, paediatric, orthopaedic and nutritional support; a free afterschool; a legal help-desk for migrants; a school of Italian and a school of English; a theatre; a boxing gym; and a space to practise yoga and ballet. In 2015, the Baobab Experience developed in Rome. A group of young volunteers reacted to the migrant 'crisis' the city was facing, with an increase of migrants arriving in Europe and transitioning to Italy in their attempts to reach other European countries. The volunteers decided to occupy and reopen a recently closed public reception centre where they provided migrants with food, short-term shelter, clothes, and psychological, medical and legal support. The Baobab centre helped more than 35,000 people between May 2015 and December 2015, when it was evicted from the squatted building. Since then, activists have carried on their activities on the street, occupying a square with tents sheltering a public canteen, some medical units and a legal help-desk.

Our analysis is based on data collected during a period spanning from 2015 to 2018 within the Horizon 2020 projects Partispace[2] and Youthblocs.[3] Twelve biographical interviews and one focus group with the activists constitute the core materials for this analysis. Although these experiences involved large communities of young people,[4] biographical interviews and focus groups were conducted mainly with activists occupying key roles in the experiences' history or internal hierarchies. Data from interviews and focus group were integrated with information collected through participant observations undertaken in some of the case studies (Làbas, Casa Bettola, and Baobab), documentary analysis on materials produced and published by the groups (such as leaflets and social media) and further informal conversations with activists. The research and analysis were undertaken in Italian, and the quotations used in this chapter have been translated into English. Data were analysed applying Ritchie and Spencer's framework approach (Ritchie and Spencer, 1994): the inquiry was carried out by considering both *a priori* concepts and research questions derived from the literature (that is, looking for emerging forms of participation among young people during the years of the crisis) and recurring themes and topics deriving from the inductive analysis of the data. The decision not to anonymise the names of the analysed experiences has been agreed with the activists but requires a brief explanation. The examples selected for this analysis were chosen in part because of their visibility in the Italian context: all of them have received wide recognition for their innovative approaches to activism, which have succeeded in engaging 'non-politicised' individuals among others. The choice to use the real names of the experiences is partially explained by this visibility, which would have prevented any attempt of anonymisation. Moreover, research participants welcome the publicising of the experiences' names, as a further opportunity for visibility and recognition. Pseudonyms have been used for the young people involved in interviews or mentioned in fieldnotes.

From the crisis to self-organisation: young people's reaction to inequalities

Several studies in the past decade have highlighted how the global economic and financial crisis of 2007–08 has had a deep impact on Italian society in relation to political participation (Passarelli and Tuorto, 2014; Bull and Pasquino, 2018). Research shows that changes in participation in the years of the crisis are not linear and have an apparently contradictory nature. On the one hand, the difficulties generated by the crisis and the subsequent austerity measures have enlarged the distance between citizens and politics (Passarelli and Tuorto, 2014). For example, in Italy, trust levels have constantly decreased over the past ten years for almost all political institutions and populist feelings have grown steadily (Shannon, 2019). However, mistrust in political institutions and outrage against the country's economic conditions have fostered an extraordinary upsurge of activism, which has manifested especially at local level through grassroots initiatives and SMOs (Giugni and Grasso, 2018; Zamponi and Bosi, 2018). These trends are extremely visible if we focus our attention on younger generations' political behaviours. Especially among young people, increasing disenchantment and disengagement from institutional politics seem to go hand by hand with a growing interest in non-institutionalised political activities (Altieri et al, 2017; De Luigi et al, 2018; Pitti, 2018).

In line with this literature, in the cases we have analysed, the crisis was the 'engine' of young people's participation. An in-depth analysis of young activists' specific interpretation of the 2008 economic crisis highlights the connection between experiences of inequality and the decision to self-organise. The consequences of the economic downturn in people's lives are presented by the young activists as the main reason that led them to participate. Occupational and economic difficulties are mentioned by Ex-OPG and Làbas activists as the main problems against which they have decided to react. Baobab's activists explain the occupation and reopening of the former public reception centre as an attempt to counteract the "social and relational crisis emerging from the economic one" (interview with P., activist at Baobab, 2018), while Casa dei Beni Comuni develops to solve the continued decrease of local institutional provision due to the cuts and the reorganisation of public services, as exemplified by this quotation:

> 'We are active in the allegedly most liveable city in Italy, where it is said that all goes well. Unfortunately, this is not the case: behind this statement, there is a social reality where the crisis is materialising not so much in terms of a decrease of income ... but in terms of a social crisis that has been affecting our territory for the last 35 years and that has a big hashtag, which is "depopulation". In the last 35 years our province has lost 15,000 people ... this is a social desertification.' (Interview with M., activist at Casa dei Beni Comuni, 2018)

Although young activists' actions address different forms of inequality generated by the crisis, all of them underline their views that the crisis is not a temporary, economic and global issue, but mainly a structural, social and local problem. From their perspectives, solutions to the problem need also to be structural, social and local, and they seek a profound shift in people's behaviours and culture. Hence, they opt for practices of self-organisation because they consider these the best way to: find sustainable and long-term solutions instead of simply trying to 'fix' an emergency; foster a deeper reactivation of social ties instead of merely answering people's immediate needs; and empower local communities, by helping them to voice their problems and elaborate shared solutions. This is exemplified by the following quotation:

> 'For us, the "collective cleaning" of the neighbourhood is not a form of welfarism, or the attempt to put a patch on a hole, but it is way to produce "collectivity" … people feel they regain possession of their own life, because they say: "This thing that was wrong before, now it is right, so it was good that we have worked together" … the idea is not to give assistance, but to create political struggle through daily practices.' (Interview with P., activist at Ex-OPG 'Je so pazzo', 2018)

The developed solutions acquire the nature of 'mutualistic' experiences of self-organisation. In social studies and political sciences, this concept refers to a specific form of grassroots mobilisation where people try to build what they claim to be right through their own contributions and resources (Ferraris, 2011; Zamponi and Bosi, 2018). Mutualistic forms of participation aim to address increasing demands for material and immaterial needs (for example, food, housing and health), but also seek to produce political changes. Indeed, what distinguishes mutualism from, for example, volunteering is its political potential: mutualism contains the aim of expressing a political vision and challenging a socioeconomic system perceived as unfair. Young activists address inequalities by proposing alternative solutions that are political and, in so doing, they seek to foster new alliances with the local population and to empower their position in relation to institutions.

From fortresses to squares: changes in youth self-organisation through social centres

In Italy, the occupation of abandoned buildings to create 'political squats' is not new. The so-called '*centri sociali*' (social centres) are forms of youth political participation with a long history in the country. Their roots can be traced back to the mid-1970s, when the *circoli del proletariato giovanile* (centers of proletarian youth) were opened throughout the country (Montagna, 2009; Genova, 2018). These spaces were 'places for meeting and building informal social networks outside schools and factories' (Genova, 2018, p 4) and they were managed by youth groups sharing an 'explicit class-rooted conflictual political identity' (Genova, 2018, p 5). Through the squatting of public spaces, youth groups expressed their concerns about the economic difficulties experienced in the country during those years, as well as about authorities' inability to provide solutions to emerging social needs. Such occupations were harshly repressed at the end of the 1970s (Mudu, 2012), but the squats that survived were turned into *centri sociali*. These became the interface of the autonomous left and anarchist movements, and developed as counter-cultural spaces. From the 1980s to the early 2000s, the activities of the *centri sociali* have mainly raised 'cultural challenges to the dominant language, to the codes that organise information and shape social practices' (Melucci, 1995, p 41) through making alternative cultural proposals. From the early 2000s, the range of activities proposed within these centres has progressively broadened to include help-desks for migrants and ethnic minorities, theatres, gyms, independent publishing houses and record labels (Mudu, 2012).

From this list of activities commonly proposed in social centres we can easily understand which kinds of 'users' traditionally frequented these spaces. First, the *centri sociali* were animated and attended by (politicised) young people who either organised or enjoyed the many cultural and social activities proposed in these spaces. Second, *centri sociali* were traditionally attended by people sharing a marginal societal position – migrants, minority ethnic groups and homeless people, as well as sex workers and drug users – who could find a welcoming environment and support through the social projects started in the political squats to address their needs. The rest of the population – that is adults, older people, families, and middle-class and non-politicised people – was rarely involved in them. The centres were portrayed by the activists and understood by the local population as a type of 'fortress': spaces having a strong counter-cultural and counter-hegemonic identity and 'governed' by alternative social rules that separated them from the rest of city (Piazza, 2018; Pitti, 2018).

The evolutions in repertoires of action during the years of the crisis have fostered changes. Mutualistic forms of participation have transformed relationships between activists and the surrounding population. Activists underline that the experiences of Casa Bettola, Casa dei Beni Comuni, Làbas, Ex OPG 'Je so pazzo' and Baobab come from the long and rich tradition of the *centri sociali*, but they also stress a symbolic and pragmatic detachment from the classic way of interpreting activism of these spaces. The novelty in these forms of self-organisation is the transformation of social centres from 'fortresses' to 'squares', by creating dialogues with local inhabitants and by turning the occupied buildings into spaces at the service of the surrounding communities, where the needs of the whole population – rather than of segments of it – are addressed. The following quotation exemplifies this:

> 'Many of us came out of the experience of a more classic social centre. We chose to close this centre because we wanted to open a wider urban experience; wider in terms of kind of intervention and internal composition. This is how Casa dei Beni Comuni was born: we defined it then and we still define it today a social centre at the service of the citizens.' (Interview with M., activist at Casa dei Beni Comuni, 2018)

Another activist explicitly uses the word 'square' to describe the new form of self-organisation: "Làbas has a big central square so opening the social centre in the abandoned building has been like giving back a square to the city" (interview with F., activist at Làbas, 2015).

This move to a 'square' occurred in Italian social centres during the historical period marked by the economic crisis and austerity. Young activists at Làbas perceived this link clearly, discussing their decisions to open, within the social centre, a shelter for homeless people. The fieldwork note describes this link:

> Antonio (activist) tells us that: 'We came from experiences in the housing struggle and our housing help-desk worked full-time: there were so many people coming to seek help to find a house. Then there was the social centre [Làbas], which had a large, unused space to put into operation. There was also always the issue of migrants. [We developed] the idea of making a sort of transit point for migrants in movement towards other cities in Europe and so we decided to open the homeless shelter organised within the centre.' (Fieldnote, June 2015)

To create the shelter, the activists decided to involve local NGOs and volunteers. They organised a city assembly to judge whether there was enough support to start such a project and launched a 'call for volunteers' to engage not only people belonging to SMOs, but also 'common people'. There seemed to be some interest in the proposal. This was perceived as an innovation for the centre, creating novel connections with local people, as explained by one young activist:

> Antonio considers the call for volunteers a real innovation and an important breakthrough moment in relation to the

classic 'recruitment' strategies of Italian social centres: 'not only in our own development as a social centre, but in the history of social centres'. According to Antonio, this 'hybrid' political practice, as he calls it, had never been experimented with before. He explains what he means by hybrid, emphasising the elements of discontinuity from the social centre's tradition: 'Usually, there is a core group of activist [the so-called "collective"] that manages the occupied space, that has the power to make political decisions and use the space. Usually, the space is like "owned" by the collective. What is happening inside this social centre is a genuine hybridisation [with local people], an innovation.' (Fieldnote, June 2015)

Providing alternatives services to (and with) the local population entails a deep change in understanding radical activism's role in society. It emerges that – in order to achieve a deep and long-term transformation of society – radical activism needs to 'be around people', to open its fortresses to non-politicised people and show them that "politics is a tool to transform what exists" (interview with P., activist at Ex-OPG 'Je So Pazzo', 2018). This is exemplified by the words of a young activist:

'So, we escort them [some local people] to the municipal council [to help them to voice a concern] and when you get this small victory, you create political capital because you have shown people that politics is a tool to transform what exists. Our idea is that it is not yet possible to start a revolution today … In this historical phase it seems rather necessary to rebuild the community bonds and the social ground on which reformist or revolutionary actions can develop. Without this work of tilling the soil from … elements of passivation and resignation, clearly nothing can be done.' (Interview with P., activist at Ex-OPG 'Je so pazzo', 2018)

The observed practices of self-organisation are based on small-scale actions and have a strong local focus. These characteristics help young activists to foster fruitful interactions with local inhabitants. In the next section, the analysis focuses on what these transformations in youth activism tell us about young people's relationship with institutions, conceived as the classic providers of those services and goods that now they try to produce by themselves.

From claiming to prefiguring: a new position towards institutions

The political transformation described in the previous section reflects a generational change in the approach to participation (Dalton, 2008) and in young people's relationship with institutions and authorities. As previously discussed, in Italy, young people have been affected by the crisis and the austerity measures more than any other generation (Bello and Cuzzocrea, 2018). The direct and everyday experience of the effects of an increasingly uneven distribution of resources between generations has developed into an 'urgency to do something' (De Luigi et al, 2018). In young Italian activists' practices of self-organisation, feelings of outrage and hope arising from conditions of structural inequality combine with new cultures of democracy (Kelly et al, 2018) where experimenting with innovative, alternative and practical solutions is not only possible, but necessary (Pitti, 2018). This is exemplified in a public declaration from Làbas:

> This is the story of a generation that wants to create relationships and open spaces to experiment with practices, languages, new ways of living the city … This is the story of a generation that wants to create its future, that wants to take back its life starting from the present by defining and pursuing concrete objectives. This is the story of a generation that wants to open political laboratories within the city, elements of anomaly in the crisis, which … wants to change what already exists in an experimental and shattering way. (Làbas public statement, 2012)

In this evolution of the *centri sociali*, it is possible to notice a non-ideological approach to politics that is typical of younger generations (Dalton, 2008). When it comes to institutionalised forms of engagement, this trend towards a non-ideological politics has been widely used to explain young people's progressive distancing from parties' ideologies. However, the non-ideological approach to politics also leads to less institutional forms of engagement and, in the case of the *centri sociali*, this approach seems to have fostered a 'pragmatic turn' in youth self-organisation. These efforts result in a type of political engagement through which young people seek to enact the new society they envision in the present. The engagement occurs through small-scale, cause-oriented and fluid actions that comply with and reflect long-term political goals. The combination of small-scale actions with long-term political goals reinvigorates young people's interest and involvement in political issues despite their scepticism with institutional politics. This political approach corresponds with what has been defined as 'prefigurative politics': that is, 'a political action, practice, movement, moment or development in which certain political ideals are experimentally actualised in the here and now rather than hoped to be realised in a distant future' (Van de Sande, 2015, p 180). According to Castells, when existing institutions fail to manage structural crisis, 'change can only take place out of the system by a transformation of power relations that starts in people's minds and develops in the forms of networks … of new actors constituting themselves as the subjects of the new history in the making' (Castells, 2012, p 228). Young activists' practices of self-organisation are utopias that 'become material force by incarnating in people's minds, by inspiring their dreams, by guiding their actions and inducing their reactions' (Castells, 2012, p 228). The following quotation makes the link between the practical actions of today showing the way to the utopias of tomorrow:

> 'Faced with the immobility of the institutions, we must show that we – that we are nobody … – are creating another model of reception [of migrants], another model of coexistence. [We are showing that] another way is possible, and we are making it, that is, [we are demonstrating that] there is this cultural possibility which starts from the desert. So today we are sowing and sowing, then we will harvest.' (Interview with P., activist at Baobab, 2018)

Hence, emerging trends in youth self-organisation in the years of the crisis foster a different relationship towards institutions. Through self-organisation, young people engage in domains that are traditionally 'institutional' by creating and providing services that are classically a task of institutions (that is, services for unemployed people, young people, homeless people, migrants and children). The stories of Casa Bettola, Casa dei Beni Comuni, Làbas, Ex OPG 'Je so pazzo' and Baobab are youth attempts to 'unpack and ground their disaffection towards institutions into projects that allow them not only to protest, but also to stop waiting for the intervention of authorities that they do not trust and to win back a power in shaping their lives and the world(s) they inhabit' (Pitti, 2018, p 119). This change of approach leads youth self-organised projects to become 'alternative institutions' in their local areas and compete with local authorities in defining what can be considered a public issue or a public service. This is explained in the following quotation:

> 'In recent years many districts ["branches" of the municipality in the neighbourhoods of the city] in Reggio Emilia have been closed. These were "institutions of proximity" that once were very important, they were a point of reference. Casa Bettola has progressively assumed a role similar to that of a district ... with people who often come to complain about difficulties ... This has led us to open the "Casa Bettola District" as a provocative, but effective gesture. We have created a new District, with the official signs, trying in some way to challenge politics.' (Interview with S., activist at Casa Bettola, 2016)

In the experiences of mutualism carried out by social centres, at stake are not only social problems and the resources to answer them, but also the politicisation of issues and needs that were previously considered of private concern (and thus requiring private solutions) or 'the discourse on these needs, their interpretations, the conflicts and the powers on their definition and recognition' (De Leonardis, 1998, p 38).

Conclusion

The chapter has analysed the transformations that youth activism has undergone during the years of the economic crisis in Italy. Practices of self-organisation within social centres emerge as forms of collective reaction to the growth of intergenerational and socioeconomic inequalities. Inspired by a mutualistic model of engagement where solidarity is combined with self-help goals (Busso and De Luigi, 2019), these practices have fostered fruitful relationships between young activists and the surrounding local communities. The autonomous provision of a variegated range of services (from libraries to medial units) has turned social centres into reference points for intergenerational contacts and socially diversified populations. Feelings of distrust towards institutions have combined with the awareness of that old solutions are no longer working. The urgency to find new solutions has led young people to experiment with alternative ideas on society through self-organisation.

In relation to the literature on unconventional practices of participation, the novelty of these new forms of self-organisation lies particularly in the new positions young people assume in relation to institutions. Traditionally unconventional forms of participation have been understood mainly as a means of protest against, or to claim via, institutions. Youth self-organised practices in the years of the crisis appear to go beyond protesting and claiming (Zamponi and Bosi, 2018). As we have argued elsewhere (Pitti, 2018), self-organisation is used to express a critique towards and to protest against authorities, but also represents a mean to 'circumnavigate' institutions that are no longer considered a useful and reliable interlocutor.

Young people's disappointment targets not only institutional solutions to the intergenerational and socioeconomic inequalities increased by the crisis, but the very definition of the situation underlying these solutions. While institutions and common discourses tend to present problems as created or harshened by the crisis and, more generally, social inequalities as effects of events and decisions beyond their control, young activists reclaim an understanding of socioeconomic and intergenerational inequalities as 'political issues', that is, as effects of conscious decisions/actions that can be solved by new conscious decisions/actions. In the analysed experiences, young people take a leading role in the repoliticisation of a series of issues – such as poverty, unemployment, migration, use of public assets – that are often depoliticised in institutional discourses, portrayed as nobody's fault and nobody's task or as mere technical issues.

Understanding inequality as a political problem emerges as a turning point in the path towards activation and empowerment of the young people involved in this chapter. This finding confirms the principle that we can elaborate solutions only if we first believe that things are modifiable and that we have the possibility and capacity to participate in this change (Arendt, 1965). In other words, disengagement is not only the effect of distrust towards institutions, but also the effect of normalising discourses (Foucault, 1975) that portray a problem as 'natural' and 'unmodifiable' (Bourdieu, 1998). Revealing the social (and thus modifiable) nature of inequalities, the connections between individual conditions and structural dynamics, and the capacity of individual and collective agency to act on existing structures of inequality, are preliminary – and yet necessary – steps towards fostering youth engagement in society, steps that social sciences have the means and the responsibility to undertake with young people.

Notes

[1] Guzman-Concha (2015) defines radical SMOs as political groups distinguished by: an agenda for drastic changes that would affect elite interests and social positions; a repertory of contention characterised by employing unconventional means; and

a counter-cultural identity that frames and justifies unconventional objectives and methods. These movements advocate for radical political and social changes, but do not seek to overthrow democracy and its institutions.

2   This project has received funding from the European Union (EU) Horizon 2020 research and innovation programme under grant agreement 649416.

3   This project has received funding from the EU Horizon 2020 research and innovation programme under the Marie Skłodowska-Curie grant 701844.

4   The informal nature of these forms of youth participation does not allow for a clear assessment of the number of young people involved in them during the study years as there is no list of participants. However, from interviews and observations we estimate that between 50 and 150 young people were involved in each experience.

References

Alteri, L., Leccardi, C. and Raffini, L. (2017) 'Youth and the reinvention of politics: new forms of participation in the age of individualization and presentification', *Partecipazione e Conflitto*, 9(3): 717–47.

Arendt, H. (1965) *On Revolution*, New York, NY: Penguin.

Barnes, S.H. and Kaase, N. (eds) (1979) Political Action: Mass Participation in Five Western Democracies, London: Sage Publications.

Bello, B.G. and Cuzzocrea, V. (2018) 'Introducing the need to study young people in contemporary Italy', *Journal of Modern Italian Studies*, 23(1): 1–7.

Bourdieu, P. (1998) *La Domination Masculine*, Paris: Seuil.

Bull, M. and Pasquino, G. (2018) 'Introduction: Italian politics in an era of recession: the end of bipolarism?', in M. Bull and G. Pasquino (eds) *Italy Transformed: Politics, Society and Institutions at the End of the Great Recession*, London: Routledge, pp 1–12.

Busso, S. and De Luigi, N. (2019) 'Civil society actors and the welfare state: a historically-based analytical framework', *Partecipazione e Conflitto*, 12(2): 259–296.

Castells, M. (2012) *Networks of Outrage and Hope: Social Movements in the Internet Age*, Cambridge: Polity Press.

Chevalier, T. (2018) 'Social citizenship of young people in Europe: a comparative institutional analysis', *Journal of Comparative Policy Analysis: Research and Practice*, 20(3): 304–23.

Dalton, R.J. (2008) *The Good Citizen. How a Younger Generation is Reshaping American Politics*, Washington, DC: CQ Press.

De Leonardis, O., Negrelli, S. and Salais, R. (eds) (2012) *Democracy and Capabilities for Voice*, Bern: Peter Lang.

De Luigi, N., Martelli, A. and Pitti, I. (2018) 'New forms of solidarity and young people: an ethnography of youth participation in Italy', in S. Pickard and J. Bessant (eds) *Young People Re-Generating Politics in Times of Crises*, Cham: Palgrave Macmillan, pp 253–71.

Ferraris, P. (2011) *Ieri e Domani: Storia Critica del Movimento Operaio e Socialista ed Emancipazione dal Presente* [Yesterday and Tomorrow: Critical History of the Worker's Movement and the Emancipation from the Present], Rome: Edizioni dell'Asino.

Foucault, M. (1975) *Surveiller et Punir*, Paris: Gallimard.

Genova, C. (2018) 'Youth activism in political squats between centri sociali and case occupate', *Societies*, 8(3): 1–25.

Giugni, M. and Grasso, M.T. (eds) (2018) *Citizens and the Crisis*, Cham: Palgrave Macmillan.

Guzman-Concha, C. (2015) 'Radical social movements in Western Europe: a configurational analysis', *Social Movement Studies*, 14(6): 668–91.

Kelly, P., Campbell, P., Harrison, L. and Hickey, C. (2018) 'Young people and the politics of outrage and hope: an introduction', in P. Kelly, P. Campbell, L. Harrison, and C. Hickey (eds) *Young People and the Politics of Outrage and Hope*, Leiden: Brill, pp 1–24.

Melucci, A. (1995) 'The process of collective identity', in H. Johnston and B. Klandermans (eds) *Social Movements and Culture*, Minneapolis, MN: University of Minnesota Press, pp 41–62.

Montagna, N. (2009) 'Italy, Centri Sociali', *The International Encyclopedia of Revolution and Protest*, https://doi.org/10.1002/9781405198073.wbierp0795

Mudu, P. (2012) 'I centri sociali italiani: verso tre decadi di occupazioni e di spazi autogestiti [Italian social centres: towards three decades of occupations and self-managed spaces]', *Partecipazione e Conflitto*, 1: 69–92.

Passarelli, G. and Tuorto, D. (2014) 'Not with my vote: turnout and the economic crisis in Italy', *Contemporary Italian Politics*, 6(2): 147–58.

Piazza, G. (2018) 'Italian social centres: conflictual political actors beyond the liberated spaces', in SqEK (ed) *Fighting for Spaces, Fighting for our Lives: Squatting Movements Today*, Münster: Edition-Assemblage, pp 284–6.

Pitti, I. (2018) *Youth and Unconventional Political Engagement*, Cham: Palgrave Macmillan.

Ritchie, J. and Spencer, A. (1994) 'Qualitative data analysis for applied policy research', in A. Bryman and R.G. Burger (eds) *Analysing Qualitative Data*, New York, NY: Taylor & Francis.

Shannon D. (2019) 'Anti-capitalism and libertarian political economy', in C. Levy and M. Adam (eds) *The Palgrave Handbook of Anarchism*, Cham: Palgrave Macmillan, pp 91–106.

Van Deth, J.W. (2014) 'A conceptual map of political participation', *Acta Politica*, 49(3): 349–67.

Van de Sande, M. (2015) 'Fighting with tools: prefiguration and radical politics in the twenty-first century', *Rethinking Marxism*, 27(2): 177–94.

Zamponi, L. and Bosi, L. (2018) 'Politicizing solidarity in times of crisis: the politics of alternative action organizations in Greece, Italy, and Spain', *American Behavioral Scientist*, 62(6): 796–815.

10

Justifying self-organisation: between inequality and critique

Anne-Lene Sand

Based on ethnographic fieldwork and the concepts of self-organisation and semi-organisation, this chapter analyses how young people from Denmark organise themselves within their leisure time. The chapter focuses on how young people design participatory possibilities for other young people mainly by themselves, but also through dialogue and collaboration with municipalities, associations and external entities. The chapter draws on Boltanski and Thévenot's (2006) pragmatic sociology and illustrates how temporal and spatial logics influence youth participatory processes. The notion of justification makes it possible to analyse participatory processes that are often taken for granted when it comes to designing participatory spaces for young people in Scandinavia. The phrase 'between inequality and critique' in the chapter title denotes an intersection between how institutional logics, on the one hand, construct unequal opportunities for young people and, on the other hand, motivate a critical thinking towards existing participatory possibilities that foster processes of empowerment that would not emerge otherwise.

Key findings

- Time and space in young people's everyday lives are hidden structures that can construct inequalities in terms of how and which participatory processes are legitimised.
- The chapter provides critical reflections about the ways in which institutions construct time and space for young people's participation and why time and space are relevant to understanding youth and complex processes of inequality.
- Adult-led participatory approaches tend to neglect young people's perspectives and ways to design participatory spaces, which consequently can result in young people losing their motivation to participate. The chapter elucidates how young people participate

through self-organised and semi-organised practices that are not adult-led.

- Young people who try to organise themselves need to justify their participatory approaches, but might be marginalised because institutionalised participatory spaces are favoured across Europe.

Introduction

> 'The biggest challenge with grassroots work is that, even if you don't want to, you become more organised. You need to organise it to a small extent, even if you want to be self-organised, but as soon as you do so, you run into an established culture … where you have to compromise your own values.' (Interview, 2015)

This quote is from an interview with a Danish man who for several years has tried to construct alternatively organised participatory possibilities for young people and adults interested in alternative cultures of movement.

Drawing on his experience of organising activities and places not affiliated with institutions, municipalities or associations, he emphasises a challenge faced by young self-organised people that concerns being forced to participate in more tightly organised activities and leisure spaces, thereby compromising their own values. Following the voices of young people who express similar challenges related to organisation and participation, this chapter explores how young people in Denmark question and push the boundaries of participatory societal structures through urban practices they design and organise themselves.

Drawing on two different ethnographic research projects, this chapter analyses the concepts of 'self-organisation' and 'semi-organisation'. Self-organisation refers to young people who organise urban and creative participatory spaces themselves (for example, concerts under bridges or raves in abandoned buildings). Semi-organisation is used to describe how young people search to define and organise participatory spaces themselves in contrast to self-organised young people who engage in dialogue with external partners such as municipalities, city planners, institutions or private entities in order to obtain advice, financial support and materials. Semi-organised practices are, for example, seen in contemporary organisations of street sport and urban cultures of movement (Sand, 2019).

In Scandinavia and elsewhere in Europe, adults have predominantly organised spaces for young people's leisure through youth organisations, formalised institutions and associations. Scandinavian associations have traditionally been significant in providing leisure possibilities for young people, with such initiatives being formally organised through democratically selected boards, annual meetings, paid membership and categorisation of members in relation to age and often gender (Kaspersen and Ottesen, 2001). Within these structural spaces, decisions about where, when, what and with whom one can participate are organised in advance (Sand, 2019).

However, the landscapes and organisation of participatory spaces are changing, and this chapter discusses the specific Scandinavian context. Recent Scandinavian studies have shown that young people are searching for flexible (Laub and Pilgaard, 2013; Sand, 2019) and alternatively organised forms of leisure participation (Sand, 2017). This emphasises the importance of understanding how young people organise themselves, what kind of participatory spaces they design and what challenges they are confronted with in relation to institutional traditions, norms and structures. A similar critical perspective on which circumstances influence young people's participation is seen in the Chapters 11 and 16 in this book.

The youth practices considered in this chapter are neither manifest political behaviours (Ekman and Amnå, 2012) nor counter-cultural in their intentions. Instead, young Danes' practices of self-organisation can be considered an example of a latent form of political participation in as much as their critique of the institutional structures that surround them entails a claim for change, a reflection on power structures and, thus, strong political potential. The use of the concept of self-organisation sheds light on how young people organise themselves. Furthermore, semi- and self-organised practices suggest how participatory spaces for young people can be constructed in the future.

The chapter provides insight into how young people design and organise participatory spaces through temporal and spatial logics, and how self- and semi-organised logics stand in contrast to the logics within formalised leisure organisations. The empirical material problematises how institutional structures, on the one hand, fail to foster creative, self-organised participatory spaces, but how, on the other hand, the lack of alternative participatory possibilities motivates young people to think differently and mobilise themselves differently. It is worth reflecting whether the lack of participatory spaces where young people can organise themselves results in unequal opportunities for these young people. Answering the following question, the chapter explores how some types of organisational spaces are valued and justified as youth spaces: which institutional challenges confront young self-organised or semi-organised people when designing spaces for participation?

The chapter is theoretically informed by the theory of justification developed by Boltanski and Thévenot (2006), which recognises the reflexive and critical capacities ordinary people use in everyday practices to denounce dominant ideologies and injustice. Principles of justification are closely linked to how, for example, people and practices are measured and legitimised as being worthy, which can lead to some logics being more dominant or legitimised than others. In this chapter, participation is understood as a critical, reflexive and alternative approach applied by young people who organise themselves. Practices of inequality are approached through Boltanski and Thévenot's concepts of 'logics' and 'tests'. Logics represent an approach to everyday life that is expressed non-verbally in the way people walk, talk, act socially and engage culturally, and how they identify themselves and choose among different types of everyday practices. The 'logics of justification' refer to the qualities that define and measure worth and can influence the processes of inequality (Boltanski and Thévenot, 2006, p 141). Tests refer to the forms of conflict that occur when people question the legitimacy of practices, as for example seen in the chapter's introductory quote, where the research participant critically reflects on the need to collaborate with established cultures. The concepts of logics and tests can help understand how young people who are self- and semi-organised experience need to justify themselves and what types of inequality traditional organisational societal structures generate, since some organisational forms are valued as more legitimate than others.

Existing perspectives on youth, participation and alternative forms of organisation

Youth researchers have argued that the tendency for societies to include young people in participatory and decision-making processes is limited, and instead an 'illusion of a youth voice' is often created (Cockburn, 2005, p 110). Relatively few young people under the age of 18 are given the opportunity to participate in political, economic, civic or social decision making. When young people are encouraged to participate, the process is usually dominated by adults (see Barber, 2009; Vromen and Collin, 2010). In a review of participation and young people in Europe, Barber describes the tendency of 'adultising' and calls for honesty about whether young people, in many situations, are being consulted in relation to their participation or are able to participate (Barber, 2009, p 38). Barber furthermore argues that top-down processes need to be analysed in order to understand both the barriers and opportunities young people, and those who work with them, are facing (Barber, 2009). In addition, research shows that young people are rarely able to influence the structures, substance or outcome of their participation (Wyn and White, 1997; Saggers, et al, 2004, p 105; Bo'sher, 2006). Johnson and colleagues (1998) analyse difficulties in reducing the effects of institutional hierarchies and pre-established positions of people with authority over children. For example, municipalities working with youth councils have little experience of working with young people in this way and may be slow to understand their needs and concerns or understand the barriers that obstruct their involvement (Johnson et al, 1998, p 247). Turner (2013) analyses how skateboarders are expected to adopt certain behavioural norms in order to participate in structural processes regarding the location and funding of public skateboarding places. According to Turner, this is a civilising process wherein skateboarders risk losing the practices that motivated them in the first place, which might result in fewer young skateboarders participating (Turner, 2013, p 1259). Turner problematises this civilising tendency, drawing on Robert Putnam's (2000) book, *Bowling Alone*, and his term 'civic broccoli', meaning that some participatory activities are 'good for you but unappealing' (Turner, 2013, p 1259).

In their article, Leccardi and Woodman (2015) emphasise that studying time and space can tell us something about young people organise themselves socially and they call for empirical studies that address time and space in young people's lives and how time and space can reveal complex processes of inequality (Leccardi and Woodman, 2015, p 718). Following Leccardi and Woodman, this chapter contains a study of bottom-up processes of participation. The chapter focuses on the 'meeting' between young people and external partners and how young people are *empowered* to create participatory spaces (Cornwall, 2004) in contrast to the spaces they are *invited* into (Brock et al, 2001; Tsekoura, 2016).

Within this chapter, the perspectives of young people are inspired by anthropological studies of youth (Amit-Talia and Wulff, 1995; Bucholtz, 2002). Anthropologist Amit argues that: 'our exploration of the dialectic between culture and youth should not be restricted to cultural constructions *by* youths. We should also be investigating the broader cultural constructions *of* youth' (Amit, 2001, p 151, emphasis in original). The dialectic entails more complicated visions and agencies of social development (Amit, 2001, p 152). This chapter does not consider inequality in relation to class or ethnicity; instead, it argues that the dialectic between practices of self-organisation and the perspective of justification can help us to understand the nature of the processes of inequality faced by some young people, and how these same processes can foster participatory possibilities.

Following young people there ... there ... and there

The empirical material represented in this chapter is based on ethnographic fieldwork carried out during two different research projects. In 2011–13, I followed young people who organised concerts and raves in urban spaces in order to understand how 38 people, one third of them female and two thirds of them male, aged 14–38, self-organised in urban space. Observing a 37-year-old doing the same as a 14-year-old led me to define youth through both age and practice, and not as a fixed age group (see Bucholtz, 2002). As I walked around different city spaces, I asked myself, "How do I position myself as a researcher in a 'social field'?" I overcame this methodological problem by having a friend accompany me during the fieldwork, and since I no longer appeared alone, I was able to observe and participate in the social practices taking place. Furthermore, my background in the musical underground culture provided a bridge to accessing young people's knowledge and experiences around their self-organised practices.

In 2015–16, I followed 18 people who applied for funding for seven projects relating to urban cultures of movement from the National Platform for Street Sports[1] (hereafter 'the Platform'). The criteria for choosing the research participants were that they were involved in a specific project, they used urban space and they were motivated to organise new spatial, temporal and social projects. Since the project organisers applied to the Platform for funding, I characterised the projects as semi-organised, as, in contrast to the self-organised projects mentioned earlier, they collaborated with external partners such as the Platform. The projects were related to skateboarding, parkour, climbing, shuffling, street soccer, street handball and urban yoga, in different Danish cities.

During the two research projects, the following methods were used: sensory participation (Pink, 2009), photography (Pink, 2007), photo-elicitation (Douglas, 2002), walk-and-talk and place interviews (Sin, 2003); a similar methodological approach can be seen in Chapter 15 of this book. The participants were ethnic Danes who came from middle-class families. The research participants were not just interested in practising skateboarding or parkour or listening to music; they were engaged in rethinking, designing, organising and building alternative spaces for their activities. It was difficult to follow young people who organised themselves since they were not affiliated with a particular institution or established context. I therefore followed them in multi-sited contexts, in line with anthropologist Ulf Hannerz's (2003) methodological term 'Being there … there … and there!'. This allowed an exploration of how the organisational, social, spatial, temporal and material aspects are related in constructing alternative forms of participation. The limitation of this methodological approach is to the difficulty in following a specific group of people over time in order to gain deeper insight into social hierarchies and relations over the long term. If studying social relationships, the methodological approach might raise ethical considerations, but the object of study was organisational processes and structures, which legitimises looking across multiple practices (see Hannerz, 2003).

The following analysis is divided into three empirical sections, which, in different ways, describe the logics that are evident to young people who organise themselves and the challenges they experience.

Justifying informal competencies

Five young men in their early twenties organised their own concerts under a bridge in the centre of a large Danish city. During a three-year period, they held three concerts in each of which up to 300 young people participated. No formalised institutions or adults were involved. The young organisers used Facebook and their social network to arrange the event socially (see Sand and Hakim-Fernandez, 2018). The concerts were free for everyone to attend, and the young men who organised the concerts sold cheap beer in order to cover the cost of renting a generator that provided electricity for the band's instruments. Organising concerts of their own led the young men to reflect on the differences between organising concerts in urban spaces and official music venues. To them, urban space provides greater participatory possibilities. Sebastian (age 24) explains:

> 'This is the first time I have carried an idea into the world in a product [that] has been so massive and aimed at so many people. It is not because I haven't had the intention, but with ideas like these, it is a bit easier to come from a place without a lot of experience and be able to do something interesting.' (Interview, 2011)

Figure 10.1: A young man rehearsing violin under the bridge

Source: Marcus Marcussen.

Figure 10.2: Young people assemble before a concert on the periphery of the city

Source: Marcus Marcussen.

Figure 10.3: At night, bands play on a 'stage' comprising a podium between the concrete pillars of a bridge

Source: Marcus Marcussen.

Sebastian feels that urban spaces, and the specific place under the bridge, provides an opportunity to gain experience in organising concerts – which is about finding bands, securing audio equipment, making visual installations, inviting people and communicating through social media. The phrase "to come from a place without a lot of experience" indicates that urban places do not require one to come from a certain formalised place in order to carry out an idea.

Mark elaborates on what this means. At 19, Mark was a pioneer in developing a self-organised underground concert space. Today he is 32 and organises one of the biggest established music scenes in Aarhus, the second largest city of Denmark. In the following dialogue, Mark links participation with formalised competencies.

Mark: 'It's about being able to support everyone, but it's a system that is aimed towards people who have certain skills. If you can create stories and illustrate that you can put the right things in play, then the chances for support are greater. It also requires discipline; when you buy an orange, then you have to remember to save the receipt for the accounts, etc. So, it's a system where you can be lost, even if you have a brilliant idea.'

Sand: 'Can you expand on how you think such formal processes can discourage self-organised processes?'

Mark: 'For example, when I have to put a new chair in a room, I have to measure it and create a diagram for the fire authorities and escape routes. Evaluations and self-evaluations also have to be sent to the state and municipality, and that time could have been spent on culture. Conversely, it shows how you can spend money responsibly, but it can be limiting.' (Interview, 2011)

From a young age, Sebastian and Mark have had experience of carrying out ideas and making musical spaces in which other young people can participate. In different ways, they explain how participation in the public music scene has been built on specific logics and requires formalised competencies linked to discipline, structure and certain types of communication. The participation also requires developing policies around security and alcohol regulations, writing evaluations and creating budgets. Justification of worth is, in this example, seen in terms of possessing specific formalised competencies that qualify for participation. The formalised and well-established music scene requires logics and restrictions that formalise the work process. Even though these ordering structures might have legitimacy, for example, when it comes to security, it is worth reflecting on whether these processes of justification can also construct participatory inequality. The problematic aspect, according to Mark, is that "it's a system that is aimed towards people who have certain skills", and, as a consequence, "it's a system where you can be lost, even if you have a brilliant idea". Instead of searching for a way to participate in the formalised musical venue, these young people test existing structures through their critical capacity to organise music differently in urban spaces. They do not just critique existing structures; they critically reflect on them. According to Boltanski and Thévenot (2006), testing aspects of everyday life makes people aware of the potential and power they have, and thereby tests become a practice of emancipation. The empirical example illustrates how reflecting on the structures surrounding them makes people capable of generating new participatory possibilities, by directing them towards emancipatory spaces.

Questioning predefined logics of time and space

In 2015, I met with three male skateboarders in Aarhus for an interview about how they organised themselves as skateboarders. The place where they had been meeting and skating for the previous 30 years had just been torn down, which forced them to organise themselves differently. They tried to organise themselves through an association, in order to get permanent indoor facilities, but ended up organising themselves in an urban space as they perceived that skateboarding was too different from the municipality's and association's organisational structure. I characterise the difference through different logics. They explained this, as follows:

Tom: 'It [being self-organised] isn't so tightly organised, and that makes it hard for the municipality, because they want to know how many members we have.'

Chris: 'We tried having registrations and had lots of people using the hall, but it was difficult getting people to sign up, and we don't have the same support from our parents that people who play football have.'

Tom: 'Applying for funding is difficult when you can't document how much a place is being used.'

Chris: 'In order to get funding, there were rules about us having to teach, but you can't teach skateboarding.'

Sand: 'Why not? '

Chris: 'We do it by skating, observing, listening, testing and learning, by clapping and asking each other, "How did you do that?"'

Tom: 'You can't get it in a line: "Kick flip, your turn, kick flip, your turn" … it is difficult explaining this to people who don't know the street culture.' (Interview, 2015)

The young men reflect that they cannot live up to the municipality's formal requirements when they want to seek funding to develop skateboarding facilities. This is because legitimising formalised participation requires assimilating the association's formalised organisational logics, which is strongly rooted within Scandinavian countries. The municipality's funding system is based on parameters related to the organisational logics within associations, which in Scandinavia require information about the number of members, the ages of members and the number of training sessions (Ibsen and Seippel, 2010). Such an association in the Scandinavian context is a formalised type of leisure organisation that can be related to different kinds of activities, for example, sports, handcrafts. The young skateboarders maintain their own logics for skating and they test traditional organisational logics, which leads to the decision to organise themselves and design participatory spaces for young people. Specifically, temporal structures, such as meeting on a specific day at a specific time and participating in training sessions, require a social hierarchical structure of trainers and members. Reacting against this process fostered motivation in the case of the skateboarders, since it encouraged them to build their own skateboarding spot at a polluted place on the periphery of town, but I also raise questions of inequality. Boltanski and Thévenot (2006) explain how tests can illustrate clashes between logics and orders of worth and be expressed in multiple ways.

> As soon as one begins to examine the constraints that bear upon disagreement and efforts at coordination, one discovers the central importance of the equivalencies and ordering principles people establish for the purpose of assessing themselves and one another. (Boltanski and Thévenot, 2006, p 65)

The meaning of equivalence is related to the way in which worth is measured. Understanding the logics and constraints related to equivalencies reveals how some participatory spaces are well suited to some, but limiting to others. And even more importantly, the empirical example illustrates how some forms of participation are valued as more legitimate than others. The skaters point to how organisational structures within associations have a certain participatory form, which for generations have served as a participatory structure to ensure young people's active participation (see Sand, 2019). But just because that organisational form has served as a participatory structure for decades, does that mean that everyone should adopt its logics and compromise their own logics? The skateboarders are critical of a specific organisational structure and they do not automatically adopt it. They instead try it out and, through experience with associational logics, they *test* the logics by comparing them with the logics within skateboarding. This situation emphasises that difficulties faced by self-organised and semi-organised youth are not related to questions of equivalence, but rather those of assimilation. Forcing people to assimilate practices within certain organisational structures raises questions of inequality: who has the right to define how, when, where and with whom to participate? Self-organised spaces provide participatory possibilities for young people who do not participate in, for example, sports, handcraft or other leisure activities organised within associations. This involves maintaining a curiosity towards new organisational logics and not judging the way in which young people test societal organisations as conflictual, but rather as an expression for emerging forms of youth participation.

Getting the right to participatory place: possibilities and constraints

The following two empirical examples illustrate how young people who design alternative places for participation are not treated on equal terms with those involved in more traditional sport and leisure activities. The photograph in Figure 10.4 was taken in 2015 at a skate park in a Danish city. During an interview, while walking with one of the founders of the skate park, we passed the depicted sign, which was attributed to the municipality and a private institution. The research participant did not question the sign, but it made me reflect on who has the right to distribute participatory places for young people, and question the logics that dominate decisions surrounding which spaces are valued and justified as suitable for young people's participation. On the one hand, the example can be understood as a way to generate alternative participatory spaces for young people who are in

Figure 10.4: A sign on the ground directed at users of a public outdoor skateboarding park in Denmark

Note: In English, the sign reads: 'It is not dangerous to walk on the ground, but do not sit down. The ground surrounding the park may still contain toxic substances from its time as a concrete factory.'

Source: Anne-Lene Sand.

need of a space. On the other hand, it raises a question about how municipalities can justify providing young people with a public space that is nevertheless polluted and restricts them in terms of how they may use it (that is, for standing or sitting). In effect, the public message is saying that it isn't dangerous to use the space as long as you do not sit down on the ground. I have observed young people who, by their own free will, have chosen polluted ground for building a space of their own, but there seems to be a difference between the participatory spaces young people choose on their own and the public spaces that are constructed *for* young people's participation.

Another example of how spaces for youth participation can be challenged is illustrated through an interview with Karsten, age 36, who is board member in a climbing association. He describes the feeling of being misunderstood when trying to establish outdoor spaces for other young climbers in an urban space.

'There must be friction in what we climb on, and therefore we came to talk about the stones. I made models that I imagined worked in practice. We had contact with a quarry. It all looked good. The stones we were going to climb were shipped to the city but, when we saw them, it was not the stones we had talked about. They were impossible to climb. The architect, who was engaged by the municipality, had changed his mind in the process, and the municipality had not informed us about it ... It is a result of how planners do not understand what climbing is and what you need from a climbing perspective. There is a lack of dialogue about "What could be great for you?" We have bombarded them with information, but we are challenged by the fact that they are used to thinking about handball goals, basketball baskets, badminton nets, timetables, etc. Many parameters play a role, but one has to consider climbing as a sport equally positioned with handball, football, etc. We are organised with 6,500 members in Denmark but climbing does not have the same history as traditional sports.' (Interview, October 2015)

Karsten, and several other research participants, experience being misunderstood when it comes to organising themselves. Karsten points specifically to the process of designing and constructing an urban space for climbing, where his specific, embodied knowledge about climbing is neglected and overlooked because other logics dominate the decision-making process. It illustrates how providing spaces for alternative participatory cultures can be influenced by a societal tendency to collaborate with more traditional organisations that promote sport or leisure activities. As Boltanski and Thévenot put it, when people do things together and must coordinate their actions, they realise when something goes wrong (Boltanski and Thévenot, 2006, p 359). Justification is about people and objects are ranked and ordered and might not be recognised met on equal premises (Boltanski and Thévenot, 2006, p 363). Returning to the interview with Karsten, a consequence of this experience is that he expresses losing the motivation to construct alternative participatory spaces. Are legitimating processes related to which participatory practices have the most members? If so, self-organised and semi-organised participatory practices cannot be treated as equal to more formal processes since their participatory logics do not operate in terms of members and fixed meetings. Following the empirical material, it may be worth considering how other parameters of quality can be defined when it comes to cultures of youth participation that accommodate the perspective of young people and adopt notions of contemporary self- and semi-organised participatory logics.

Conclusion

Based on two ethnographic fieldwork studies, this chapter focuses on how young people from Denmark organise themselves in their leisure time. Through the concepts of self-organisation and semi-organisation, the chapter focuses on the participatory processes that young people construct *for* other young people mainly by themselves, but also through dialogue and collaboration with municipalities, associations and external entities. The research participants are characterised by a strong drive towards constructing participatory opportunities for skateboarding, climbing or musical events in urban environments. The chapter analyses young people's experience of how their self-organised practices are not understood or equally respected in line with boarder and popular leisure activities.

Theoretically the chapter draws on Boltanski's and Thévenot's (2006) pragmatic and reflexive sociology, and explores how temporal and spatial logics influence youth participatory processes. The notion of justification makes it possible to analyse participatory processes that are often taken for granted when it comes to constructing participatory leisure spaces for young people in Europe. The words 'between inequality and critique' in the chapter title denote an intersection between how institutional logics, on the one hand, construct unequal opportunities for young people and, on the other hand, foster a motivation to maintain critical thinking surrounding participatory possibilities, which in turn fosters processes of empowerment that would not emerge otherwise.

In the context of self-organised initiatives, inequality is not related to the traditional aspects of inequality (for example, ethnicity, class or educational background) but rather to the processes between the people who organise themselves and the institutional structures that surround them. The analysis points to the specific conditions of inequality, which are easily overlooked in discussions of youth inequality. The primary problem is the tendency to compare and measure self-organised and semi-organised participatory processes with institutional logics, which constructs unequal processes of worth and legitimisation since the young people who organise themselves experience being misunderstood and forced to compromise their participatory approach. More specifically, the young people experience formalised institutional spaces that devalue their alternative organisational logics and they are required to assimilate formalised organisational structures, formalised logics or formalised competencies, thereby compromising the logics essential to their own participatory practices.

This chapter indicates the need for future research to explore how temporal and spatial structures can construct inequality. Furthermore, this chapter reveals an important practice development potential related to young people's participation that calls for new approaches that support alternatively organised participatory practices. Finally, it is interesting to reflect on the extent to which legitimate leisure structures in Scandinavian and other European societies influence participatory practices. But how can participatory spaces for self-organised processes be developed when an essential logic within self-organised cultures is a do-it-yourself rather than a formalised approach?

Note

[1] The National Platform for Street Sports is a Danish non-political initiative supported by the Nordea Foundation with funding worth 15 million Danish krone over two periods (2015–18 and 2018–21). The aim of the Platform is to support novel and innovating initiatives for street sports in Denmark. Children, young people and adults can make an application under one of the following categories: nails and screws; National Street Sports Day; capacity and network; the joker (http://gadeidraet.dk).

References

Amit, V. (2001) 'The study of youth culture: why it's marginal but doesn't need to be so', *EUROPEA: Journal of the Europeanists*, 7: 145–54.

Amit-Talia, V. and Wulff, H. (1995) *Youth Cultures: A Cross-Cultural Perspective*, London: Routledge.

Barber, T. (2009) 'Participation, citizenship and well-being: engaging with young people, making a difference', *YOUNG*, 17(1), 25–40, https://doi.org/10.1177/110330880801700103

Boltanski, L. and Thévenot, L. (2006) *On Justification: Economies of Worth*, Princeton, NJ and Oxford: Princeton University Press.

Bo'sher, L. (2006) 'Where are the priorities? Where is the action?', *Children, Youth and Environments*, 16(2): 338–47.

Brock, K., Cornwall, A. and Gaventa, J. (2001) *Power, Knowledge and Political Spaces in the Framing of Poverty Policy*, IDS Working Paper 143, Brighton: Institute of Development Studies.

Bucholtz, M. (2002) 'Youth and cultural practice', *Annual Review of Anthropology*, 31(1): 525–52, https://doi.org/10.1146/annurev. anthro.31.040402.085443

Cockburn, T. (2005) 'Children's participation in social policy: inclusion, chimera or authenticity?', *Social Policy and Society*, 4(2): 109–19.

Cornwall, A. (2004) 'Spaces for transformation? Reflections on issues of power and difference in participation in development', in S. Hickey and G. Mohan (eds) *Participation: From Tyranny to Transformation*, London: Zed Books, pp 75–91.

Douglas, H. (2002) 'Talking about pictures: a case of photo elicitation', *Visual Studies*, 17(1): 13–26.

Ekman, J. and Amnå, E. (2012) 'Political participation and civil engagement: towards a new typology', *Human Affairs*, 22(3), 283–300, https://doi.org/10.2478/s13374-012-0024-1

Hannerz, U. (2003) 'Being there … and there … and there!', *Ethnography*, 4(2): 201–16.

Ibsen, B. and Seippel, Ø. (2010) 'Voluntary organised sport in Denmark and Norway', Sport in Society, 13(4): 593–608, https://doi.org/ 10.1080/17430431003616266

Johnson, V., Ivan-Smith, E., Gordon, G., Pridmore, P. and Scott, P. (1998) *Stepping Forward: Children and Young People's Participation in the Development Process*, London: Intermediate Technology Publications.

Kaspersen, L.B. and Ottesen, L. (2001) 'Associationalism for 150 years and still alive and kicking: some reflections on Danish civil society', *Critical Review of International Social and Political Philosophy*, 4(1): 105–130.

Laub, T.B. and Pilgaard, M. (2013) *Sports Participation in Denmark 2011*, Copenhagen: Danish Institute for Sports Studies.

Leccardi, C. and Woodman, D. (2015) 'Time and space in youth studies', in J. Wyn and H. Cahill (eds) *Handbook of Children and Youth Studies*, New York, NY: Springer, pp 705–21.

Matthews, H. (2001) 'Citizenship, youth councils and young people's participation', *Journal of Youth Studies*, 4(3): 299–318, doi: 10.1080/13676260120075464

Pink, S. (2007) *Doing Visual Ethnography: Images, Media and Representation in Research*, London: Sage Publications.

Pink, S. (2009) *Doing Sensory Ethnography*, London: Sage Publications.

Putnam, R.D. (2000) *Bowling Alone: The Collapse and Revival of American Community*, New York, NY: Simon & Schuster.

Saggers, S., Palmer, D., Royce, P., Wilson, L. and Charlton, A. (2004) *Alive and Motivated: Young People, Participation and Local Government*, Canberra: National Youth Affairs Research Scheme.

Sand, A.-L. (2017) 'Jamming with urban rhythms: improvisatorial place-making among Danish youth', *YOUNG*, 25(3), 286–304, https://doi.org/10.1177/1103308816671611

Sand, A.-L. (2019) 'Skal fritiden være i faste rammer? Fritidsorganisatoriske potentialer mellem planlægning og planløshed', *Dansk Sociologi*, 30, 1–29.

Sand, A.-L. and Hakim-Fernandez, N. (2018) 'Ephemeral socialities: social navigation among young Danes', *Kult-Ur*, 5(9): 57–80.

Sin, C.H. (2003) 'Interviewing in "place": the socio-spatial construction of interview data', *Area*, 35(3): 205–312.

Tsekoura, M. (2016) 'Spaces for youth participation and youth empowerment: case studies from the UK and Greece', *YOUNG*, 24(4): 326–341, https://doi.org/10.1177/1103308815618505

Turner, D. (2013) 'The civilized skateboarder and the sport funding hegemony: a case study of alternative sport', *Sport in Society*, 16(10): 1248–65, https://doi.org/10.1080/17430437.2013.821256

Vromen, A. and Collin, P. (2010) 'Everyday youth participation? Contrasting views from Australian policymakers and young people', *YOUNG*, 18(1): 97–112, https://doi.org/10.1177/110330880901800107

Wyn, J. and White, R. (1997) *Rethinking Youth*, London: Sage Publications.

11

Advocacy and participation: young people with autism spectrum disorder and their experiences with statutory casework

Cecilie K. Moesby-Jensen

This chapter addresses how a group of young people with autism spectrum disorder (ASD) experience their contact with statutory caseworkers from Danish social services departments, drawing on insights from social phenomenology and focusing on their lived experiences. The point of departure is a study that aimed to investigate how these vulnerable youths viewed the possibility of influencing their life situations. This is ultimately a question of participation: do young people with ASD feel properly understood, included and involved in the decision-making processes regarding important life issues? In this chapter, advocacy is seen as a necessary condition to ensure the participation and the rights of these young people. The chapter shows that violations of their guaranteed participation and rights are quite common, and this calls for stronger advocacy to be exercised by statutory caseworkers, as well as by other types of advocates.

Key findings

- Young people with ASD are particularly vulnerable in their meetings with statutory caseworkers due to their diagnosis-related challenges with communication and social interaction. These challenges are often not recognised or addressed by the statutory caseworkers during the meetings.
- The same diagnosis-related challenges that put these young people in contact with the social services system in the first place also place them at risk in the very system that is supposed to help them, and their problems often intensify, multiply, persist or evolve rather than get resolved. Hence, particular care should be taken to ensure

genuine participatory decision-making processes, supported by adequate advocacy, in the work with these young people.

- According to the study, personal advocates of these young people play an important role in the participatory decision-making processes of social services departments. Statutory caseworkers themselves, however, often fail in their role as advocates.
- Several young people participating in the study did not experience genuine participation in the decision-making processes with statutory caseworkers, even with regard to crucial issues in their lives, and violations of their rights were shown to be quite common and widespread.

Introduction

Since the mid-1990s, there has been a significant increase in the number of children and young people diagnosed with ASD worldwide (Timimi and McCabe, 2016). This increase has also been seen in Denmark (National Board of Health, 2014). Consequently, there has also been an increase in the number of young people with ASD who apply for support from Danish social services departments (Moesby-Jensen, 2019). ASD is a neurodevelopmental disorder that manifests in diagnosis-related functional impairments and challenges that vary greatly in both content and severity (APA, 2013). According to DSM 5 (*The Diagnostic and Statistical Manual of Mental Disorders*, 5th edition), people with ASD have core difficulties in two main areas: communicative skills and social interaction, and repetitive and restrictive behaviour (APA, 2013). However, various other diagnosis-related challenges are common, and different co-diagnoses often occur as well. Accordingly, people with ASD remain a group with a mixed spectrum of vulnerabilities. Research has shown that children and young people in vulnerable positions are often not involved in the casework concerning their own lives (Williamson and Butler, 1995; Sinclair, 1998; Thomas and O'Kane, 1999; Thomas, 2000; Vis and Thomas, 2009). Accordingly, Sinclair (2004) suggests that they are rarely perceived as 'participating actors'. In the case of young people with disabilities, research has shown that discrimination and oppression often take place on the grounds of both age and disability (Martin and Franklin, 2009; Hultman et al, 2017), and there is a tendency to disregard young people's strengths and abilities (Martin and Franklin 2009). Furthermore, young people with disabilities often feel pressured to present themselves as vulnerable based on their impairments and to stress 'the negative consequences of the impairment' (Hultman et al,

2017). Research has also shown that young people and children with communication impairments or complex needs are considerably less involved than their peers in the processes of decision making about their life situations (Martin and Franklin, 2009). However, we know very little about how young people with ASD in particular experience their meetings with statutory caseworkers with regard to decision-making processes that concern important aspects of their lives (Moesby-Jensen, 2019). This chapter aims to help fill this gap, drawing on a study based on 21 qualitative, semi-structured interviews with young people diagnosed with ASD. These interviews, conducted in Denmark in 2017, focused on how this group experienced their possibilities of participating in decision-making processes with statutory caseworkers in Danish social services departments. This chapter develops its themes, drawing on the intersection between youth, disability and social work research.

ASD: a particular vulnerability

It is important to acknowledge that people with ASD share a particular vulnerability, which is linked to the specific challenges described by and determining the diagnosis itself. These can be manifold and express themselves in different ways. However, the main distinguishing feature of ASD consists in having an impaired and disordered communicative ability, to such a degree that it radically influences and changes the person's development and life. Communicative ability concerns the capacities to engage in verbal and non-verbal reciprocity with others; to adjust and align to and show sensibility to others; and to successfully and actively participate in the continuously running mutual test of understanding that is at play in conversation and interaction, and so on. Impaired communicative ability is a basic condition of existence for a person with ASD, who faces a particular vulnerability in general, and a specific vulnerability in relation to statutory casework that is also relevant to the thematic at hand in this chapter. As stated earlier, research has shown that neurotypical young people certainly face challenges in relation to statutory casework, because they have problems with communicating (for example, expressing themselves in a precise manner; they sometimes misunderstand or are misunderstood by others), or because of their youth, cognitive level, and/or lack of education. However, this is far from being the same problematic as that of young persons with ASD, and to think otherwise is to disregard their particular life situation and their diagnosis-specific challenges, which often manifest themselves as quite severe functional impairments. Moreover, since ASD is a so-called hidden disability not visible to the eye, it is often overlooked. Hence, for statutory caseworkers interacting with people with ASD, considerations and inspiration from ASD-specific pedagogy seem highly relevant and even necessary, if the caseworkers want to interact with these young people in a meaningful and dignified manner. An important part of the contribution of this chapter is thus to emphasise that young people with ASD have certain challenges that make them particularly vulnerable in the context of bureaucratically organised social work, and hence, of statutory casework itself.

Statutory casework in Denmark

The social system in Denmark is characterised by universalism, as well as by offering specialised support and services to people with disabilities (Ministry of Social Affairs and Integration, 2011). In order to obtain disability aid, citizens with an impairment must apply for support in the social services department in the municipality where they reside. To apply for personal help and care services, financial support, special needs education and so on, a citizen must get in touch with a statutory caseworker in a social services department, which is also often the case for young people with ASD. According to Danish legislation, the purpose of statutory casework in regard to this population is to provide support to ensure that they 'achieve the same opportunities for personal development, good health and independent adulthood as their peers' (Social Services Act No. 573 of 2005 [SSA], section 46).[1] Moreover, Danish law – as well as the United Nations Convention on the Rights of the Child (UNCRC) and the United Nations Convention on the Rights of Persons with Disabilities (UNCRPD), both of which Denmark has ratified – all ensure these young people's right to be heard and involved in decision-making processes regarding their lives (SSA, 46(3); UNCRC, Articles 12, 13 and 17 ; UNCRPD, Articles 7 and 3; see also Chapter 13 in this book). Bound and informed by the SSA, the statutory caseworker formally determines whether or not citizens are entitled to the support they have applied for. In these decision-making processes, personal convictions and institutional logics influence the judgment of the statutory caseworker. Also, facilitating shared decision-making processes that lead up to the final formal decision is ultimately part of the responsibility of the caseworker, who must determine and ensure the right measure of advocacy for the citizen. As Healy remarks, the unique role of statutory caseworkers is to 'recognize and balance their legal and helping responsibilities' (Healy,

2012, p 84). This role is practised in a bureaucratic context,[2] where control, power, social policies and economic rationality affect and obscure the statutory caseworker's opportunity to recognise and assist the individual applying for help (Lipsky, 2010). Statutory casework is, as remarked elsewhere, a twilight zone, where both the legitimate and illegitimate exercise of power and administration are at work (Järvinen et al, 2003). Lipsky frames this by elaborating the conditions under which street-level bureaucrats operate, saying that they are torn between unendurable demands from service users regarding responsiveness and efficiency, and demands from politicians and department managers in the municipalities regarding efficient allocation of public services, since resources are limited. Due to these incompatible pressures, front-line staff tend to develop shortcuts, coping strategies and defence mechanisms in response to the endless demand for services, lofty organisational goals, competing policy objectives, scarce resources, piles of pending cases and work-related stress (Lipsky, 2010).

On participation and advocacy

It is generally acknowledged that participation and shared decision-making processes are closely related to ideas of democracy and citizenship;[3] the concept of participation is also closely connected to ideas of dignity and equality, and implies that human beings, in spite of their possible differences, are included and recognised and should have the opportunity to take part in civil society and to influence their own lives. The concept of participation can be said to have two basic components: it implies that somebody is actively taking part in something, and that the participant has some degree of influence (Thomas, 2007). In this chapter, advocacy is understood as a necessary condition to ensure the participation and rights of young people with ASD. Dalrymple and Boylan's (2009) thoughts on advocacy are useful to understand how the young people in the study perceived the social interaction and communication that took place in their meetings with statutory caseworkers. According to Dalrymple and Boylan (2009), advocacy can have several meanings, but overall it implies the act of giving voice to vulnerable groups in society and of speaking in support of their concerns or needs. Advocacy may be understood as the act of making sure that people who have a voice are heard, or the act of helping people who have difficulties voicing their own concerns or needs, or as giving voice to those who do not have a voice. Advocacy can serve to diminish the effects of asymmetric power, perhaps in particular in situations where clients are involuntary (Lipsky,

2010) and have nowhere else to go; it can be used to describe and understand the interaction between children and youth in vulnerable positions and social welfare employees and health and educational providers. Advocacy also makes it possible to challenge social, health and educational organisations, and the professionals working in them, in a way that highlights marginalising and discriminating practices (Dalrymple and Boylan, 2009).

About the study

Drawing on insights from social phenomenology (Schutz, 1970), the qualitative study conducted in 2017 focused on the lived experiences of a selected group of young people diagnosed with ASD (Moesby-Jensen, 2019). The study design included 21 individual semi-structured interviews with young people between the ages of 17 and 26 years. The interviews dealt with questions and issues of participation and the decision-making processes that took place in relation to respondents' meetings and dealings with statutory caseworkers. The criterion for participation in the study was that the respondent had, or had previously had, a statutory caseworker with whom they met face to face. Respondents were recruited through the staff at a special needs school attended by some of the young people, or through staff at a supported housing facility where some of them lived. The individual interviews varied in length and lasted between 20 and 60 minutes. The setting of the interview was either at the participant's home (a supported living facility) or at the Specially Planned Youth Education School (SPYES) they were attending. A SPYES is a special needs educational facility for young people who are not able to complete secondary education under typical circumstances and who are under the age of 25. In Denmark, young people with special needs have a legal right to receive a youth education that is individually adapted to them; it is formative, but does not formally qualify them for further education or later occupation (Ministry of Children and Education, 2018).

The ethical considerations in this study were linked to the careful and explicit preparation and support of each of the young participants, to aligning expectations, and to creating a 'comfortable' environment around each interview session. The aim was to secure a controlled, predictable context and to avoid sensory overload, allowing participants to tell their stories as freely as possible. To ensure this, several measures and precautions were taken, with particular consideration to and inspiration from specific ASD pedagogy. These considerations affected the whole approach and included a written invitation sent to all accepting participants detailing the purpose of the study, the identity of the interviewer (the current author), the nature of the participation, the duration of the interview and the study, and so on. Furthermore, there was information about consent (Freedman, 2001), anonymity, withdrawal from the study and confidentiality, and it was made explicit that the interview would be recorded digitally (Iacono and Murray, 2003). Finally, the written invitation also explained what would be discussed during the interview, and an interview guide was provided beforehand so that the participants would have prior knowledge of the questions posed (Fayette and Bond, 2018). The professionals working with the participants were involved in improving the appropriateness of the questions. The methods and interview setting were also discussed with them (Morris, 2003; Milton, 2012), and they played a crucial role in informing, coordinating and preparing the young people before the actual interviews. While many of these considerations are, at least on the surface, quite common, the intention in the overall approach was to ensure predictability, structure and clarity for the young people, thus making participation easier, more pleasant and less stressful. Similar intention, attention and care applied to the interviews. These were conducted using a visual structure by having the written invitation laid out on the table between us, together with the declaration of consent and the interview guide. Moreover, verbal and non-verbal communication was adapted to suit each participant. The young people participating in the study all had verbal language abilities and were cognitively within or above the normal range in terms of IQ. However, they had very different impairments and abilities, and almost half of the participants also had another diagnosis – mostly depression and/or (social) anxiety; hence they were, as is characteristic, a heterogeneous group, and sensibility to this was part of the approach. All of the participants were in the process of leaving home and choosing an education and a future path in the labour market, and they came from different areas of Denmark. Most of them had different kinds of support services in their everyday lives, for instance, housing support, a personal assistant or another (welfare) professional to help them cope with practical and/or social problems and challenges. At the time of the interview, 19 of the interviewees were attending (or had already attended) an SPYES. Nineteen of the participants were male, and although most of those who are diagnosed with ASD are men[4] (Loomes et al, 2017), women were under-represented in this study. After the interviews, the recorded audio files were fully transcribed and a qualitative content analysis was conducted using NVivo 12 to search out prominent themes and general patterns (Brinkmann and Kvale, 2015).

Experiences of recognition

Despite the fact that the young people's experiences of their meetings and dealings with statutory caseworkers were mostly of a negative sort, some also told stories of caseworkers who were dedicated and understood their needs, and had made huge efforts to help them in a way that was relevant and meaningful for them. These were experiences of 'being seen and heard', of being respected and being perceived as equal human beings. Their stories of recognition were particularly related to communication and social interaction that were useful and resulted in relevant decisions concerning important life issues in regard to such things as supported housing, special needs education and assistance in taking part in social interactions outside their homes. These stories can be interpreted as experiences of actual participatory decision making (Hart, 1992). Further, they can be interpreted as instances in which the statutory caseworkers acted as the young persons' advocates by making sure that their voices were being heard, that they were not being made 'socially invisible', as Honneth (1995) phrases it, that they were supported in voicing their concerns or needs (Boylan and Dalrymple, 2009), and that they were able to have a say in influencing their own lives. In one such interview, Carl[5] expressed how he had experienced dedication and understanding from his former statutory caseworker, who was successful in creating genuine participation. He described feeling included in a decision-making process involving something that he himself viewed as an important life decision:

> 'He [the caseworker] was super capable, really good … he was interested in my situation and he listened. He understood the kind of person that I am, and he understood me. That was really nice. He showed great understanding for me. It was like he knew what I wanted without I knew it myself [sic]. The best thing that ever happened for me was when he suggested that I moved [sic] to a supported housing facility.' (Carl, male, age 26)

There were other similar stories about statutory caseworkers who succeeded in their role as advocates and who in a relevant way provided information about special needs education or other matters of importance, who initiated shared decision-making processes, and who were supportive of the young people when they voiced their own thoughts. Malthe's story was an illustration of this, and documents how advocacy was of tremendous importance to him:

> 'She helped me get into an education [special needs school] … she does everything to help me … She has worked in the social services department for a while, so she knows how to make things go faster and get the desired outcome. She is very pleasant to be with … she has done things that I am very pleased she could do.' (Malthe, male, age 23)

Malthe clearly felt understood and recognised. He emphasised the caseworker's ability to act within the bureaucracy of the social services department and her willingness to advocate for him. Similar points were expressed by a few other participants in the study, but this was not a common occurrence in the narratives.

Communication and social interaction

More frequently, interviewees shared stories and experiences of discomfort in their interactions with caseworkers. Several participants explained that they were often nervous or afraid of saying something wrong when talking to their statutory caseworker; they were unsure of what to say and when to present their own point of view, and felt insecure about how to express their views.

> 'I have to take in a lot of information, and I have to give a lot of information as well, and I have to do this in a strange place with people that I do not know very well. In such a situation, it is really hard to think of the right things to say, and actually say them too. Both things can be a big challenge. To find out what to say and then also try to find a moment in the conversation, when it is possible to say what I want. Yeah, to be in a completely strange place and have nothing to fall back on if you suddenly feel uncomfortable or something, that can be really stressful. This situation can make it very difficult to say what you want.' (Victor, male, age 20)

Victor's description of the meetings illustrates the importance of context, specifically how it was very difficult for him to understand, communicate and interact with the caseworker in the unfamiliar setting of the social services department and how this poses a threat to participation. This was a common experience among the participants in the study that may be intensified by the limitations of language skills that people with ASD can experience; basically it is the core challenge of those with impaired communicative skills and social interaction skills that is at play here, making it difficult for the participants to understand, to express verbally what they want, and to express themselves non-verbally through facial expressions, eye contact and so on. Impaired communicative skills make it difficult for those with ASD to understand other people's body language and the meaning of different vocal tones.[6] While communicative reciprocity is generally challenging for those with ASD, there might also be a delay in response (latency) when participating in a conversation (Donohue et al, 2012), creating problems in communication and social interaction with other people (APA, 2013). For a conversation to succeed, there must be a running test of understanding between the two parties involved, which is a process of continual alignment. This process entirely depends on an overall sensibility towards each other by the two parties involved, making a conversation a delicate and fragile process that is actually quite unlikely, and while such conversation and understanding is made more likely by communicative skills, impairment in these skills renders conversation, understanding and participation quite difficult. The study showed that communicative challenges played a crucial and constrictive role in the participants' social interaction with the caseworkers, as stories about such challenges were common and numerous. Statutory caseworkers have a very special responsibility here, and many of the violations, that is, many of the cases of non-participation that came to light in the study, originated in instances where impairment in communication was disregarded for various reasons. It remains almost paradoxical that the very reason why young people with ASD come into contact with statutory caseworkers – namely their diagnosis-related challenges with communicative and social interaction – makes them even more vulnerable in the interaction with the caseworkers in the social services departments that are supposed to help them.

Denial of voice

Lack of responsiveness, recognition and understanding was a recurring problem in the young people's narratives, and many of them told stories of instances in which the statutory caseworker did not listen to what they said, did not show understanding for or patience with their perspective, or did not show any empathy:

'I experience her as very annoying … I often feel that she doesn't really listen to the things we say … she really just wants to hear what she wants to hear.' (Storm, male, age 19)

Storm's perception of the communication with his statutory caseworker was a clear example of interactions that lacked a participatory element, and he consistently experienced the denial of having a voice. Most of the participants told stories about meetings where they had experienced not being taken seriously or given a voice. Magnus said:

'If it was a meeting about what kind of education I should take, and I said, "I would like this", then they did not really listen. Then they might say, "Well that's not for you, you should do this instead … you're not, we don't think … you're probably not fit for that."' (Magnus, male, age 25)

This is an example of a citizen who experienced being made socially invisible in a disrespectful manner, his self-insight being seriously questioned and his perception of reality regarding his own abilities concerning choice of an education being degraded; finally, he experienced that the caseworker entirely pushed her own agenda. Now, while there is no reason to doubt that Magnus did in fact experience all these things, we do not know the other side of the story, or the full story regarding these situations. However, a citizen being left with such impressions of disregard for participation at a minimum suggests that the statutory caseworkers have a problem with explaining and communicating their positions, even more so if the narrated situations did in fact play out in the manner described. This form of violation would then be an example of how some of the young people were not recognised as equal citizens with formal individual autonomy and civil rights. Without passing judgment on particular instances, this study remains full of similar stories, and they are substantiated and corroborated by related research and findings within disability research (Priestley, 2000; Martin and Franklin, 2009; Landsdown, 2010; Hultman et al, 2019) and the research field of vulnerable children and youth (Williamson and Butler, 1995; Sinclair, 1998, 2004; Thomas and O'Kane, 1999; Thomas, 2000; Vis and Thomas, 2009; Jensen, 2014). These studies all show that young people and children in vulnerable positions, according to themselves, are very often not heard or involved in decision making about their own lives. Further, the experiences described in the interviews also corroborate research that shows that even though caseworkers say that they wish to involve children with disabilities, they actually exclude them from participating in the decision-making processes with the argument that the impairment does not allow the children the capacity to make informed decisions (Hultman et al, 2019). Finally, these findings are in line with those of researchers who argue that young people and children with communication impairments are less likely to be involved in decision-making processes than their peers (Martin and Franklin, 2009).

The importance of advocacy

All of the participants in this study, irrespective of their different social and communication skills and life experiences, emphasised the importance of having a personal advocate when meeting with a statutory caseworker. An advocate is someone who aids, supports and helps look out for their interests, and who would perhaps afterwards be able to help remember and reconstruct what was said and decided. In the Danish context, a person can bring an advocate to such meetings; they do not need to have special training and could be a parent, a residential youth worker, a welfare professional, a personal assistant or similar. Some non-governmental organisations have advocacy services that young people can use free of charge.

The participants in the study often described the advocate as a 'middleman', who could act as a translator between the statutory caseworker and themselves. Johan explained why he always brought his personal assistant from the supported housing facility where he lived when he attended meetings:

> 'Well, it's like, if there is something that I don't understand, then he can be a kind of, how to put it, be a middleman. And if I say something that he [the statutory caseworker] doesn't get, then he can kind of translate … I think that it is really nice. Sometimes he can also explain things better than I can.' (Johan, male, age 23)

Only a few of the participants had experiences of attending meetings alone, and only a few of them expressed being comfortable participating in meetings by themselves. They explained their strong need for advocacy with their life situations, and attributed it to being a young person in transition into adulthood and therefore inexperienced in interacting in the complex bureaucratic setting of social services departments. They stressed the importance of being heard and seen and thus having the potential to influence their own lives and, finally, with reference to their diagnosis-related impairment(s), many explicitly expressed being 'uneasy' and 'uncomfortable' meeting with the caseworker alone, or they used similar and even stronger words in relation to their descriptions.

George described how two advocates, his mother and a representative from his school, played an important role in the decision-making process regarding his application to move into a supported housing facility. He described the immense struggle with the statutory caseworker to grant him the supported housing, where he would be able to get the help he needed in order to live more independently:

> 'We had a huge battle about permitting me to move to a supported living facility … Me and my mom and then someone from the school … we had to make sure that I was in the target group for the right disability paragraph [in the law]. Apparently, there are different disability paragraphs … We started applying when I was 18 and I think I got it when I turned 21 … and I could only stay there until I turned 23.' (George, male, age 22)

George and all the other participants in the study explained how their advocates outside the social services departments played an important role, both in regard to getting in touch with statutory caseworkers, and subsequently in gaining access to the services and support efforts they needed, which could only be granted by a statutory caseworker. However, despite having a more personal advocate present at these meetings, many of the young people in the study were careful not to go into intense discussions with the caseworkers because they believed it could result in unwanted consequences regarding their chances of getting the help and support that they needed. Thomas explained why he tried to avoid such discussions:

> 'Yes, that's the reason too, they control if you can live here [residential housing for young people with special needs]. So you do not want to get in a heated discussion with them.' (Thomas, male, age 23)

As this quote illustrates, Thomas was aware of the asymmetric power relation between himself as a young service user – and as Lipsky has phrased it, as an involuntary client – and the statutory caseworker, who is a municipality-backed employee with the power to make formal decisions based on their interpretation of the SSA. Thomas' reactions and other similar stories point to a certain type or instance of non-participation where vulnerable persons hold back their views in order not to have a fallout with the statutory caseworkers because they fear the consequences of being too forward or even confrontational as they try to meet their own life interests.

The need for advocacy for young people with ASD, such as those in this study, is closely linked to the fact that interaction with social services departments requires and demands certain communication skills and social skills in order to make the interaction succeed or even function. Even establishing and maintaining contact with statutory caseworkers, who change jobs frequently, was a major issue and problem for many participants and often resulted in a complete breakdown of communication, with a range of differing consequences. Very often a personal advocate seemed indispensable to counteract the variety of impairments experienced by the person with ASD at all levels of interaction in order to secure proper participation in the decision-making processes.

In the study, personal advocates played a pivotal role in ensuring that the voices of the participants were heard, and hence in promoting the desired change (Dalrymple and Boylan, 2013) in their lives. They empowered participants to be able to participate in decision-making processes. Ideally, advocates take on the role of empowering and enabling young people to ensure that they understand the issues at hand, and to make sure that their rights and views are respected and that their wishes are heard and considered (Dalrymple and Boylan, 2009, p 90). From the stories shared in the study, the benefits of advocacy had to do with the act of someone speaking up for them when they had difficulties speaking up for themselves, and with the act of supporting them to speak up for themselves and persuading the statutory caseworkers to listen. The advocacy noted in the study moved on a continuum from active to passive depending on the degree of the youth's own participation in the advocacy work (Dalrymple and Boylan, 2013). The study also showed that the advocacy and support could take place either before a meeting, serving a preparatory function; during a meeting; or as a debriefing after a meeting. The study also suggests that, without these types of personal advocacy, social services departments risk producing and reproducing even greater inequality for a particular group of citizens. Not all young people with ASD have an advocate, or an advocate with deep knowledge about the particular person they are assisting, with the dedication, means and resources (time, educational level, capacity) to accompany that person, continually participate in the meetings, make convincing arguments and be a dignified support to a young person. Those who do not have access to such an advocate can experience great difficulties interacting with the system and can even get lost in it, since they will remain excluded from participation and will likely not get the help they need.

Conclusion

Knowledge about how young people with ASD experience meetings with statutory caseworkers, and their stories about participation in the decision-making processes regarding important life issues, can inform and qualify the way in which statutory caseworkers think, act and handle their interactions and practices with this population. The present study indicates that most young people with ASD do not feel comfortable in the social interactions with caseworkers and that the continued presence of a capable, more personal, advocate is of major importance in order to ensure that these young people have the opportunity to voice their views. Statutory caseworkers themselves far too often fail to act as advocates for this vulnerable group, and there should be an increased awareness as to how they can act in order to secure proper participation. Statutory caseworkers must embrace their own role as advocates to help promote these young people's rights and interests in a way that is characterised by recognition, so that they are included in the decision-making processes in a dignified manner. Moreover, case workers need to ensure that other advocates can support these young people in having a voice. As of now, in the Danish context, the possibility of participating in decision-making processes for young people with ASD seems quite limited. More attention should be devoted to their diagnosis-related impairments and challenges, and much can be gained by letting communication and social interaction be inspired by insights from ASD-specific pedagogics that can promote (mutual) understanding and participation. Social services departments should adapt their casework practices and approaches when working with children and young people with ASD, and communicate and interact with them in a different way than with their (neurotypical) peers. In line with Shakespeare (2015), I believe that 'if we listen to the voices of children and young people with disabilities [then] we will be more likely to treat them as equals, attend to their needs and promote their rights' (p xi). In the end, this is about democratic and societal inclusion and participation, and all citizens leading lives they can actively influence and that they find meaningful.

Notes

[1] The Social Service Act (*Lov om Social Service*) No. 573 of 2005. Available from: https://www.retsinformation.dk/Forms/R0710.aspx?id=20372

[2] This point, and many more in this chapter, is further substantiated and elaborated elsewhere, as this study is thematically and empirically related to and interlinked with a group of other texts and studies on children and young people with ASD and social work that mutually enlighten each other (most notably Moesby-Jensen 2019; Moesby-Jensen and Moesby-Jensen, 2016, 2017, 2019). Among other things, these studies critically examine themes such as participation and violation in relation to statutory casework, drawing on Max Weber, Zygmunt Baumann, Axel Honneth, Pierre Bourdieu and Michael Lipsky, to name but a few. The possible sources of failed advocacy and failed shared decision making remain many and complex.

[3] See Chapters 8 and 13 in this book for a discussion on young people's participation in decision making.

[4] Approximately one out of three diagnosed with ASD is female.

[5] All the young people appear with fictional names.

[6] NIDCH (National Institute on Deafness and Other Communication Disorders), https://www.nidcd.nih.gov/health/autism-spectrum-disorder-communication-problems-children

References

AMA (American Psychiatric Association) (2013) *Diagnostic and Statistical Manual of Mental Disorders* (5th edn), Washington, DC: American Psychiatric Association Press.

Brinkmann, S. and Kvale, S. (2015) *InterViews: Learning the Craft of Qualitative Research Interviewing*, Thousand Oaks, CA: Sage Publications.

Dalrymple, J. and Boylan, J. (2009) *Understanding Advocacy for Children and Young People*, New York, NY: McGraw-Hill.

Dalrymple, J. and Boylan, J. (2013) *Effective Advocacy in Social Work*, London: Sage Publications.

Donohue, M.M., Casey, L.B., Bicard, D.F. and Bicard, S.E. (2012) 'Effect of differential reinforcement of short latencies on response latency, task completion, and accuracy of an adolescent with autism', *Education and Training in Autism Developmental Disabilities*, 47(1): 97–108.

Fayette, R. and Bond, C. (2018) 'A systematic literature review of qualitative research methods for eliciting the views of young people with ASD about their educational experiences', *European Journal of Special Needs Education*, 33(3): 349–65.

Freedman, R.I. (2001) 'Ethical challenges in the conduct of research involving persons with mental retardation', *Mental Retardation*, 39: 130–41.

Hart, R.A. (1992) *Children's Participation: From Tokenism to Citizenship*, Innocenti Essay No. 4, Florence: UNICEF Office of Research.

Healy, K. (2012) *Social Work Methods and Skills: The Essential Foundations of Practice*, Basingstoke: Palgrave Macmillan.

Honneth, A. (1995) *The Struggle for Recognition: The Moral Grammar of Social Conflicts*, Cambridge: Polity Press.

Hultman, L., Pergert, P. and Forinder, U. (2017) 'Reluctant participation – the experiences of adolescents with disabilities of meetings with social workers regarding their right to receive personal assistance', *European Journal of Social Work*, 20(4): 509–21.

Hultman, L., Forinder, U., Öhrvall, A., Pergert, P. and Fugl-Meyer, K. (2019) 'Elusive participation – social workers' experience of the participation of children with disabilities in LSS assessments', *Scandinavian Journal of Disability Research*, 21(1): 38–48.

Jensen, B.S. (2014) 'Involvement of vulnerable children and young people in social work - genuine involvement or symbolic rhetoric?' PhD thesis. Aalborg University, Denmark.

Järvinen, M., Larsen, J.E. and Mortensen, N. (eds) (2003) *Det Magtfulde Møde Mellem System og Klient*, Aarhus: Aarhus Universitetsforlag.

Lacono, T. and Murray, V. (2003) 'Issues of informed consent in conducting medical research involving people with intellectual disability', *Journal of Applied Research in Intellectual Disabilities*, 16(1): 41–51.

Lansdown, G. (2010) 'The realisation of children's participation rights', in B. Percy-Smith and N. Thomas (eds) *A Handbook of Children and Young People's Participation: Perspectives from Theory and Practice*, Abingdon: Routledge, pp 11–23.

Lipsky, M. (2010) *Street-Level Bureaucracy: Dilemmas of the Individual in Public Services* (2nd edn), New York, NY: Russell Sage Foundation.

Loomes, R., Hull, L., Polmear, W. and Locke, M. (2017) 'What is the male-to-female ratio in autism spectrum disorder? A systematic review and meta-analysis', *Journal of the American Academy of Child & Adolescent Psychiatry*, 56(6): 466–74.

Martin, K. and Franklin, A. (2009) 'Disabled children and participation in the UK: reality or rhetoric?', in B. Percy-Smith and N. Thomas (eds) *A Handbook of Children and Young People's Participation: Perspectives from Theory and Practice*, Abingdon: Routledge, pp 98–104.

Milton, D. E. (2012) 'On the ontological status of autism: the "double empathy problem"', *Disability & Society*, 27(6): 883–7.

Ministry of Children and Education (2018) 'Om særligt tilrettelagt ungdomsuddannelse (STU)', Ministry of Children and Education, [online]. Available from: https://uvm.dk/saerligt-tilrettelagt-ungdomsuddannelse/om-stu [Accessed 20 November 2018].

Ministry of Social Affairs and Integration (2011) *Social Policy in Denmark*, Copenhagen: Ministry of Social Affairs and Integration. Available from: www.oim.dk/media/14947/social-policy-in-denmark.pdf

Moesby-Jensen, C.K. (2019) 'Unge med autismespektrumforstyrrelser og deres møder med myndighedsrådgivere', in C.K. Moesby-Jensen (ed) *Diagnoser i Myndighedsarbejde: Børn og Unge med Autisme eller ADHD*, Frederiksberg: Samfundslitteratur, pp 205–26.

Moesby-Jensen, C.K. and Moesby-Jensen, T. (2016) 'Om kategorisering og symbolsk magtudøvelse i socialt arbejde: myten om de ressourcestærke forældre til børn med neuro-psykiatriske diagnoser', *Sociologisk Forskning*, 53(4): 371–95.

Moesby-Jensen, C.K. and Moesby-Jensen, T. (2017) 'Lydighedsetik og bureaukratisk grusomhed: refleksioner over det tværprofessionelle samarbejde mellem myndighedssagsbehandlere og PPR-ansatte', in C.K. Moesby-Jensen (ed) *Når Professioner Samarbejder: Praksis med Udsatte Børn og Unge*, Frederiksberg: Samfundslitteratur, pp 213–41.

Moesby-Jensen, C.K. and Moesby-Jensen, T. (2019) 'Vilkår og praksis i det socialfaglige myndighedsarbejde omkring børn med autismespektrumforstyrrelser eller ADHD', in C.K. Moesby-Jensen (ed) *Diagnoser i Myndighedsarbejde: Børn og Unge med Autisme eller ADHD*, Frederiksberg: Samfundslitteratur, pp 137–76.

Morris, J. (2003) 'Including all children: finding out about the experiences of children with communication and/or cognitive impairments', *Children & Society*, 17(5): 337–48.

National Board of Health (Sundhedsstyrelsen) (2014) *National Klinisk Retningslinje for Udredning og Behandling af ADHD hos Børn og Unge: Med Fokus på Diagnoserne 'Forstyrrelse af Aktivitet og Opmærksomhed' og 'Opmærksomhedsforstyrrelse uden Hyperaktivitet' i Henhold til ICD10*, Copenhagen: Sundhedsstyrelsen.

Schutz, A. (1970) *On Phenomenology and Social Relations*, Chicago, IL: University of Chicago Press.

Shakespeare, T. (2015) 'Foreword', in R. Traustadóttir, B. Ytterhus, S.T. Egilson and B. Berg (eds) *Childhood and Disability in Nordic Countries: Being, Becoming, Belonging*, Basingstoke: Palgrave Macmillan, p ix.

Sinclair, R. (1998) 'Involving children in planning their care', *Child and Family Social Work* 3(2): 137–42.

Sinclair, R. (2004) 'Participation in practice: making it meaningful, effective and sustainable', *Children & Society*, 18(2): 106–18.

Thomas, N. (2000) *Children, Family and the State: Decision-Making and Child Participation*, Bristol: Policy Press.

Thomas, N. (2007) 'Towards a theory of children's participation', *International Journal of Children's Rights*, 15(2): 199–218.

Thomas, N. and O'Kane, C. (1999) 'Children's participation in reviews and planning meetings when they are looked after "in middle childhood"', *Child & Family Social Work*, 4(3): 221–30.

Timimi, S. and McCabe, B. (2016) 'What have we learned from the science of autism', in K. Runswick-Cole, R. Mallet and S. Timimi (eds) *Re-Thinking Autism: Diagnosis, Identity and Equality*, London: Jessica Kingsley.

Vis, S.A. and Thomas, N. (2009) 'Beyond talking – children's participation in Norwegian care and protection cases', *European Journal of Social Work*, 12(2): 155–68.

Williamson, H. and Butler, I. (1995) 'No one ever listens to us: interviewing children and young people', in C. Cloke and M. Davies (eds) *Participation and Empowerment in Child Protection*, Chichester: John Wiley & Sons, pp 61–79.

12

Young people seeking asylum: voice and activism in a 'hostile environment'

Gráinne McMahon and Rhetta Moran

This chapter sets out the grassroots activism of a group of four young people aged 24–29 who were seeking asylum in the UK's 'hostile environment'. Moving away from normative definitions of political participation as the formal activities of citizens, the analysis draws upon second wave feminist and Classical Marxist understandings of collective action. The chapter argues that by 'speaking bitterness' and creating 'language from below' in order to craft a play to depict dramaturgically their lived realities, the young people formed collective action and did politics 'differently'. They engaged in biographically meaningful, 'personal-political' and 'political-personal' activism that focused on the particular needs of their wider group. They also made 'democracy anew' by practising democracy informally and in alternative, co-equal, meaningful and purposeful ways, within a hostile environment that 'others' them and alienates them from political and social participation.

Key findings

- Alienated from formal political processes, and isolated by an increasingly populist and right-leaning democracy, the young activists aspired to form a collective to do politics 'differently'.
- Using methods of co-production embedded within the organisation, the young activists engaged in biographically meaningful, 'personal-political' and 'political-personal' collective action that resonated deeply with feminist and Classical Marxist politics, focusing on the particular needs of their wider group.
- In making 'democracy anew', the young activists utilised many tools of collective action, and found voice and collectivism despite, and perhaps because of, the hostile environment. Their grassroots activism was practising democracy differently.

Introduction

Over the seven years since it first (re)surfaced in 2012 to describe the UK government's political intention towards net migration into the UK (Kirkup and Robert, 2012), the phrase 'hostile environment' has become everyday coinage while the conditions of the hostile environment are ubiquitous. The hostile environment refers to the conditions within which migrants and those seeking asylum survive in the UK and includes measures to prohibit legal working, enforce destitution, and limit access to housing, healthcare and bank accounts. It is 'characterised by a system of citizen-on-citizen immigration checks ... astronomically high immigration application fees, the continued policy of indefinite detention, the Byzantine complexity of the rules, the enforced separation of some families, the infamous "Go Home" vans and more' (Yeo, 2018). The hostile environment is also, however, being exposed by sections of civil society (see, for example, JCWI, n.d.) and challenged by 'non-citizens' (Taylor and Busby, 2019).

This chapter offers first a context-setting impression by briefly sketching historical, political and cultural events instrumental in creating this socio-political landscape in the UK and the deleterious effects of the UK's hostile environment on the young people who co-produced the current research – young people seeking asylum in Britain (herein: young activists[1]). The chapter then sets out the ways in which the young activists came together and found voice within, despite, and perhaps even because of, the hostile environment. The research, part of the Europe-wide PARTISPACE study, explored the spaces and styles of young people's social and political participation. In order to understand, and celebrate, the young people's activism within a state-driven and openly racist political climate, the chapter moves away from dominant understandings of political participation as a set of activities carried out by private citizens to influence decision making and the business of governance (Nie and Verba, 1972) and draws upon second wave feminist (Rowbotham, 1986; Young, 1989; Phillips, 1991) and Classical Marxist (Gluckstein, 2014) perspectives on collective action and political participation.

The UK's 'hostile environment'

Despite migration and the movement of peoples being a long-standing phenomenon, myriad migration laws and policies (United Nations Department of Economic and Social Affairs, 2017), anti-immigration sentiments (Connor and Krogstad, 2018) and anti-migration policies are growing internationally (Human Rights Watch, 2019). In the UK in 2012, when Theresa May, then Home Secretary of the incumbent Conservative and Liberal Democrat coalition government, announced "We're going to give illegal migrants a really hostile reception" (Kirkup and Robert, 2012), the 'hostile environment' policy publicly (re)surfaced in that national context. However, this process of separating out migrants, and treating them differently, through state actions that cultivate and then apply legally defined categories to them, has been in place ever since people began to flee pogroms and/or search for work in large numbers.

Following a 30-year period of economic decline (Holmes, 1988), the Aliens Act 1905 first introduced immigration control and registration into the UK, but only for those without visible means of support. A Conservative MP who at the time likened those targeted to 'diseased cattle' (Foot, 1965, p 89) sought to dehumanise migrants, just like the Nazis in the 1930s and 1940s when they defined Jewish and other people as 'parasitic vermin' (United States Holocaust Memorial Museum, n.d.). Despite the British state making war on the Nazis, British MPs continued to call for a further tightening of immigration controls against people 'scurrying' (Foot 1965, p 221) and, in the immediate aftermath of the Second World War, efforts to control the level and nature of legal migration continued.

By 1948, the newly created United Nations General Assembly defined the UK's post-war treatment of the displaced people arriving as workers as 'an official policy of discrimination' (Holmes, 1988, p 210). That did not, however, deter the British Labour Cabinet Committee recommending in 1951 that future immigration controls would 'as a general rule, be more or less confined to coloured persons' (Miles and Phizacklea, 1987, pp 148–9). Continuing to make and apply law according to people's perceived 'race', the 1962 Commonwealth Immigrants Bill restricted entry by Commonwealth citizens. In effect, 'immigration' now meant 'black immigration' (Corporate Watch, 2018) and the same Conservative administration that authored this 'cruel and brutal anti-colour legislation' (Shand-Baptiste, 2019, quoting former Labour leader Hugh Gaitskell) hosted MP Enoch Powell who warned in 1968 that there would be a race war if 'coloured' migration was not controlled. It would be 30 years before the state released the MI5 report that revealed the role of fascists in supporting Powell at that time (Norton Taylor and Milne, 1999).

Today's immigration system is based on the Immigration Act 1971 that followed, downgrading Commonwealth citizens to the status of 'foreigner', preparing the ground for Margaret Thatcher's infamous

1978 statement that 'people are really rather afraid that this country might be swamped by people with a different culture' (quoted in Trilling, 2013). The asylum procedure in the UK that, according to Amnesty International in 1999 had produced a 'culture of disbelief' (*The Guardian*, 1999), also enabled, shortly after the 9/11 terrorist attacks in the US, the Asylum Act 2002, which legalised the eviction of people failed by the asylum system into destitution and barred people seeking asylum from working legally (Moran, 2003). At the same time, the then Prime Minister Tony Blair announced his desire to halve immigration (Dean, 2012), signalling state-level rejection of the 1951 Refugee Convention principles, even though most of the newest arrivals to the UK were European; de facto, refugees had become key scapegoats to appease anti-migrant voters.

The ideological terrain developed over the past 20 years has included a sustained media campaign that equates 'asylum' with 'scum' (Dean, 2012), attacks on civil rights (O'Cinneide, 2018), increasing anti-Muslim rhetoric (Poynting and Mason, 2007), and the rise of far-right violence and electoral profile (Smith and Shifrin, 2019). Government-led policy and practice produced the 'Go Home' vans (Hattenstone, 2018); the threat of 'voluntarily' returning people to their countries of origin or facing arrest, which infiltrated the third sector (RAPAR, 2018; Taylor and Busby, 2019); the high-profile immigration raids that demonstrated the state's arsenal against immigration (Tyler, 2018); and the failure of that same state arsenal, as exemplified in the suffocation of 39 people in a container in October 2019 (Kelly, 2019).

The current study

Despite these alarming political and cultural shifts, there has been a long-standing interplay between anti-migrant law and anti-racist mobilisation. For example, in 1970s Britain the Grunwick Strikers of 1976 worked with anti-racists to form the Anti-Nazi League in 1978 (Sabbagh, 2018; Chaudhary, 2019). This became the precursor to Britain's current anti-fascist united front, Unite Against Fascism (Holborow, 2019), which is supported by all major party political organisations in the UK. Anti-fascist mobilisation persists (see, for example, Copsey, 2016) and more recently movements contesting the hostile environment have grown (for example, England, 2019). This resistance is crucial in order to prevent the politically embedded hostile environment – sanctioned by a 'full-blown state racism' (Burnett, 2016, p 20) independent of party political agenda – from taking root culturally (Burnett, 2016). It is within this context of active and sustained resistance that the current study took place. Exploring the work using theories of collective action, and thinking of collective action as a 'particular form of politics' (West, 2013, p 28) and making of democracy (Blee, 2012), enables an understanding of the motivations underpinning the young activists' participation in and engagement with the project, and their intended outcomes (McMahon et al, 2018).

The organisation that took part in the current study, Refugee and Asylum Participatory Action Research (RAPAR), is a Manchester-based human rights organisation working with people at risk of having their rights denied. RAPAR is a long-standing casework, research and campaigning collective that co-creates and co-produces research and public-facing campaigns about issues that are identified by and important to its members who are seeking asylum. Though they have myriad backgrounds and experiences, RAPAR's members seeking leave to remain in the UK[2] share in common the experience of displacement from their home countries and the reluctance and/or refusal of the UK state to extend them safety and asylum. YoungRAPAR is a long-standing group comprising RAPAR members under 30, and it is this group (four young activists, aged 24–29) who took part in the PARTISPACE work, using the principles of participatory action research embedded within the work of the organisation (Moran et al, 2006; Moran and Lavalette, 2016). All of the young activists in the study had had an asylum claim rejected by the state or had been living in the UK 'undocumented' for a long period of time.

Living in the hostile environment: 'the system'

At the beginning of the research, a colleague introduced the chapter's co-authors to discuss the PARTISPACE project and the participatory action research part of the project. When the co-authors agreed in principle in their initial meeting to co-create a participatory project with the young people in RAPAR, they met immediately with the then existing members of YoungRAPAR. The members of YoungRAPAR had been working with RAPAR (asylum casework) and seeing each other there socially for varying lengths of time. All of the young members were enthusiastic about becoming involved in a research project about young people's participation.

The project began with an open question posed to the group: 'What does the word participation mean to you?' First, the young activists explored and shared the meaning/s of the English word 'participation' in their mother tongues: 'kosala nakati' (Lingala) and 'شومیلتی' (Urdu), which mean, 'I am joining in'. The group then discussed the relationships of those meanings with the term 'belonging', the action of taking part in something with others, and the experience of being a part of 'something'. One young member said: 'In my country, we say, one finger can't wash the face, if it is all five, we can wash the face" (said in Linguala and then translated). Very quickly, however, the group discussion became about how the young activists felt unable to participate. They said that they were not allowed to take part in paid work or to access higher education, and that they felt like they were always 'waiting' for something.

Here the group utilised Voloshinov's (1986 [1929]) theory of 'language creation from below' (Moran and Butler, 2001). This Classical Marxist theoretical framework explains how existence comes to be reflected in 'sign' through the process of social intercourse: the material medium of language. Voloshinov counters a number of positions in his text, including individual subjectivism (that the meaning of the word is exclusively determined by the speaker, as argued by von Humbolt), abstract objectivism (that the meaning of the word is exclusively determined by the context and there is no meaning invested by the speaker, as argued by Saussure), and post-structuralist theories of language as represented by Derrida and Foucault. Through their adherence to Althusser's mechanical materialism, which separates base (the economic organisation of society) from superstructure (ideology, political structures and so on) (Harman, 1986), Derrida and Foucault extend Saussure's arguments by abstracting the meanings of words from their material base. Voloshinov, in contrast, extends the meaning of language beyond that of the relationships between the structure, sound and meaning of words that are perceived as existing within a closed system that is abstracted from the material world (Callinicos, 1990).

Further, Voloshinov pre-emptively counters the idea that reality is given directly to the subject on the grounds that consciousness has a direct access to reality and exists separately from words or signifiers (again, see Derrida). The framework does this by making explicit the role of language as the material medium between the socioeconomic conditions within which people are surviving and the individual human psyche. For Voloshinov, the definition of a thing depends on its historical situation and its contextual boundaries: the words, already existent within the given time period and the given social group, make up the repertoire of speech forms for ideological communication. Therefore, things that exist do not inevitably come to the attention of society. For something to become the object, or the theme, of a sign, it must first become meaningful between people within the social group – it must acquire an 'interindividual significance'. As it does so, the theme acquires social value:

> In order for any item, from whatever domain of reality it may come, to enter the social purview of the group and elicit ideological reaction it must be associated with the vital socioeconomic prerequisites of the particular group's existence: it must somehow, if only obliquely, make contact with the bases of the group's material life. (Voloshinov, 1986 [1929], p 22)

By harnessing these tools of language creation, the young activists' early discussions revealed that they used the term 'the system' to refer to the totality of structures within which they live and the climate of the hostile environment. They were acutely aware of the constraints that 'the system' places on them in terms of a precarious status ("Still hanging around, I can't do anything, I'm helpless") and limitations on their ability to participate widely. They referred to participation as "being listened to, being accepted, being treated equally" at the same time as knowing that they are: deliberately isolated, "They put you far away from everyone" (see also Moran, 2003); disparaged, "A lot of people think they are higher status, hierarchy, you are an asylum seeker and I am not" (see also Dean, 2012); and stigmatised, "Because I am different" (see Goffman, 1963, for a discussion of stigma and the 'situation of the individual who is disqualified from full social acceptance' [p 9]).

The group's early discussions were also about the impacts of the asylum process, and the political climate of the hostile environment, on the young activists' daily lives. They reported feeling: scared, "On the bus, sometimes stop, police get on, big men, I will feel OHHHHHH, very scared"; targeted, "I go some shop, security looking, looking, and then around and then go back and they think, stolen something, I do not feel good inside"; depressed, "I am so sad, crying, every day crying"; humiliated, "I came with big courage, I say, 'Let me go there.' I queued for one-and-a-half hours. I was very shamed"; anxious about being detained or even deported, "sick with worry" the night before a reporting appointment; and being forced to remain in a precarious and liminal state as they wait for a decision on their claim, "The uncertainty is like floating on the water … we might get rescued but it is a waiting game", which can take up to 20 years to come through (Lyons, 2018).

The system in this case was twofold. First, it included the bodies, agencies and structures of decision making and regulation that govern the asylum-seeking process – the Border Agency, security agencies, housing agencies and the police, for example. Second, these 'systems of authority' also included an ideology of 'othering' ("They do not want 'us' here. They make us wait and wait") and less tangible sets of beliefs, values and 'interpretive frameworks that rationalise the distribution and exercise of the authority and provide the "vocabularies of motive"' (Snow and Soule, 2010, p 9) on which the system relies. Mills (1940) considered these 'vocabularies of motive' as a context-specific way for systems and structures to rationalise, and then implement, regulations and procedures and, importantly, to punish their violation. In this respect, vocabularies of motive, alongside what Cohen (2006, p 57) calls the 'dehumanising Newspeak of immigration controls', enable the hostile environment to exist, operate, sustain and continue to suppress. In naming their fears of harassment, isolation, destitution, and, ultimately, deportation, the young activists underscored the ways in which they understood the atmosphere of the hostile environment to enable their othering and oppression, and the reason that they felt unable to participate, politically or socially, in wider society.

Making the 'Faceless' seen and heard

After the discussions about the meanings of 'participation' for the young activists, and barriers to participation, they moved quickly to creating a project that would involve public dialogue and consciousness raising about 'the system'. At this stage of the study, the chapter's co-authors (the 'professional researchers') had handed the research space over to the young activists and had begun to play more of an observational and supportive role in the work as the young activists discussed among themselves their ideas for a project. At the beginning of the project, the co-authors had been clear that the project would utilise the participatory methods that are used throughout the organisation, inspired by Freire's and Fals-Borda's work and the philosophy that social science research should ensure that the everyday experiences and struggles of the poor, oppressed, and marginalised are moved from the periphery of social inquiry to the centre (Hordan, 2008). As the young activists were familiar with this way of working, they did not need any instruction on how such a methodology 'worked' or what it meant, and were reassured from the outset that the project 'belonged' to them. In the same way, the young activists were immediately comfortable with being co-researchers in the work. Co-research in its turn was framed as a 'participatory method of research that situates participants as joint contributors and investigators to the findings of a research project [and which] validates and privileges the experiences of participants, making them experts and therefore co-researchers and collaborators in the process of gathering and interpreting data' (Boylorn, 2008, p 599). The young activists' ease and unanimity in deciding to create a co-researched awareness-raising project derived from their motivation to participate in wider society, an acute alertness to the inequalities they had experienced because of hostile environment, (see also Chapter 2 in this book), and to be active politically despite their awareness of barriers to their participation and dominant public opinion (Dean, 2012).

For this group of young activists, utilising a conventional definition of political participation to refer to activities carried out by a private citizen to influence decision making and governance (Nie and Verba, 1972) is therefore limited in a number of ways. First, the implication that political participation takes a particular, universal form concerned only with the formal political realm does not address the subtleties around the access of marginalised groups to participation. Second, conventional definitions of political participation rely on notions of citizenship that mean belonging, legally, to a national state, and thereby exclude refugees, even those with asylum. The traditional and formal democratic processes available to 'citizens' are not available to people seeking asylum, even after they have been granted 'leave to remain' (leave to remain does not imply citizenship in the UK). In addition, and importantly, the idea of the 'private citizen' is based upon traditional activities concerned with achieving the 'common good' for all citizens that requires a setting aside of needs that are not common to all (Young, 1998). In other words, normative understandings of citizenship and the 'citizen' do not apply to a group for whom traditional and mainstream routes to political participation are neither accessible nor desirable and which sits at the very margins of democratic citizenship (McMahon et al, 2018).

Moreover, the young activists expressed a profound distrust in the political system, fear of the immigration system, and a strong desire to do things 'differently'. They were keenly aware that they form part of a marginalised, stigmatised and 'othered' group (Goffman, 1963) – broadly categorised as 'asylum seekers' in the hostile environment – and initiated their project with the aim of interacting with the public in order to profile their own understandings of their group's lived experiences. By overcoming the 'invisibility' of the realities of their existence that dominates in the public domain, they wanted to generate a dialogue within and about the hostile environment that manufactures and sustains conditions of inequality and injustice. In this way, the very acts of collectivising, activating and naming their fears are themselves forms of protest against a 'system' predicated on dispersal (Moran, 2003; Glorius et al, 2016) and isolation (Gower, 2020).

"It is because of your society that we fade into the background"

The young activists' discussion about the form of the work resulted in a decision to write, perform and film a play, reflecting the power of art and film in activism and awareness raising (see Chapters 3 and 15 in this book) that dramaturgically depicted the lived experiences of being displaced, disbelieved, boundaried, othered, and made to feel out of place in the UK's hostile environment. Drawing upon their discussions exploring participation, marginalisation and vilification, one YoungRAPAR member offered to prepare a script. 'Faceless', the short play that he wrote, was also, largely, directed and produced by him, while three others performed it. Its key aim was public dissemination – to redress dominant public opinion about asylum that the young activists linked so clearly with the hostile political environment – and it featured the 'faceless' person seeking asylum and a 'stranger' to whom 'Faceless' is at first invisible. The play starts:

> Someone sits alone, with a blurred face. Many people walk by without taking notice. Another stranger walks by, but back-steps – confused.

Stranger: 'Am I seeing things?'
             (Approaches Faceless)
Stranger: 'Hello? Is someone there?'
Faceless: 'I am ... here.'
Stranger: 'Who said that? I'm not – oh, I think I see you! Yes, I see you now!'
Faceless: 'That's further than most can perceive.'
Stranger: 'Why?'
Faceless: 'We are mostly invisible to the average person; but see us, some can ... some can.'
Stranger: 'But why is this? Why do you make yourself invisible?'
Faceless: 'We don't. Rather, it is you.'
Stranger: (Shakes head confused). 'I don't ...'
Faceless: 'Your society makes us invisible. It is because of your society that we fade into the background.'

Participation, collective action and a new democracy

The young activists continued to talk throughout the project about their experiences as young people seeking asylum and their motivation to depict their experiences to the public. Both during rehearsals and the filming of the play, their conversations focused on the meanings of the text of the play and what its words represented and depicted, and they continually adjusted the script to embrace different perspectives and emotions, returning to ideas about participation and activism, and reflecting on learning. 'Data' in the project comprised materials co-created within the group, including mind-maps exploring the meanings of participation, the young activists' notes on discussions and ideas, the play's script itself and ideas around the play, and the copious fieldnotes compiled by the co-authors on the conversations and reflections in the group. The learning was co-analysed within the group in the frequent reflective sessions that took place throughout the work. The analysis explored the young people's meaning making and learning about participation in general, being and becoming politically active, finding a collective voice, and engaging in activism, and identified key points of learning, for example, participation as personal politics and doing politics differently.

'Faceless' the play underscores the ways in which the young activists feel, and are made to feel, invisible and ashamed of their existence, and the pain and fear they feel because of their alienation and precarity. The play is an example of youth-led community activism by young people seeking asylum in the UK. Their exploration of their experiences and their terms for describing aspects of their daily lives – fear, shame, waiting, hiding, confused, anxious, sad, lost, lonely, hopeless, weak, non-existent, voiceless, abandoned, to name a few – represent the hostile environment that Theresa May worked to embed during her tenure as Home Secretary (Kirkup and Robert, 2012). During the research, group members referred to feeling unwelcome, unwanted, invisible and 'outside'. In one group session when the young activists were naming words to express their frequent feelings, one of the members said: "Scared. That's such an obvious one. Why has no one said it already?" Another responded: "Because that is our daily life." During the making of 'Faceless', the hostile environment was both silent and explicit. The young activists frequently became upset, frustrated, and anxious, particularly when scenes emphasised the invisibility of the refugee and the impact of invisibility (and 'disposability', Tyler, 2018) on their lived lives.

Making a collective space for personal-political politics

The young activists' work involved spending a great deal of time together and they met at least once per week, over a period of several months, to talk, share their experiences and concerns, and find their common meanings. The conversations generally began with catch-up chats between the members of the group, including the chapter's co-authors, to talk about what had been taking place in everyone's previous week. Some of the young activists had particular experiences to report (for example, a 'signing' at a Home Office reporting centre, which is a legal requirement when an asylum claim is in progress, or a case update). More often, however, these conversations were about how the young activists had been feeling over the previous week. In this respect, they were taking part in the feminist practice of 'speaking bitterness' (Mitchell, 1971) where 'speaking bitterness' is the 'bringing to consciousness of the virtually unconscious oppression; one person's realisation of an injustice brings to mind other injustices for the whole group' (Mitchell, 1971, p 62) and the naming of what is often perceived as private problems in the group in contexts where oppression manifests in the 'repression of words' (Mitchell, 1971, p 62). Part of the young activists' work, then, was forging and protecting a collective space where they could speak freely and safely and where, using Volosinov's framework, they could create through and for the play, a language for their oppression.

The community in this respect becomes all of the people who use the same set of signs – words – for ideological communication but who do not necessarily imbue the sign – the word – with the same meaning. The acutely impoverished and multi-translocated group that made up 'Faceless' selected words about their lived experiences of inequality – injustice, fear, 'the system', and 'always waiting' – and their meanings for these words emerged over time, in between moments of silence, thought and reflection. Often buried deeply inside individual psyches, through the collective research processes that developed, the words became voiced with their meanings, shared between the young activists and then publicly asserted by screening their film of their situated utterances, spoken by specific characters within a discrete context in the play. As the work progressed, and when 'Faceless' was being filmed, the group did not shy away from depicting the profound emotional reality of their experiences. A line from the script reads, 'We struggle with ways to cope. We lose animation. We become lifeless. We feel like machines', tapping into Goodwin et al's (2001) idea of mobilising the symbolic power of language and emotion, rather than just argument alone, in political and collective action.

In harnessing Classical Marxist and second-wave feminist tools of collective action – consciousness raising as making the hidden visible and 'speaking bitterness' as the basis of collectivism (Mitchell 1971) – the young activists' participation became biographically meaningful and politically relevant in the hostile environment. In other words, their very personal experiences became the basis for their 'personal is political' action (see Hanisch's [1970] work for one of the first uses of this term, although Hanisch did not herself coin the phrase) where the work was autobiographical (McMahon et al, 2020) and where the 'political' (referring to power relations) was rooted in personal experiences and common, systemic struggles. Hanisch further argued that consciousness-raising 'analytical sessions are a form of political action' (Hanisch, 1970) and that 'one of the first things we discover in these groups is that personal problems are political problems' (Hanisch, 1970). She concluded that '[t]here are no personal solutions at this time. There is only collective action for a collective solution' (Hanisch, 1970). Understanding about this dialectic that renders the political-personal was palpably demonstrated throughout the current study as those seeking asylum understood, interrogated and challenged the impact of the political landscape on their personal and group lives.[3]

Voice and activism in hostile environment

The young activists – as all young people seeking asylum in the hostile environment – are 'the dispossessed' where 'being dispossessed refers to processes and ideologies by which persons are disowned and abjected by normative and normalizing powers that define cultural ineligibility' (Butler and Athanasiou, 2013, p 2; see also Tyler, 2013). The hostile environment did not come about in a political and cultural vacuum and manifests in daily lives and realities because those seeking asylum are marginalised, vilified, displaced, made to feel out of place, and kept in enforced conditions of isolation, inequality and extreme poverty. However, being dispossessed is not countered simply by appropriation and by (re)gaining material assets in some way; rather, dispossession is the symbolic and embodied deprivation of safety, identity, freedom and autonomy. The most common adjectives used by the young activists to describe their deepest needs were 'safe' and 'free': "to be safe and to be free".

Grassroots activism, often 'thought of as an ancillary to democratic politics [or] as serving a conduit into electoral politics' (Blee, 2012, pp 3–4), brought about new opportunities for the young activists' democratic participation. In doing so, it also challenged normative ideas of democracy that equate democracy only with governance and neglect the 'democratising effects of grassroots political action' (Blee, 2012, p 4). In the absence of access to formal institutions of politics, or indeed a belief in such processes, the young 'Faceless' people engaged in politics in alternative ways that were co-equal, meaningful and purposeful to them (Walther, 2018; McMahon et al, 2020). In this sense, the grassroots activism of the group was concerned with making 'democracy and anew' (Blee, 2012) and practising democracy differently (what Étienne Balibar referred to as a democracy 'beneath and beyond the state'). This the young people achieved by committing to both individual and collective agency (Callinicos, 2009) within the organisation and involving 'all members in the co-production of knowledge, theory and practice' (Moran and Lavalette, 2016, p 118) where marginalised voices were centred (Moran and Lavalette, 2016; Percy-Smith et al, 2019). Activism as democracy became a co-produced process concerned with people collecting, deliberating and working together to bring about change.

Notes

[1] The chapter uses this terminology to refer to the young people who took part in the work for two reasons: first, the young people identified as activists during the work and, second, to move away from the idea that 'asylum seeker' captures the extent of the young people's identities and existences. The term 'young activists' ascribes agency and purpose to the young people's work. The chapter per se reverts to 'young people'/'young people seeking asylum' in more general discussions and as appropriate.

[2] Leave to remain ('refugee status') or permanent residency are immigration statuses granted to an individual who does not have the right 'of abode' in the UK but who has been admitted to the UK for a specific or permanent time, and who is then free to take up employment or higher education.

[3] See also the work of Young (1989, 1990), Phillips (1993) and Rowbotham (1986) for discussions of democracies of group difference that lie 'outside the conventionally political sphere' (Phillips, 1993, p 80).

References

Blee, K. (2012) *Democracy in the Making*, Oxford: Oxford University Press.

Boylorn, R. (2008) 'Participants as co-researchers', in L. Given (ed) *The Sage Encyclopedia of Qualitative Research Methods*, London: Sage Publications, pp 599–601.

Burnett, J. (2016) *Racial Violence and the Brexit State*, London: Institute of Race Relations. Available from: www.irr.org.uk/app/uploads/2016/11/Racial-violence-and-the-Brexit-state-final.pdf

Butler, J. and Athanasiou, A. (2013) *Dispossession: The Performative in the Political*, Cambridge: Polity Press.

Callinicos, A. (1990) *Against Postmodernism: A Marxist Critique*, Cambridge: Polity Press.

Callinicos, A. (2009) *Making History: Agency, Structure, and Change in Social Theory*, Chicago, IL: Haymarket Books.

Chaudhary, V. (2019) 'Forty years on, Southall demands justice for killing of Blair Peach', *The Guardian*, 21 April. Available from: www.theguardian.com/uk-news/2019/apr/21/southall-demands-justice-killing-of-blair-peach-1979

Cohen, S. (2006) *Deportation is Freedom: The Orwellian World of Immigration Controls*, London: Jessica Kingsley.

Connor, P. and Krogstad, J.M. (2018) 'Many worldwide oppose more migration – both into and out of their countries', Pew Research Centre, [online] 10 December. Available from: www.pewresearch.org/fact-tank/2018/12/10/many-worldwide-oppose-more-migration-both-into-and-out-of-their-countries

Copsey, N. (2016) 'Crossing borders: anti-fascist action and transnational anti-fascist militancy in the 1990s', *Contemporary European History*, 25(4): 707–27.

Corporate Watch (2018) *The UK Border Regime: A Critical Guide*, London: Corporate Watch.

Dean, M. (2012) *Democracy Under Attack: How the Media Distort Policy and Politics*, Bristol: Policy Press.

England, C. (2019) 'Power beyond borders: climate activists target the hostile environment', *Novara Media*, [online] 30 July. Available from: https://novaramedia.com/2019/07/30/power-beyond-borders-climate-activists-target-the-hostile-environment

Foot, P. (1965) *Immigration and Race in British Politics*, London: Penguin.

Glorius, B., Doomernik, J. and Darling, J. (2016) 'Asylum in austere times: instability, privatization and experimentation within the UK asylum dispersal system', *Journal of Refugee Studies*, 29(4): 483–505.

Gluckstein, D. (2014) 'Classical Marxism and the question of reformism', *International Socialism*, 143, [online] 26 June.

Goffman, E. (1963) *Stigma: Notes on the Management of Spoiled Identity*, London: Penguin.

Goodwin, J., Jasper, J.M. and Polletta, F. (2001) *Passionate Politics: Emotions and Social Movements*, Chicago, IL, University of Chicago Press.

Gower, M. (2020) *Asylum Seekers: The Permission to Work Policy*, Briefing Paper No. 1908, London: House of Commons Library.

Hanisch, C. (1970) 'The personal is political', in S. Firestone *Notes From the Second Year: Women's Liberation. Major Writings of the Radical Feminists*, New York, NY: Radical Feminism.

Harman, C. (1986) 'Base and superstructure', *International Socialism*, 2(32): 3–44.

Hattenstone, S. (2018) 'Why was the scheme behind May's "Go Home" vans called Operation Vaken?', *The Guardian*, 26 April. Available from: www.theguardian.com/commentisfree/2018/apr/26/theresa-may-go-home-vans-operation-vaken-ukip

Holborow, P. (2019) 'The anti-Nazi league and its lessons for today', *International Socialism*, 163, [online] 1 July.

Holmes, C. (1988) *John Bull's Island: Immigration and British Society, 1871–1971*, Basingstoke: Palgrave Macmillan.

Hordan, S. (2008) 'Participatory action research (PAR)', in L. Given (ed) *The Sage Encyclopedia of Qualitative Research Methods*, London: Sage Publications, pp 601–4.

Human Rights Watch (2019) World Report 2019: Rights Trends in European Union. [online] Available from: https://www.hrw.org/world-report/2019/country-chapters/european-union

JCWI (Joint Council for the Welfare of Immigrants) (n.d.) 'Ending the hostile environment', JCWI, [online]. Available from: www.jcwi.org.uk/pages/category/ending-the-hostile-environment

Kelly, A. (2019) 'The 39 people who died in the lorry were victims. Why does the law treat them as criminals?', *The Guardian*, 29 October. Available from: www.theguardian.com/commentisfree/2019/oct/29/39-people-lorry-victims-law-criminals-immigration-slavery

Kirkup, J. and Robert, W. (2012) Theresa May interview: 'We're going to give illegal migrants a really hostile reception', *The Telegraph*, 25 May. Available from: www.telegraph.co.uk/news/0/theresa-may-interview-going-give-illegal-migrants-really-hostile/

Lyons, K. (2018) 'Revealed: asylum seekers' 20-year wait for Home Office ruling', *The Guardian*, 17 August. Available from: www.theguardian.com/uk-news/2018/aug/17/revealed-asylum-seekers-20-year-wait-for-home-office-ruling

McMahon, G., Percy-Smith, B., Thomas, N., Bečević, Z., Liljeholm Hansson, S. and Forkby, T. (2018) *Young People's Participation: Learning from Action Research in Eight European Cities*, PARTISPACE Working Paper D5.3 Evaluation of Participatory Action Research, [online]. Available from: http://doi.org/10.5281/zenodo.1240227

McMahon, G., Liljeholm Hansson, S., von Schwanenflügel, L., Lütgens, J. and Ilardo, M. (2020) 'Participation biographies: meaning-making, identity-work and the self', in A. Walther, J. Batsleer, P. Loncle and A. Pohl (eds) *Young People and the Struggle for Participation: Contested Practices, Power and Pedagogies in Public Space*, Abingdon: Routledge, pp 161–75.

Miles, R. and Phizacklea, A. (1987) *White Man's Country*, London: Pluto Press.

Mills, C.W. (1940) 'Situated actions and vocabularies of motive', *American Sociological Review*, 5(6): 904–13.

Mitchell, J. (1971) *Woman's Estate*, London: Penguin.

Moran, R. (2003) 'From dispersal to destitution: dialectical methods in participatory action research with people seeking asylum', Paper presented at the international conference Policy and Politics in a Globalising World, University of Bristol, Bristol, 24 July.

Moran, R. and Butler, D. (2001) 'Whose health profile?', *Critical Public Health*, 11(1): 59–74.

Moran, R. and Lavalette, M. (2016) 'Co-production workers, volunteers and people seeking asylum – "popular social work" in action in Britain', in C. Williams and M. J. Graham (eds) *Social Work in a Diverse Society: Transformative Practice with Black and Minority Ethnic Individuals and Communities*, Bristol: Policy Press, pp 109–26.

Moran, R., Mohamed, Z. and Lovel, H. (2006) 'Breaking the silence: participatory research processes about health with Somali refugee people seeking asylum', in B. Temple and R. Moran (eds) *Doing Research with Refugees: Issues and Guidelines*, Bristol: Policy Press, pp 55–74.

Nie, N. and Verba, S. (1972) *Participation in America*, New York, NY: Harper & Row.

Norton Taylor, R. and Milne, S. (1999) 'Racism: extremists led Powell marches', *The Guardian*. 1 January. Available from: www.theguardian.com/uk/1999/jan/01/richardnortontaylor2

O'Cinneide, C. (2018) 'How well does the UK's democracy protect human rights and civil liberties?', Democratic Audit, [online] 28 November. Available from: www.democraticaudit.com/2018/11/28/how-well-does-the-uks-democracy-protect-human-rights-and-civil-liberties

Percy-Smith, B., McMahon, G. and Thomas, N. (2019) 'Recognition, inclusion and democracy: learning from action research with young people', *Educational Action Research*, 27(3): 347–61.

Phillips, A. (1991) *Engendering Democracy*, Cambridge: Polity Press.

Phillips, A. (1993) *Democracy and Difference*, Cambridge: Polity Press.

Poynting, S. and Mason, V. (2007) 'The resistible rise of Islamophobia: anti-Muslim racism in the UK and Australia before 11 September 2001', *Journal of Sociology*, 43(1): 61–86.

RAPAR (Refugee and Asylum Participatory Action Research) (2018) 'There's no such thing as "voluntary" returns', RAPAR, [online] 3 April. Available from: http://raparuk.weebly.com/theresnosuchthingasvoluntaryreturns.html

Rowbotham, S. (1986) 'Feminism and democracy', in D. Held and C. Pollitt (eds) *New Forms of Democracy*, London: Sage Publications, pp 85–6.

Sabbagh, D. (2018) 'Anti-Nazi League founders call for new national campaign', *The Guardian*, 15 August. Available from: www.theguardian.com/world/2018/aug/15/anti-nazi-league-founders-call-for-new-national-campaign

Shand-Baptiste, K. (2019) 'The UK's immigration system is ideologically broken', *The Independent*, 8 October. Available from: www.independent.co.uk/voices/windrush-dexter-bristol-death-scandal-immigration-home-office-a9146221.html

Smith, M. and Shifrin, T. (2019) 'Fascism and the far right in Europe: country by country guide, 2019', Dream Deferred, [online] 19 May. Available from: www.dreamdeferred.org.uk/2019/05/2019-update-fascism-and-the-far-right-in-europe-country-by-country-part-1

Snow, D.A. and Soule, S.A. (2010) *A Primer on Social Movements*, New York, NY: W.W. Norton.

Taylor, D. and Busby, M. (2019) 'Home Office pays religious groups to help deport rough sleepers', *The Guardian*, 5 November. Available from: www.theguardian.com/uk-news/2019/nov/05/home-office-pays-religious-groups-to-help-deport-rough-sleepers#:~:text=Religious%20and%20community%20organisations%20have,in%20most%20cases%20rough%20sleepers

The Guardian (1999) 'Editorial: A prime piece of cheek', *The Guardian*, 24 August. Available from: www.theguardian.com/politics/1999/aug/24/labour.labour1997to99

Trilling, D. (2013) *Thatcher: The PM who Brought Racism in from the Cold*, London: Verso Books.

Tyler, I. (2013) *Revolting Subjects: Social Abjection and Resistance in Neoliberal Britain*, London: Zed Books.

Tyler, I. (2018) 'Deportation nation: Theresa May's hostile environment', *Journal for the Study of British Cultures*, 25(1).

United Nations Department of Economic and Social Affairs (2017) *International Migration Policies: Data Booklet*, New York, NY: United Nations Department of Economic and Social Affairs.

United States Holocaust Memorial Museum (n.d.) 'Victims of the Nazi era: Nazi racial ideology', Holocaust Encyclopedia, [online]. Available from: https://encyclopedia.ushmm.org/content/en/article/victims-of-the-nazi-era-nazi-racial-ideology

Voloshinov, V.N. (1986 [1929]) *Marxism and the Philosophy of Language*, Cambridge, MA: Harvard University Press.

Walther, A. (2018) *Re-Thinking Youth Participation – Contributions of PARTISPACE*, PARTISPACE Working Paper June 2018, [online]. Available from: http://partispace.eu/cms/wp-content/uploads/2018/06/PARTISPACE-Working-paper-re-thinking-youth-participation.pdf

West, D. (2013) *Social Movements in Global Politics*, Cambridge: Polity Press.

Yeo, C. (2018) 'Briefing: what is the hostile environment, where does it come from, who does it affect?', Free Movement, [online] 1 May. Available from: www.freemovement.org.uk/briefing-what-is-the-hostile-environment-where-does-it-come-from-who-does-it-affect

Young, I.M. (1989) 'Polity and group difference: a critique of the ideal of universal citizenship', *Ethics*, 99(2): 250–74.

Young, I.M. (1990) *Justice and the Politics of Difference*, Princeton, NJ: Princeton University Press.

Young, I.M. (1998) 'Polity and group difference: a critique of the ideal of universal citizenship', in A. Phillips (ed) *Feminism and Politics*, Oxford: Oxford University Press, pp 401–29.

PART IV

New opportunities for young people's participation: facilitating new forms of youth participation

13

Meaningful, effective and sustainable? Challenges for children and young people's participation

E. Kay M. Tisdall

Children and young people's participation activities continue to grow, galvanised by the United Nations Convention on the Rights of the Child (UNCRC).[1] As the activities have proliferated, so has a list of common barriers and problems for children and young people's participation in collective decision making, from tokenism and lack of impact on decision making, to some children and young people being over-consulted while others are marginalised. While this list is frustratingly familiar, certain activities seem to address all or most of these barriers and problems. These examples provide potential learning tools, to examine *why* they have apparently done so. One such example is youth-led research projects, which involve a core group of children and young people, over a set amount of time, with facilitating adults and organisations. This chapter considers how the young researchers and projects claim credibility and legitimacy through processes of knowledge production. By emphasising expertise, these projects resist perennial critiques of children and young people's participation being unrepresentative. But they create inequalities for those with less time, interest or commitment for in-depth involvement. The chapter concludes that such projects are not radical in challenging the norms of legitimacy and credibility but can be so in positioning children and young people as knowledge producers.

Key findings

- Youth-led research projects position young researchers as knowledge producers.
- Young researchers bring expertise to the projects and develop expertise and knowledge through the projects. This leads to credibility and legitimacy claims for both the young researchers and the projects.

- Such claims can lead to demonstrable impacts on service and policy decision making, as documented by several examples.
- The intensive involvement required of young people involved as researchers may exclude those with less time, commitment and interest.

Introduction

For those working in participation in the children's human rights field, there is a very familiar narrative (McMellon and Tisdall, 2020). It begins with recognising the impetus of the UNCRC, which puts forward children's rights to participation. These participation rights are described as 'innovative' and 'radical', changing traditional views of children as vulnerable, innocent and dependent to perceptions of children as social and political actors, who can express agency and competency. As the most ratified of all human rights treaties (to date, all member states but the US have ratified), the UNCRC requires children's participation rights to be realised.

The narrative continues with tributes to the legislative and policy changes to recognise these rights, both for children and young people's involvement in decision making about themselves individually and when they join together to influence collective decision making. In terms of the latter, there have been a plethora of projects and activities, ranging from children's engagement in neighbourhood planning (Wood, 2015) to young people's contributions to international meetings.[2] Yet the rhetoric and promotion have not consistently led to meaningful, effective and sustainable participation by children and young people. All too often, their participation does not influence decision making but can be tokenistic and side-lined by adult systems and attitudes. There is a significant implementation gap between the rights set out in the UNCRC and realising these rights for children and young people.

While this narrative has been both familiar and remarkably consistent over the past 30 years since UNCRC ratification, there are successes where children and young people's participation does seem to influence collective decision making. The successes provide opportunities for learning: *why* are these activities able to overcome the familiar challenges and barriers?

Some of the most successful activities involve a core group of children and young people working over a set amount of time, through a process of inquiry. They have control over deciding or refining the inquiry's focus, the methodology of the inquiry, the analysis and the ensuing recommendations and solutions. This type of working has different labels (each with their implications; see Tisdall, 2013), ranging from co-production or co-design, participatory action research or child-led or youth-led research. But, even with these differences in labels, the examples are united by a similar positioning of children and young people as knowledge producers. As such, the children and young people involved have the legitimacy and credibility to influence decision makers and decision making. This chapter investigates such positioning and claims in more depth, with attention to potential inequalities. The term youth-led research is used here, as this phrase underlines the claims to knowledge, legitimacy and credibility (Cuevas-Parra and Tisdall, 2019a).

The chapter first reviews the relevant debates around children and young people's participation from a human rights' perspective and how youth-led research has developed as one answer to recognising children and young people's rights to participate. Using three examples, the chapter explores the positions and claims of youth-led research in terms of knowledge production, legitimacy and credibility. The chapter concludes that the projects do not disturb the ageism inherent in the UNCRC's participation rights, but the projects are radical in claiming the legitimacy and credibility of young people as knowledge producers.

Young people's participation in the human rights field

The touchstone for children and young people's participation in the human rights field is the UNCRC and particularly Article 12(1):

> States Parties shall assure to the child who is capable of forming his or her own views the right to express those views freely in all matters affecting the child, the views of the child being given due weight in accordance with the age and maturity of the child.

Other rights typically categorised as participation rights in the UNCRC are Article 13 (freedom of expression), Article 14 (freedom of thought, conscience and religion), Article 15 (freedom of association and peaceful assembly) and Article 17 (access to information).

Participation is not a word that is included in Article 12(1) itself. The United Nations (UN) Committee on the Rights of the Child provides a description of it:

> This term has evolved and is now widely used to describe ongoing processes, which include information-sharing

and dialogue between children and adults based on mutual respect, and in which children can learn how their views and those of adults are taken into account and shape the outcome of such processes. (2009, p 3)

As has been analysed both legally and in practice, Article 12 is a modest and qualified right (Tisdall, 2015; Daly, 2018). Article 12(1) is a very far away from a child having the right to choose, to make their own decision and for self-determination more generally. Instead, a child's views should be part of decision making, given 'due weight', but their views are not necessarily decisive. In international human rights legislation, such a qualified participation right is only given to children. It is contained in Article 12(1) of the UNCRC and, after lobbying, was also modified for inclusion in the later UN Convention on the Rights of Persons with Disabilities (Article 7(3)).

This very modest participation right underlines that children, and young people who are classified as children,[3] do not have full political rights for engagement. This has been critiqued over time by a range of scholars, from the more philosophical (Wall and Dar, 2011; Cook, 2013) to the more practical (Wyness, 2001). It underlines that below a certain age, children and young people are prohibited or constrained from many of the political rights adults can exercise, including voting and standing for political office. Often the creation of children and young people's participation activities are justified as necessary, particular and special, *because* children and young people do not have the full range of civil and political human rights recognised for adults (Wyness, 2001; Wall and Dar, 2011). Thus the UNCRC, and related practices and policy, do recognise children and young people's participation rights but only up to a certain, non-political point.

Across the globe, participation activities have faced very similar challenges over recent decades (see overviews in Percy-Smith and Thomas, 2010; Lundy, 2018; McMellon and Tisdall, 2020). All too often, children and young people provide their energy and ideas to influence services, policies and other decisions but are involved too late or too peripherally in the decision-making process, so their views have no demonstrable influence on the decision making and children and young people receive minimal to no feedback on the decisions (see, for example, Austin, 2010; Kallio and Häkli, 2011; African Child Policy Forum, 2015; Collins et al, 2016). Children and young people's participation is often precarious in its staffing and funding, with activities ending while the children and young people are still wanting to continue and their influencing agendas unfinished (Le

Borgne, 2016). Adults often raise concerns about who is included or excluded in participation activities: that certain groups of children and young people have been excluded; that participating children and young people are unrepresentative of others; and that only 'elite' children and young people are involved (see, for example, Matthews and Limb, 2003; McGinley and Grieve, 2010; Augsberger et al, 2018). The list is considerable and consistent across widely different contexts.

While this list is very familiar, a number of young people's participation activities *do* seem to be having an influence on decision making at a collective level and some commentators give attention to *why* such activities may be doing so (for example, Shier et al, 2014; Tisdall et al, 2014; Crowley, 2015; Le Borgne and Tisdall, 2017). A particular set of examples involves a core group of young people coming together over a particular issue, developing their ideas on the problems, the evidence and the solutions, and bringing these ideas to the (adult) decisions makers in order to influence change. Adults support these groups, typically by providing an adult facilitator, logistical support and resources to meet, but the projects remain youth-led rather than co-research with adults. Examples include: an evaluation of the Children's Commissioner for Wales (Cook et al, 2008); the Youth Alcohol Commission (Young Scot, n.d.) and the Young Commission for iRights, in Scotland; and globally in such countries as Bangladesh, Brazil, Chile, Ghana and Romania (see Cuevas-Parra and Tisdall, 2019b). These projects make particular claims to the knowledge production by the young people and the resulting legitimacy and credibility.

To discuss these claims, this chapter considers certain examples in more depth, where internal and external research have been undertaken and the research includes the views of the young researchers as well as other stakeholders. These examples are:

- Voice against Violence (VAV)[4]: a group of eight young experts supported by the Scottish Government to influence the National Domestic Abuse Delivery Plan for Children and Young People, with subsequent follow on projects (Houghton, 2013, 2015, 2018);
- Young Edinburgh Action (YEA): annual participatory action research projects of between six to 15 young people, which are part of the City of Edinburgh Council's youth participation strategy (McMellon and Mitchell, 2016; Macdonald et al, 2018; McMellon and Mitchell, 2018; see also Chapter 3);
- child-led research in Bangladesh, Jordan and Lebanon: World Vision developed a series of child-led research projects, with three selected

for a research study (Cuevas-Parra, 2018; Cuevas-Parra and Tisdall, 2019a, 2019b).[5]

In all these projects, young people were aged 12 and older. The phrase 'young researchers' is used to refer to the young people in the projects' core groups. This phrase picks up the preferences of young people in Cuevas-Parra's research (see Cuevas-Parra, 2018). Here, the young people saw their identity as 'young' as a source of pride, a positive adjunct to the term 'researcher'. This chapter continues with this phrase, as it emphasises the issues of research and knowledge production that are explored in this chapter.

Knowledge production

Youth-led research positions the young researchers as knowledgeable and the research results as valuable knowledge. These perceptions were found throughout the three examples; the perceptions were held by virtually all parties – from the young researchers themselves, to the facilitators and organisations supporting them, to potential decision makers.

Young researchers were perceived as knowledgeable because they brought particular knowledge *as young people* to the research. Young people were described as better able than adults to identify research agendas relevant and important for their own contexts and for those of other young people. For example, a VAV young researcher put forward their expertise: '"We are the experts, we lived it, we know what worked and what didn't"' (quoted in Houghton, 2015, p 240). Even when young people have been recruited to a particular project, with parameters already set for the research focus, the young researchers reported having an important role in further refinement. For example, in Jordan and Lebanon, young people were recruited to a project on the local experiences of young refugees from the Syrian conflict. While this focus was already set, the young researchers determinedly included refugees' schooling experiences about discrimination and bullying in the project's research agenda. This had not been the focus of previous research undertaken by adults. Thus, the contextual experiences of young people led their research to identify topics not necessarily prioritised for adults and these topics had important policy and practice implications.

The young researchers were perceived by themselves and by others as better researchers with other young people than adult researchers would be. They were described as particularly good at recruiting other young people to be research participants because they had peer and community networks not accessible to adult researchers. They were discussed as better able to communicate with other young people, in ways that young participants would better understand. Particularly in the research undertaken by Cuevas-Parra (2018) in Bangladesh, Jordan and Lebanon, the young researchers' own experiences were described as crucial resources for data analysis. For example, one young researcher explained:

> 'We discovered issues that were covered or hidden, and we brought them into the light and exposed them to the public. We explained in detail the things that affect children.' (Quoted in Cuevas-Parra and Tisdall, 2019b, p 6)

Further, the young researchers discussed how they used their own personal experiences as research data and to help them understand the data they had collected more broadly. These contributions from young researchers, as young people, led to quality in terms of both content and process.

In these ways, young researchers were perceived as improving the focus of the research, the data collection and the analysis, compared to adult researchers. Further, the projects increased young researchers' knowledge, both in terms of content and skills. Taken together, the young researchers claimed expertise, which led to increased impact of their findings on decision making (Houghton, 2018).

Legitimacy and credibility

The aspects of legitimacy and credibility in knowledge production, and associated expertise of the young researchers, gave both the research and the young researchers certain legitimacy and credibility. This is exemplified by a staff member describing young researchers presenting their report to a government minister: "'They [young researchers] did it so well because they were talking about the things they researched themselves. They owned the information. Everything they said was so natural'" (quoted in Cuevas-Parra, 2018, p 292). The young researchers had a claim to be heard because they were talking about the research they had done. Further, the young researchers had done so 'naturally', with ownership of the information. This relates to the very frequent assertion by both young researchers and the adults supporting them, that this was youth-led research, with key decisions controlled by the young researchers throughout.

The excerpt in the previous paragraph makes claims for the young researchers and their research's legitimacy and credibility. Legitimacy has been extensively theorised and researched in a number of social science disciplines, including and notably within political science and social psychology (see Johnson et al, 2006 for an overview). Suchman's seminal definition of legitimacy, from an organisational perspective, captures key elements: 'a generalized perception or assumption that the actions of an entity are desirable, proper or appropriate within some socially constructed system of norms, values, beliefs and definitions' (1995, p 574). Within research, as a particular socially constructed system, legitimacy is perceived in certain specific ways. When considering how research does or does not influence decision making, Cash and colleagues (2003) define legitimacy as 'how fair an information producing process is and whether it considers appropriate values, concerns, and perspectives of different actors' (p 2). They distinguish this from credibility, which is 'how to create authoritative, believable and trusted information' so that an actor 'perceives information as meeting standards of plausibility and technical adequacy' (p 4). Thus legitimacy and credibility in research appeal to fair, authoritative and believable information that is valued by the collective audience (Suchman, 1995; Johnson et al, 2006). The literature points to the social construction of legitimacy and credibility but that, by constructing something as legitimate and credible, it asserts that it is right morally and technically (Johnson et al 2006).

All the examples of youth-led research made claims to legitimacy, on several bases. As with many youth participation activities, a claim was made that young people (and especially children) were frequently excluded in practice or by law from collective decision making (see, for example, Tisdall, 2012; Houghton, 2018). Thus particular activities were requested and extra effort was needed to have mechanisms so young people were heard on decisions that affect them. One YEA young researcher expanded on such reasons for involving young people:

> 'Young people are those who are going to be affected by decisions which are made now so it is very important that we take an interest in influencing decisions on issues that are important to us and our future. We are also those who will become decision-makers in the future, and by practising and engaging with a similar process we are equipping ourselves to make stronger decisions when it becomes out turn.' (Quoted in Macdonald et al, 2018, p 1)

As evident within this quotation, such activities made an appeal to recognising young people as current community members, service consumers and future decision makers. Thus the legitimacy of youth-led research was claimed because it included an otherwise excluded group of people, it would lead to better decisions and it would help train people for the future.

For youth-led research, this was further particularised by the young people's expertise and experiences. As evidenced earlier, the young researchers were seen as improving the quality and content of the research they undertook. All the examples reached out to other young people as research participants, thus ensuring the knowledge generated included a range of young people. All these elements were legitimisation claims. The research processes undertaken by these examples were claimed to be credible because they were rigorous throughout. For example, young researchers in both YEA and the child-led research detailed with pride the creation of sound research instruments (such as questionnaires and interview schedules), refined through group discussions. They make credibility claims for their findings, based on who they involved as research participants and their analytical processes, so that they have produced authoritative and trusted knowledge. Their confidence in their analysis relates to Lincoln and Guba's (1985) definition of credibility for qualitative research, which appeals to research participants and others with similar experiences perceiving the results as credible. The young researchers, and those supporting them, combined assertions of research rigour and informed results to assert credibility.

Further, when the young researchers presented the research themselves (whether in writing or in person) to broader audiences, such presentations furthered the credibility dimension of authenticity as suggested by the earlier quotation. One young researcher took this further in terms of emotional authenticity:

> 'When we were writing the report, I did not expect too many things but [I hoped] at least to do something that can touch people's hearts, their feelings. I wrote a quote and felt this quote touched me, and I was sure that it could touch other people.' (Quoted in Cuevas-Parra and Tisdall 2019a, p 9)

The young researchers were thus combining the emotional claims from their own experiences with the scientific claims of research's plausibility and technical adequacy, with the aim of influencing decision makers.

Across all the projects, such claims to legitimacy and credibility were persuasive to at least some decision makers and some policy decisions. For example, VAV influenced Scottish Government decision making dramatically, with specified funding for all local government areas to employ specialist workers for children affected by domestic abuse (Houghton, 2018). YEA identified a service gap, leading to new sex education post (Macdonald et al, 2018). The child-led research in Bangladesh encouraged local administrators and community leaders to promote birth certification as well as using existing birth certificates to address child labour and child marriage (Cuevas-Parra, 2018). The young researchers and the research projects were seen as legitimate and credible sources of expertise and knowledge, which influenced (adult) attitudes, policies and services.

Such claims, however, were not always accepted. Their precariousness was exemplified in certain external questioning whether the research was truly youth-led, thus querying its authenticity. The young researchers in all three examples noted the vital role supporting adults and organisations had within their projects, in terms of providing practical and emotional support. But they asserted that they had made the key decisions about the process and outcomes. As summarised by one young researcher, ' "Yes, no one telling us what to do, our own priorities, our own words"' (quoted in Houghton, 2018, p 85).

One of the greatest threats to both legitimacy and credibility for children and young people's participation generally are queries about young people's representativeness. As discussed earlier, the criticisms are frequently that collective participation activities privilege the elite, such as the more socioeconomically advantaged and those more educationally fluent, and that their participation is selective, often without an underlying democratic process, so that the young people have no accountability to young people more generally (Turkie, 2010). As such, young people involved in such activities are neither demographically nor democratically representative and their views can thus be dismissed in collective decision making.

To a certain extent, youth-led research side-steps such critiques because young people are involved because of their expertise, not their representativeness. As detailed previously, young people were involved in these projects initially because of their contextual and personal experiences. These experiences were valued as bringing particular expertise to the research. Further, young people developed research skills and substantive knowledge personally and collectively through the youth-led research, so by the end of the process they and the project were credible. When young people were able to demonstrate this with decision makers, often most effectively because of dialogical relationships with decision makers (see Houghton, 2018; McMellon and Mitchell, 2018), they and the research had demonstrable impacts in terms of decisions.

But claims to 'expert' representation are not always successful generally (see Arnesen and Peters, 2017) nor in the youth participation field (Ross et al, 2018). The projects here buttressed themselves in several ways. Supporting organisations and adults explicitly sought certain diversity among young researchers, through the recruitment and selection process. For example, the child-led research in Bangladesh, Jordan and Lebanon ensured a balance of girls and boys, in contexts of local gender hierarchies (Cuevas-Parra, 2018). VAV undertook recruitment across Scotland, with care to ensure diversity as well as experience (Houghton, 2018). Both the Bangladeshi and YEA groups were self-selected, by the young people's interest in being involved, but both projects arose from large-scale consultative activities with a wider group of young people (the Bangladesh project arose from long-standing local Child Forums, while YEA has 'gatherings' that identify annual priorities for action groups). Therefore problem identification and the resulting research topics emerged from a more demographically inclusive group with an element of 'voting' democratically for priorities. Furthermore, young researchers and their projects often reached out to a broader range of young people, with the explicit intent to be more inclusive demographically. For example, in developing their recommendations on sex education in schools, the YEA action group undertook a questionnaire survey with young people across several Edinburgh secondary schools (see YEA and CRFR, 2015; Ross et al, 2018). Thus a more diverse demographic group of young people were involved as research participants. Such means of selection, problem identification and participant reach are commonly used in participation activities more generally, to deal with queries about young people's representativeness, with some success.

These combined efforts addressed certain inequalities across young people, in terms of opportunities to be engaged in meaningful participation activities and to have their views influence collective decision making. But certain inequalities persisted despite all of these efforts. All the projects explicitly avoided recruiting from elite groups and groupings, with supporting staff reaching out to a range of young people from more socioeconomically disadvantaged backgrounds. Care was taken by certain projects to reach out to young people with other background characteristics who are often excluded in their community contexts – such as YEA's explicit reaching out to young people with disabilities, LGBTI young people and care-experienced young people. These efforts were successful. But the young researchers could still face criticism of being the 'elite': as they gained skills and knowledge, particularly in policies and interaction with adult decision makers, they risked being considered too 'professionalised' and no longer authentically expressing the views of young people. They were young people who could find the time and had the commitment and interest to be involved, whereas other young people lacking one or more of these elements might not be involved. Nairn and colleagues (2006) powerfully evidence, in the New Zealand context, how young people were well represented from more 'hard to reach' or 'disadvantaged' and more 'elite' backgrounds across a range of participation activities: it was the 'excluded middle' who were not even identified as missing by adult organisers, let alone involved. The inequalities of youth participation within youth-led research projects, and particularly as young researchers, were not necessarily the standard concerns of elitism of schooling performance and socioeconomic background. Instead, there were inequalities of time, commitment and interest and, once again, the 'excluded middle' of young people risked not being involved.

Thus the youth-led research projects and the young researchers were able to make claims to legitimacy and credibility, in terms of their experience, expertise and research process. These claims were contested and contestable, as demonstrated by the frequency of their defence of young researchers' representativeness.

Conclusion

The projects used as examples here have different labels – youth-led research, participatory action research, co-production or co-design – but they were united by certain processes and claims. Practically, they all were time-limited, they involved a core group of young people with supporting adults, and they involved an in-depth inquiry by the young people. The young people had time and space to work together as a collective. There was an adult commitment for young people to take the lead in key decisions, throughout the whole project, with support from adult facilitators, organisations and the funding to do so. Further, these adults and their organisations scaffolded young people's connections with adult decision makers, making it more likely that the youth-led research would influence the decision makers and have an impact on decisions.

With these elements, the projects were able to address several of the challenges and barriers so often found in youth participation activities – and particularly to have demonstrable impacts on decision making. Their success can be attributed to the projects recasting the positioning of young researchers and the projects, so that young people were perceived as experts and as generators of knowledge. The young people were persuasive in presenting their findings, recommendations and solutions to decision makers, often in dialogue with decision makers, leading to decisions incorporating some or all of the young people's recommendations. While none of these projects achieved all of its desired policy or practice changes, the examples all affected decisions that mattered to the young people involved.

This repositioning of young people as expert knowledge producers was underpinned by claims to legitimacy and credibility, explored in this chapter. The young people's own personal and contextual experiences created both legitimacy (in terms of young people being fairly included and heard) and credibility (in terms of the young researchers' expertise and believability). The processes of core group selection assisted with legitimacy while the wider reach to other young people aided both legitimacy and credibility. The processes of topic focus, in-depth inquiry and systematic analysis aligned themselves with social science claims to credibility, as producing authoritative and trusted information (Cash et al, 2003; Blaikie, 2009).

The claims to legitimacy and credibility were not without their tensions. The projects struggled with the perennial critique of youth participation that the young people involved were unrepresentative. The projects addressed some of these criticisms through directed selection and outreach activities, but their focus on a core group of young people left them unable to represent fully the diversity of young people in any one community demographically and they were not backed by a democratic representational process. Participation activities are frequently criticised for privileging elite young people, whether in terms of academic performance and/or socioeconomic background. This was avoided in the projects discussed here, although the projects led to other inequalities, particularly in terms of the 'excluded middle' of young people who were neither the privileged elite nor from disadvantaged groups, but rather the 'ordinary' young people who were not encouraged to be involved. To be in the core group of young people required considerable time, interest and commitment, which is not the preserve of all young people. Thus, this type of participation activity creates and perpetuates its own inequalities across young people, just not the standard ones of elitism and socioeconomic advantage.

Such projects are radical in questioning the legitimacy and credibility boundaries of knowledge production – as other adult groups are doing (see Cahill, 2007; Campbell and Vanderhoven, 2016). They do so by questioning and stretching these boundaries, of what counts as 'good research', well-grounded findings and informed recommendations. They are potentially radical *within* these boundaries as they seek to gain a 'place at the table', to be one among others with credibility and legitimacy, to become valued stakeholders within governance. They are not particularly radical in questioning the 'table', the fundamentals of how decisions are made and governance undertaken, compared with other forms of youth participation documented in this book (see Chapters 2 and 9). They are not overtly political action nor radical activism, disturbing the requirements of the UNCRC's participation rights. Such projects thus risk, as do other participatory governance attempts, co-option by the already powerful, thus closing off of other options and smothering dissent. But in the short term such forms facilitate young people to powerfully influence decisions that affect young people collectively. In the long term, they can legitimate more broadly young people's participation, bolstering norms, values and beliefs so that young people's participation is not an innovation but an embedded, expected, legitimate and credible social practice. Youth-led research is proving an effective way to claim the legitimacy and credibility of young people as knowledge producers, as a route to ensuring that children's participation rights are realised in collective decision making.

Acknowledgements

The chapter is based on collaborations with children, young people and adult partners. These include projects funded by the British Academy, Economic and Social Research Council (ESRC)/UK Research and Innovation (R451265206, RES-189-25-0174, RES-451-26-0685, ES/T001399/1, ES/S004351/1) and Knowledge Exchange funds from the University of Edinburgh and the ESRC Impact Acceleration Account, the European Research Council, the European Union's Rights, Equality and Citizenship Programme (2014–20), the Foundation of Canadian Studies, the Leverhulme Trust, the Royal Society of Edinburgh and the Social Sciences and Humanities Research Council of Canada and in partnership with World Vision International.

Notes
[1] Young people involved in this chapter's empirical examples are mostly between the ages of 12 and 18. They are referred to as young people or young researchers. More generally, the chapter refers to children and young people in the participation

field, which is framed by the UNCRC. However, the UNCRC uses the term child only.

2   For example, see www.wvi.org/child-participation/publication/ideas-action-children-and-young-people-june-global-moment

3   Under Article 1 of the UNCRC, and for the purposes of the UNCRC, a child is defined as 'every human being below the age of eighteen years unless, under the law applicable to the child, majority is attained earlier'.

4   See www.voiceagainstviolence.org.uk

5   I have had differing involvement in the projects, which has given me insight into how they work and given me the chance to meet some of the young people involved. For VAV, I and the Centre for Research on Families and Relationships (CRFR) supported as 'a critical friend' and hosted the project respectively. For Young Edinburgh Action, we had an evolving partnership that included the making of 'YEA: It's a film' and supported YEA young people in training researchers. I also supported several master's students to undertake independent research about YEA. For the work with World Vision, I was supervisor for the PhD research on the projects and then co-wrote certain later publications with Cuevas-Parra on this at his invitation.

References

African Child Policy Forum (2015) *A Study on Child Participation in Eastern Africa*, Addis Ababa: African Child Policy Forum. Available from: https://app.box.com/s/agbasad14dvxuakgtxxnk96czxdyn7v1 [Accessed 14 February 2019].

Arnesen, S. and Peters, Y. (2017) 'The legitimacy of representation', *Comparative Political Studies*, 51(7): 868–99.

Augsberger, A., Collins, M.E., Gecker, W. and Dougher, M. (2018) 'Youth civic engagement', *Journal of Adolescent Research*, 33(2): 187–208.

Austin, S.L. (2010) 'Children's participation in citizenship and governance', in B. Percy-Smith and N. Thomas (eds) *A Handbook of Children and Young People's Participation*, Abingdon: Routledge, pp 245–53.

Blaikie, N. (2009) *Designing Social Research*, Cambridge: Polity Press.

Cahill, C. (2007) 'The personal is political: developing new subjectivities through participatory action research', *Gender, Place & Culture*, 1(4): 267–92.

Campbell, H. and Vanderhoven, D. (2016) *Knowledge That Matters*, N8 Research Partnership, [online]. Available from: www.n8research.org.uk/research-focus/co-production/ [Accessed 3 November 2020].

Cash, D., Clark, W.C., Alcock, F., Dickson, N.E. and Jager, J. (2003) *Salience, Credibility, Legitimacy and Boundaries: Linking Research, Access and Decision Making*, KSG Working Papers Series, 2003, Digital Access to Scholarship at Harvard [online]. Available from: https://dash.harvard.edu/bitstream/handle/1/32067415/Salience_credibility.pdf?sequence=4 [Accessed 6 December 2019].

Collins, M.E., Augsberger, A. and Gecker, W. (2016) 'Youth councils in municipal government', *Children and Youth Services Review*, 65: 140–7.

Cook, J., France, H., Hillman, J., Jenkins, C., Michael, L., Pearson, T., Pugh-Dungey, R., Richards, J., Sawyers, B., Taylor, M., Cook, M., Crowley, A. and Thomas, N. (2008) *Evaluating the Children's Commissioner for Wales*, Welsh Parliament, [online]. Available from: www.assembly.wales/NAfW%20Documents/cc-001eng.pdf%20-%2015122008/cc-001eng-English.pdf [Accessed 8 November 2019].

Cook, P. (2013) 'Against a minimum voting age', *Critical Review of International Social and Political Philosophy*, 16(3): 439–58.

Crowley, A. (2015) 'Is anyone listening – the impact of children's participation on public policy', *International Journal of Children's Rights*, 23: 602–21.

Cuevas-Parra, P. (2018) 'Exploring child-led research: case studies from Bangladesh, Lebanon and Jordan', PhD thesis, University of Edinburgh, Edinburgh, UK, [online]. Available from: www.era.lib.ed.ac.uk/handle/1842/33057 [Accessed 9 January 2019].

Cuevas-Parra, P. and Tisdall, E.K.M. (2019a) 'Child-led research', *Social Sciences*, 8(2): 44, doi: 10.3390/socsci8020044

Cuevas-Parra, P. and Tisdall, E.K.M. (2019b) *Child-Led Research: From Participating in Research to Leading It*, London: World Vision International.

Daly, A. (2018) *Children, Autonomy and the Courts*, Leiden: Brill/Nijhoff.

Houghton, C. (2013) 'Voice against violence', PhD thesis, Warwick University, Warwick, UK.

Houghton, C. (2015) 'Young people's perspectives on participatory ethics', *Child Abuse Review*, 24(4): 235–48.

Houghton, C. (2018) 'Voice, agency, power', in S. Holt, C. Øverlien and J. Devaney (eds) *Responding to Domestic Violence*, London: Jessica Kingsley, pp 77–96.

Johnson, C., Dowd, T.J. and Ridgeway, C.L. (2006) 'Legitimacy as a social process', *Annual Review Sociology*, 32: 53–78.

Kallio, K.P. and Häkli, J. (2011) 'Tracing children's politics', *Political Geography*, 30: 99–109.

Le Borgne, C. (2016) 'Implementing children's participation at the community level', Doctoral dissertation, University of Edinburgh, Edinburgh, UK.

Le Borgne, C. and Tisdall, E.K.M. (2017) 'Children's participation', *Social Inclusion*, 5(3): 122–30.

Lincoln, Y.S. and Guba, E.G. (1985) *Naturalistic Inquiry*, London; Sage Publications.

Lundy, L. (2018) 'In defence of tokenism?', *Childhood*, 25(3): 340–54.

Macdonald, S., Eltiraifi, M., Stark, C., Paton, A., Jamieson-MacKenzie, I., Dempsie, K. and Watt, M. (2018) *Young Edinburgh Action Presents … YEA We Can*, CRFR Research Briefing No. 92, Edinburgh: CRFR. Available from: https://era.ed.ac.uk/handle/1842/35633 [Accessed 6 December 2019].

Matthews, H. and Limb, M. (2003) 'Another white elephant?', *Space and Polity*, 7(2): 173–92.

McGinley, B. and Grieve, A. (2010) 'Maintaining the status quo?', in B. Percy-Smith and N. Thomas (eds) *A Handbook of Children and Young People's Participation*, Abingdon: Routledge, pp 254–61.

McMellon, C. and Mitchell, M. (2016) Young Edinburgh Action: reinvigorating young people's participation in Edinburgh, CRFR Research Briefing 85, Available from: era.ed.ac.uk/bitstream/handle/1842/16875/CRFR%20briefing%2085.pdf?sequence=1&isAllowed=y [Accessed 3 November 2020]

McMellon, C. and Mitchell, M. (2018) 'Participatory action research and young people', in J. Ravenscroft and L. Hamilton (eds) *Building Research Design in Education*, London: Bloomsbury, pp 172–95.

McMellon, C. and Tisdall, E.K.M. (2020) 'Children and young people's participation rights: looking backwards and moving forwards', *International Journal of Children's Rights*, 28(1): 157–82.

Nairn, K., Sligo, J. and Freeman, C. (2006) 'Polarizing participation in local government', *Children, Youth and Environments*, 16(2): 248–71.

Percy-Smith, B. and Thomas, N. (eds) (2010) *A Handbook of Children and Young People's Participation*, Abingdon: Routledge.

Ross, C., Kerridge, E. and Woodhouse, A. (2018) *The Impact of Children and Young People's Participation on Policy Making*, Edinburgh: Scottish Government. Available from: www.gov.scot/publications/impact-children-young-peoples-participation-policy-making [Accessed 8 November 2019].

Shier, H., Méndez, M.H., Centeno, M., Arróliga, I. and González, M. (2014) 'How children and young people influence policy-makers: lessons from Nicaragua', *Children & Society*, 28(1): 1–14.

Suchman, M. (1995) 'Managing legitimacy: strategic and institutional approaches', *Academic Management Review*, 20(3): 571–610.

Tisdall, E.K.M. (2012) 'Taking forward children and young people's participation', in M. Hill, G. Head, A. Lockyer, B. Reid and R. Taylor (eds) *Children's Services: Working Together*, Harlow: Pearson Press, pp 151–62.

Tisdall, E.K.M. (2013) 'The transformation of participation?', *Global Studies of Childhood*, 3(2): 183–93.

Tisdall, E.K.M. (2015) 'Children and young people's participation', in W. Vandenhole, E. Desmet, D. Reynaert and S. Lembrechts (eds) *Routledge International Handbook of Children's Rights Studies*, Abingdon: Routledge, pp 185–200.

Tisdall, E.K.M., Gadda, A.M. and Butler, U.M. (eds) (2014) *Children and Young People's Participation and its Transformative Potential: Learning from Across Countries*, Basingstoke: Palgrave Macmillan.

Turkie, A. (2010) 'More than crumbs from the table', in B. Percy-Smith and N. Thomas (eds) *A Handbook of Children and Young People's Participation*, Abingdon: Routledge, pp 262–269.

UN Committee on the Rights of the Child (2009) 'General comment no. 12 (2009): The right of the child to be heard', UNCRC, [online]. Available from: https://www2.ohchr.org/english/bodies/crc/docs/AdvanceVersions/CRC-C-GC-12.pdf [Accessed 30 May 2019].

Wall, J. and Dar, A. (2011) 'Children's political representation: the right to make a difference', *International Journal of Children's Rights*, 19(4): 595–612.

Wood, J. (2015) 'Children and planning: to what extent does the Scottish town planning system facilitate the UN Convention on the Rights of the Child', *Planning Practice & Research*, 30(2): 139–59.

Wyness, M. (2001) 'Children, childhood and political participation: case studies of young people's councils', *International Journal of Children's Rights*, 9(3): 193–212.

YEA (Young Edinburgh Action) and CRFR (Centre for Research on Families and Relationships) (2015) 'YEA: It's a film', University of Edinburgh, [online]. Available from: https://media.ed.ac.uk/media/Young+Edinburgh+Action/1_etof4nna [Accessed 8 August 2019].

Young Scot (n.d.) 'Building the boat: young people as co-producers of policy', Young Scot, [online]. Available from: www.youngscot.net/what-we-do/key-documents/building-the-boat.aspx [Accessed 8 August 2019].

14

Journey mapping as a method to make sense of participation

Anne Mette W. Nielsen and Maria Bruselius-Jensen

This chapter explores how journey mapping as a qualitative research method allows young people on the edge of society to reflect on and make sense of their engagement in different youth projects. The method provides young people with the time, space and means to explore the participatory activities they engage in and to map the multiple ways they interact with the often messy, multi-sensual and frictional youth life on the edge of society. This approach to journey mapping is inspired by cultural researcher Roz Stewart-Hall (hereafter and in the References quoted as Hall). She developed the method to address a critique of how project evaluations seldom carried any meaningful insights into what makes a difference to the participants as well as in broader explorations of what it means to be a young person on the edge of society (Hall, 2005).

Key findings

- Journey mapping is a way to invite young people on the edge of society to (re)define and negotiate that which makes sense to them when they engage in participatory activities.
- The method emphasises the significance of a space for young people on the edge of society to reflect on their engagement and participation in adult-led programmes.
- The method promotes a multiplicity of insights into youth lives on the edge of society rather than a unifying overview.
- The method argues that this multiplicity can lead to new questions and understandings of what matters, when young people on the edge of society engage in participatory activities.
- The method can easily be employed in arenas other than research, in order to increase and strengthen knowledge exchanges between professionals and young people on the edge of society.

Qualitative, participatory-driven research methods

Qualitative, participatory-driven research methods are at the core of much research with children and young people. Spanning a highly diverse field, participatory methods are characterised by an emphasis on doing research *with* children and young people rather than *on* them, both as a way to generate unique types of data and to understand better the meanings, realities and experiences of children and young people. Nevertheless, the field has gained new experiential energy over the past few decades, with digital cameras, digital recorders, smart phones, iPads, computers and a variety of visual and audio production software becoming available and integrated into the everyday practices of adult researchers, children and young people. This expansion of the field goes along with a revitalised awareness of possibilities to go beyond consultation and to embrace participatory modes in which children and young people are engaged in more reciprocal ways of collaborating – for example, with adult researchers (Fielding, 2010).

Journey mapping is an example of a participatory-driven qualitative research method with children and young people, placing itself in line with a number of visually based methods such as timelines (for example, Adriansen, 2012; see also Chapter 3 in this book), participatory video (for example Milne et al, 2012) and snap log (for example, Bramming, 2009). They are all characterised by using different visual strategies to document social reality (Pauwels, 2015) and to explore significant experiences, transactions and affects (Bagnoli, 2009). At the same time, journey mapping differs from these methods by not limiting the adult researcher, children and young people to specific ways of structuring or mediating the material, for example, through timelines or video, respectively. Instead, the method invites the adult researcher, children and young people into a space of reflection that can take many directions, encouraging a rather open examination of *what* elements appear significant and *how* they appear significant within a given process or projects as well as in children's and young people's everyday lives.

'On the edge' as a position produced through complex transactions

The chapter shares empirical data from two studies. The first study (2015–17) follows young people (aged 14–29) on the edge of society, who took part in different art and cultural projects in various areas/neighbourhoods of Denmark (Nielsen and Sørensen, 2017). The second study (2018–ongoing) follows a youth project supporting young people from deprived neighbourhoods in Copenhagen to influence and shape their local communities. The first study involved 11 journey maps conducted as individual interviews. The second study involved 19 journey maps conducted individually or in groups of two to six young people.

Both studies are characterised by involving what we here define as 'youth on the edge of society'. The concept emphasises young people being 'on the edge' as produced through complex transactions between the young people and the agents, discourses and contextual settings surrounding them (Sletten and Hyggen, 2013; Katznelson et al, 2015; Nielsen and Sørensen, 2017). Thus it points to a broader and more dynamic definition of 'the edge of society' than the classical understanding closely connected to socioeconomic background (for example, Willis, 1977). Though still encompassing structural inequalities, the concept reflects new demands of social and cultural inclusion based on norms and values that more and more young people find to be out of reach (Harsløf and Malmberg-Heimonen, 2014). These demands have been described as processes of 'hard individualization' (Hermann, 2007) or a new 'performance culture' (Sørensen et al, 2013), oriented by comparison, ranking and assessment. They are not exclusively anchored in the arena of formal education (Jackson, 2006; Biesta, 2009), but appear in a number of other arenas defining young people's lives such as friendship, family and leisure time (Sørensen et al, 2013). At the same time – due to the obvious metaphorical pitfalls of the concept – it is important to emphasise that processes of social stabilisation of the lives of youth on the edge of society cannot be understood only in terms of more inclusion ('normalisation') or increased exclusion ('losing the grip') along an axis of centre–periphery. Social stabilisation for these young people also involves new forms of social integration, belonging and communities *in* the periphery (Nielsen and Sørensen, 2017).

Our use of journey mapping in two qualitative studies

Our use of journey mapping is inspired by cultural researcher Roz Stewart-Hall, who has used the method in her evaluations of a number of community arts projects in the UK. She developed the method in the early 2000s as a critique of an evaluation practice that seldom provided any meaningful insights into what it meant to participate to those involved (Hall, 2015). It was a critique that emphasised how evaluations had a tendency to focus on already defined measures and criteria (the number of participants, their transitions into education or employment and so on) and provided hardly any understanding of the quality or significance of the experiences to the participants. Thus these evaluations not only failed to create any substantial knowledge exchanges between projects and participants, but also failed to provide any new perspectives on what kind of challenges participants were facing in their lives and how their participation in the projects played into these challenges. Based on this critique, Stewart-Hall suggested the use of journey mapping as one way of allowing participants the time and space to reflect on their participation and what it meant to them (Hall, 2015). This emphasis on journey mapping as a space of reflection underlines *meaning* as a contingent *making* that appears depending on what comes into mind (at that exact time) in a participant's life as well as on the approach the participant decides to follow. In that sense, the method also points to transformative learning as core in participation processes not least – as pointed out in Chapter 16 in this book – for young people at risk of marginalisation. Our use of journey mapping thus differs from how the method is understood in fields such as design and management, and in relation to customer and consumer studies, where it is seen as a way to gain insights into 'what leads to what' in a process (Følstad and Kvale, 2018). It is less about uncovering the steps in a given process than about the multiple ways meaningful participation unfolds.

In both studies, we use journey mapping as a way to explore the qualities of what it means to young people themselves to be a young person on the edge of society, and how participation in different youth projects can make a difference in their lives. We begin our exploration by asking the young people in the studies to make a journey map of the events and elements they find to be the most important in the youth projects they are or have been part of (Box 14.1). The mapping is followed by a dialogue, where the young people unfold the map and describe what the different elements mean to them. The dialogue involves clarifying-type questions from us as researchers and often, in the cases where other participants are present, comments from the latter.

The participants create their journey maps on a large piece of paper (either A3, A2 or A1). They are provided with the time they need to reflect on what elements they want to include, and they are free to choose any kind of format. In both studies, this methodological openness leads to a variety of expressions from brainstorms, timelines, drawings, lists of words and categorisations of significant events to montage-like images and illustrations of 'life paths' and so on (Figure 14.1). The methodological openness encourages participants

---

Box 14.1 Example of a guideline for a journey-mapping process with young people in deprived social housing in Copenhagen, Denmark (translated from the original Danish)

Introduction

We are about to create a journey map. It's a way to share what you think has been the most important elements for you in your participation in the project. It is called a journey map because it is similar to what we do when we return from a trip and tell others what we have experienced. You can include elements from the whole period of the project or part of it, or even include earlier experiences that are significant in order to understand what it means to participate in a project like this. You get a piece of paper and pens. You can use whatever expression and format you'd like and take the time you need. When you're done, we will talk about the journey map together.

Follow-up questions for dialogue (if needed)

Why did you participate?

What did you do in the project?

How does it make a difference for you?

Additional mapping

If you look forward, how do you imagine using the experience you had in the project in the future? (please use some time to reflect on this in part of your journey map).

---

to decide whether they want to include past or future experiences not directly related to their participation in a specific youth project, emphasise a specific time period or moment in the project *or* use the overall time frame of their participation in a project as the temporal boundary of their map. This means that the final maps involve very different temporalities (Figure 14.1).

In the follow-up dialogue, the map provides the young people with concrete examples from which to unfold and negotiate their experiences, as well as reflect on more inaccessible, abstract or tacit elements they have not necessarily talked about (in this way) before. The dialogue around the map also invites them to take apart, connect, supplement or create other kinds of adjustments to the map, while they go through its elements. This in-built morphability may disturb such categories as relevance, structure and other (convenient) conventions from the structured or semi-structured research interview, but serves not only to secure the method's openness to what comes into mind and to how it can be expressed, but also to include the meanings that appear in the mutual reflection process between the young people and the researcher. The latter allows the young people to take part in an initial analytical process that otherwise often remains unavailable to them.

In both studies we finish the dialogue by asking the participants to make reflections on the future and add them to their maps. In the first study we ask: 'What do you imagine to be the most important elements from this project that you bring with you to other arenas in the future?' In the second: 'If you look forward, how do you imagine using these experiences in the future?' The dialogue ends with a brief talk about this part of the map.

Three examples of the benefits of journey mapping

In this section we present three examples of how young people use journey mapping to explore and communicate a great variety of aspects in their participation in different projects. The three examples have been chosen based on the differences in how the mappings approach format, time and space.

Concerning ethical aspects, the examples have been anonymised to safeguard privacy in agreement with the participants. The participants have been informed that their journey maps and the follow-up dialogue will be used in a research project and have accepted that the maps and their stories will be used in academic publications. The interpretations following the depictions are based on the subsequent discussions with the participants (as discussed earlier).

Mapping the relationship between affect, place and time in participation

The first journey map is by a young woman, Sofie, aged 20. In her map she explores the significant events in her almost two year-long participation in a visual arts project for young people who are outside of employment, education and training (Figure 14.1).

Sophie divides her journey map into four frames. The first frame focuses on a long period of isolation and loneliness at home before starting in the project. The second frame emphasises the nervousness she felt when she arrived at the project the first day. The third frame shares how she continued to feel lonely during her first four months

Figure 14.1: The first four frames of Sofie's journey map

in the project. The fourth frame illustrates the loving feelings she experiences when integrating with the other participants and the artist working with the group. In the map, the young woman uses a strong narrative structure of beginning, middle and end, which makes the story of the different stages of affect that she has gone through over the past four years accessible for an outsider even without the follow-up dialogue. Nevertheless, the dialogue gives her a chance to unfold what contributed to the change and how affect, time and place play together in her participation:

Sofie: 'Well, I think this might be the first couple of months at the project. Probably.'

Interviewer: 'When was that?'

Sofie: 'It's almost two years since I started. And before I started, I just thought, that it was yet another place where it would go wrong or not as I would have liked it to go. So, I was quite afraid of it. I thought, that there was not much hope to find there, right. And then I remember … [silence].'

Interviewer:	'Is that what happens in the second frame?'
Sofie:	'Yes, it is.'
Interviewer:	'Will you tell a little about the first frame? Is that you?'
Sofie:	'Yes.'
Interviewer:	'Alone in a room?'
Sofie:	'Yes.'
Interviewer:	'Is it also a "room" in your mind?'
Sofie:	'Yes, probably also that. Because I wasn't alone, but I felt so ... And the first couple of months, four months maybe – I thought, "What am I doing here?" There wasn't much to learn. I was so anxious I couldn't communicate with people. So that probably also stopped me from befriending anyone in the beginning.'
Interviewer:	'What happened then?'
Sofie:	'Well, it is probably because at this place you just need to find out that you can be everything you are. Also the bad parts. You don't get scolded for the bad parts and don't get told: "Get yourself together."' It means that I have come to believe more in myself, because I have realised I haven't been looked upon as anything special.' (Interview, Sofie, 2016)

The young woman's juxtapositioning of scenarios ascribes equal importance and affective intensity to the experiences they reflect, thereby exploring the variety of actualities and meanings drawn from her participation. In the first frame, she circles around long years of hopelessness and of feeling alone before beginning at the project. In the second frame, she shares an intense moment of extreme nervousness, when standing in front of the project's entrance door on her first day. The third frame witnesses her continual feeling of being situated in a place outside the project's community. Finally, in the last frame, she sums up the past one-and-a-half years as a period during which the project becomes a community she can belong to and take part in.

In a final reflection of what she imagines bringing with her from the project and into the future, she reveals how the absence of being able to give form to the future also terrifies her, despite her readiness to move on and her feeling of support from the community at the project (Figure 14.2).

More than anything else, Sofie's journey map reflects how affect, time and place play together in the overall compositions of the past (and

Figure 14.2: Last frame of Sofie's journey map

future) in young people's lived lives and form their (non-)participation in youth projects as well as in other formal and informal arenas.

The composition of an immense and inaccessible chaos

Whereas Sofie's journey map used an almost clichéd clearness to express the former loneliness of her youth life, other maps in the same study appear chaotic and almost inaccessible, mirroring the fragmented life on the edge of society, where most life-orienting coordinates have imploded (both in time and place). This is the case in a journey map by Isaam, aged 25, who participated in a theatre play about homelessness (Figure 14.3).

In the dialogue following the creation of his journey map, Isaam unfolds and interprets the map for the interviewer. He begins by talking about the open book and the houses arising from it, in the lower middle part of his map:

Isaam: 'It is the story about the street, we're telling. Once
                upon a time in the streets …'
Interviewer: 'Yes?'

Figure 14.3: Isaam's journey map

Isaam: '... It is important for people to understand what happens in the streets, because what happens there is not for the fun. It will be your children that will get hurt one day, because they stood in the wrong spot, and the streets haven't been cleaned. Because nobody took care of the streets, nobody cares about the streets. They let them rot and suddenly a hate arises in the streets and things happen and that is a pity, that should not happen, that ought not to happen. I think the city should be torn down, bombed, burned down completely and then just let the trees grow, so we can walk between them, man. I think it's ugly to look at the grey buildings sometimes. I think: "Fuck off. I grew up in concrete. It is not ... I don't want it, man."'

Interviewer: 'And what is this?' [Interviewer points further up on the journey map]

Isaam: 'It is a mic.'

Interviewer: 'Is it your song?'

Isaam: 'Yes.'
Interviewer: 'Why was that important?'
Isaam: 'It felt good to get it out. Well … but honestly, it …
                  I think it is like some of these mornings you have,
                  right, where you see the sunrise and you just see life
                  in a different way. Even though you know that life is
                  shit you have just done something that made more
                  than sense. And then … You know, you get motivated
                  to continue.' (Interview, Isaam, 2016)

In the fragmented journey map, Isaam makes sense of his participation in the play drawing not on a distant past – as Sofie did – but on his everyday whereabouts as homeless in the streets of Copenhagen. In his unfolding of the map, the maltreatment on the streets resembles the story he tells elsewhere in the interview of being left alone with an intense fear and hopelessness from a very young age. The map helps Isaam to put into words how utterly wrong and at the same time justified he feels about the hate he has inside. He is clear about his participation in the play not changing anything in this life situation in itself. However, he also stresses how his participation in the project has brought sense into his life, giving him the ability to speak up about it to a broader public.

While the benefits of journey mapping in Sofie's case had to do with the map's ability to let her condense and stretch time and place in relation to the emotions connected to her participation, the benefits of journey mapping in case of Isaam's story are linked to the method's ability to let him give form to something that has lost all form (and sense). It becomes clear through his map and his unfolding of it that the openness and flexibility of the method – without its predefined form and structure – allows him to make a harsh critique of how youth lives are left to implode. By allowing the map to be without an overall structure, the method offers Isaam access to sharing how this lack of order and structure is experienced in his everyday life on the edge of society.

What do young people talk about when they talk about community?

The last example is from the study of young people participating in the formation of a community action group in a deprived Copenhagen neighbourhood. While the project itself talks about a 'community' in the singular, a comparative reading of several journey maps by young people

Figure 14.4: Examples of small, project-defined communities. Danish text says: 1. Courage, happiness, unity, common cause. 2. Meet new young people

participating in the project permits a more differentiated understanding of how they experience the very concept of 'community'. A reading across journey maps shows that the young people participating in the project experience not *one*, but *three* kinds of community, each of a very different quality, through their participation: a small, project-defined community; a larger, local community; and a big, societal community.

The young people describe the first kind of community (a small, project-defined community) as a cheerful and warm community, where they experience being *with* new people they meet through the activities they take part in (Figure 14.4). It is a community defined by unity, energy and the possibility of meeting other young people.

The second kind of community (a larger, local community) is illustrated by the young people as a community where they are in front of and lead a change process. It is a community that the young people define as one they make a change *for* (not *with*, as was the case in the first kind). Across different journey maps, the young people position themselves as leaders of a change process and as people who make a difference for their community through activities such as cultural events and public meetings (Figure 14.5).

Figure 14.5: Examples of larger, local communities. Danish text says: 1. Welcome to a ghetto, welfare support, Islam, immigrants, integration, crime. 2. Help other young people – make a difference

The third kind of community (a big, societal community) appears in the young people's journey maps as an audience, *in front* of which the young people stand. In the follow-up dialogues, they explain this part of their project participation as highly significant moments where they get to represent both their 'close community' and 'the local community' in front of a wider public. They describe these moments as possibilities to change how a surrounding society looks on them and their friends as well as the place they live (Figure 14.6).

The differences between the three kinds of community are revealed in the kind of prepositions used (visually illustrated or written out) across the maps. Prepositions as grammatical indications telling us about how relations between people (and things, places and time) are understood to express how people are located in relation to others as well as to movements and causes (for example, who is acting and who is acted upon). An analytical approach comparing several journey maps by young people in the same project – preferably in a group dialogue with young people themselves – can draw attention to the qualities of different participatory positionings of young people and how they are supported in activities within the same project. This shows how the method not only allows young people to identify the significant experiences in projects they often care highly about, but also provides them with the possibility to create strong visual insights that transgress and differentiate project discourses (in this case a rather simplistic logic about 'community' as a singular).

What kind of mapping is journey mapping and why does it matter?

In the three case examples described in the previous section, the 'map' is a highly flexible and even morphable format. This quality provides

Figure 14.6: Examples of big, societal communities

young people on the edge of society with a chance to overwrite and renegotiate not only their own preconceptions, but also the discourses of the projects they participate in as well as the policy making that often sets the defining horizons for these projects. In that sense, journey mapping can be said to do away with participation being directed towards specific outcomes as well as with narrow categorisations of what it means to be a young person on the edge of society.

The emphasis on an open-ended mapping of participatory processes challenges any associations to scalable maps such as the cartographic map with its longitudes, latitudes, altitudes and fixed scalability. Instead, journey maps can be understood as small overviews of lived life where events, actions and feelings can be both condensed and stretched in time, can reach far back in time and/or into other arenas of a life, and get reinterpreted in the light of current events and actions.

Albeit challenging to analyse – as in the case of Isaam's map – the method gains its strength from its ability to share how multiple temporal and spatial connections play in the lives and participatory patterns of young people on the edge of society. We suggest that we can understand its potential through French philosopher and anthropologist Latour, who argues that this built-in heterogeneity permits new insights while maintaining that it is an illusion to represent anything in a totality (not least something as complex as a youth life on the edge of society as in this case) and through a single gaze (Latour and Hermant, 2006). Introducing the concept of 'oligopticon' (combining the Greek word *oligo* meaning 'few' and the word *opticon* meaning 'overview'), Latour underlines how overviews are not necessarily defined by a unified, singular view, but also can be understood as multiple 'seeing *little* and seeing it *well*', thereby permitting us to take a new look at theoretical questions involving different materials, relations and scales (Latour, 2010).

Journey mapping, understood as a creation of multiple overviews, emphasises the importance of inviting young people to visit, reflect on, reconsider and reinterpret the many meanings of their project participation, and contributes to a production of 'the edge of society' as a heterogeneous place of being. The method thereby challenges policy-driving categories such as the influential NEET (Not in Education, Employment or Training) category that have a tendency to reduce the complexities of being at 'the edge of society' to a singular experience:

> Being outside education or without work may not be the most immediate or important challenge facing a young person, and it is necessary to unpick the NEET category in order to understand the needs of those with specific circumstances. (Simmons et al, 2014a, p 579)

In this quote, Simmons and colleagues suggest the NEET category (used in the UK) as a reductive pitfall, which contributes to veiling the challenges faced by young people on the edge of society. The risk is that projects dedicated to improving the lives of young people on the edge end up being evaluated by parameters that at best do not make any sense to the young people themselves and at worst foreground and ascribe value to activities that make no positive difference for them (Finlay et al, 2010; Simmons et al, 2014b).

In our use of journey mapping as exemplified in this chapter, we found that the method offered young people a way to explore some of the answers to the important questions and challenges they are facing 'on the edge'. It promoted a way to avoid a focus on a project's capacity to mould young people into the norms and values of a surrounding society – preventing young people from doing specific things (for example, committing a crime, or quitting school or a job) or make them do certain things (for example, do better in school, find a job). Instead, the method promotes what Australian art and education scholar Anna Hickey-Moody (2013) defines as aesthetic, and often multimodal, critical reflections that can amplify young people's understanding of what their life looks like and what makes a difference to them (as well as our knowledge of it as researchers or as practitioners and project owners):

> In line with critical theory we insist on an ongoing exploration of how we can understand and work with the arts in art education not as technologies for social control, but as methods that create new scapes and sensitivities, new ways of knowing and being. (Hickey-Moody, 2013, p 1)

In this extract, Hickey-Moody emphasises the necessity for theory to avoid supporting the creation of social interventions (in this case art) as 'technologies for social control'. Instead, she suggests that we evaluate and research projects that work with young people on the edge of society not based on how well the projects do in relation to the baselines of a policy discourse, but on how well they enable young people to articulate new understandings of their lives and create new belongings and communities based on their own premises.

Final remarks: four qualities of journey mapping

We finalise by summing up four main qualities of journey mapping.

First is the participatory aspect of the method, where the young people give form to their own interpretation of the processes they have been part of. This youth perspective on participation offers knowledge of the diverse and rich ways in which young people on the edge of society experience participation and how this participation may help to negotiate and redefine their positions on the edge of society. Just like Tisdall's approach in Chapter 11, journey mapping recognises young people as generators of knowledge in their own right.

Second, the method emphasises the significance of a space to reflect on participation (make a stop, think, go back, give form, think again, for example). Both the reflective and productive character of journey mapping creates a sense of ownership, where the young people get to set the agenda for the follow-up dialogue and define their interpretations – manifested in interventions by the interviewer when needed.

Third, journey mapping composes the object (the participation of the young person in a given project or process), creating heterogenous 'little overviews' that can be understood as oligopticons rather than as synthesised and universal. This underlines how meaning making is an aesthetically informed activity that has to do with producing or coding as well as interpreting or decoding (for example, Hayles, 2012; Nielsen and Cortsen, 2018).

Fourth, journey mapping is a method that can quite easily increase knowledge exchanges between professionals and young people on the edge of society about how they experience their participation. Thus the method challenges the understanding of what 'impact' means and who or what is affecting whom. That question is at the centre of Stewart-Hall's critique of most evaluations being based on unhelpful sets of assumptions about who is in need of transformation (Hall, 2015). Stewart-Hall draws on cultural researcher Francois Matarasso, who problematises 'impact' as a concept that indicates that something/someone puts its mark on something/someone else 'like a die impressing itself on a blank' (Matarasso, 2015, p 5). The concept of 'impact' implicitly maintains an acting agent and a passive receiver, thus predefining who it is in a given situation that needs to be improved or developed. However, in our studies, the young people's journey maps show that the events foregrounded by the young people as significant are the ones where they perceive themselves as agents with a high level of impact on the projects, both influencing what happens during their participation and also taking responsibility for it (Nielsen and Sørensen, 2018). Thus journey mapping as a creation of oligopticons introduced into young people's participatory processes is a welcome opportunity to uncover the nuances in how impact is to be understood in projects working with young people on the edge of society, not as a one-sided cause and effect, but as processes.

References

Adriansen, H.K. (2012) 'Timeline interviews: a tool for conducting life history research', *Qualitative Studies*, 3(1): 40–55.

Bagnoli, A. (2009) 'Beyond the standard interview: the use of graphic elicitation and arts-based methods', *Qualitative Research*, 9(5): 547–70.

Biesta, G. (2009) 'Good education in an age of measurement: on the need to reconnect with the question of purpose in education', *Educational Assessment, Evaluation and Accountability*, 21(1): 33–46.

Bramming, P., Hansen, B.G. and Olesen, K.G. (2009) 'SnapLog – en performativ forskningsteknologi, eller hvad grævlingelorten fortæller om lærertrivsel' [SnapLog – a performative research technology, or what the shit of a badger tells about a teacher's well-being], *Tidsskrift for Arbejdsliv*, 11(4): 24 –37.

Fielding, M. (2010) 'The radical potential of student voice: creating spaces for restless encounters', *The International Journal of Emotional Education*, 2(1): 61–73.

Finlay, I., Sheridan, M., McKay, J. and Nudzor, H. (2010) 'Young people on the margins: in need of more choices and more chances in twenty-first century Scotland', *British Educational Research Journal*, 36(5): 851–67.

Følstad, A. and Kvale, K. (2018) 'Customer journeys: a systematic literature review', *Journal of Service Theory and Practice*, 28(2): 196–227.

Hall, R. (2005) *The Value of Visual Exploration: Understanding Cultural Activities with Young People*, West Bromwich: The Public.

Hall, R. (2015) 'Evaluation for meaningful (ex)change', Paper presented at A Different Game: Young People Working with Art and Artists, 2015 Engage International Conference, Glasgow, 19–20 November.

Harsløf, I. and Malmberg-Heimonen, I. (2014) 'Tiltak mot marginalisering i livsfasen fra ung til voksen' [Preventing marginalization in the transition from youth to adulthood], in Hammer, T. and Hyggen, C. (eds) *Ung Voksen Utenfor: Mestring og Marginalisering på vei til Voksenliv*, Oslo: Gyldendal Akademisk.

Hayles, K. (2012) *How We Think*, Chicago, IL: University of Chicago Press.

Hermann, S. (2007) *Magt & Oplysning: Folkeskolen 1950-2006* [Power & Enlightenment: The Public School 1959–2006], Copenhagen: Forlaget Unge Pædagoger.

Hickey-Moody, A. (2013) *Youth, Arts and Education: Reassembling Subjectivity Through Affect*, Abingdon: Routledge.

Jackson, C. (2006) *Lads and Ladettes in School: Gender and a Fear of Failure*, Maidenhead: Open University Press/McGraw-Hill Education.

Katznelson, N., Jørgensen, H. D. and Sørensen, N.U. (2015) *Hvem er de Unge på Kanten af det Danske Samfund?* [Who are the Young People on the Edge of the Danish Society], Aalborg: Aalborg Universitetsforlag.

Latour, B. (2010) 'Steps toward the writing of a compositionist manifesto', *New Literary History*, 41: 471 –90.

Latour, B. and Hermant, E. (2006) *Paris: Invisible City*, Paris: La Découverte/Les Empêcheurs de Penser en Rond. Available from: www.bruno-latour.fr/sites/default/files/downloads/viii_paris-city-gb.pdf [Accessed 11 December 2019].

Matarasso, F. (2015) 'Music and social change: intentions and outcomes', Paper presented at the first International Symposium of the SIMM (Social Impact of Making Music) Research Centre of the Ghent University Association , Ghent, Belgium, 6 October. Available from: https://arestlessart.files.wordpress.com/2015/10/2015-music-and-social-change.pdf

Milne, E.-J., Mitchell, C. and de Lange, N. (2012) *Handbook of Participatory Video*, New York, NY/Plymouth: AltaMira Press.

Nielsen, A.M and Sørensen, N.U. (2017) *Når Kunst gør en Forskel: Unges Deltagelse i Kunst- og Kulturprojekter som Alternativ Arena for Social Indsats Indsats* [When Art Makes a Difference: Young People's Participation in Art and Cultural Projects as an Arena for Social Work], Aalborg: Aalborg Universitetsforlag.

Nielsen, A.W. and Cortsen, R.P. (2018) 'Artistic makings as a method of inquiry in higher education', in B. Lund and S. Arndt (eds) *The Creative University*, Rotterdam/Boston, MA: Sense Publishers, pp 31–49.

Nielsen, A.W. and Sørensen, N.U. (2018) 'Journey mapping som forskningsmetode' [Journey mapping as research method], in M. Pless and N.U. Sørensen (eds) *Ungeperspektiver som Metodisk Tilgang i Ungdomsforskningen*, Aalborg: Aalborg Universitetsforlag, pp 39–62.

Pauwels, L. (2015) 'Participatory' visual research revisited: a critical-constructive assessment of epistemological, methodological and social activist tenets', *Ethnography*, 16(1): 95–117.

Simmons, R., Russell, L. and Thompson, R. (2014a) 'Young people and labour market marginality: findings from a longitudinal ethnographic study', *Journal of Youth Studies*, 17(5): 577–91.

Simmons, R., Thompson, R. and Russell, L. (2014b) *Education Work and Social Change*, Basingstoke: Palgrave Macmillan.

Sletten, M. and Hyggen, C. (2013) *Ungdom, Frafall og Marginalisering Marginalisering* [Youth, School Fall Out and Marginalization], Oslo: Det Norske Forskningsråd.

Sørensen, N.U., Hutters, C., Katznelson, N. and Juul, T.M. (2013) *Unges Motivation og Læring: 12 Eksperter om Motivationskrisen i Uddannelsessystemet Uddannelsessystemet* [Youth Motivation and Learning: 12 Experts about the Crisis of Motivation in the Educational System], Copenhagen: Hans Reitzels Forlag.

Willis, P. (1977) *Learning to Labor: How Working Class Kids get Working Class Jobs*, New York, NY: Colombia University Press.

15

Playful walks: a methodological approach for analysing the embodied citizenship of young people in the countryside

Claire Levy

Working with visual and playful multimedia methods, this chapter focuses on what this approach can offer youth studies and qualitative research. The research, which took place in summer 2017 in a rural town in the UK, aimed to explore how young people in the countryside engage with their localities through the visual and the non-verbal. By understanding playfulness as subversion (Bakhtin, 1984; Sutton-Smith, 2009), the chapter foregrounds a way to access forms of participation outside institutional, state activity. The chapter seeks to subvert the over-focus of youth research on urban experience, producing a deeper narrative of youth citizenship in the countryside. Analysis shows how these methods reconfigure the power relationships between them and the researcher by offering greater scope for autonomy within the research process. The multimedia methodology also affords the opportunity to reveal its processes to readers without hiding their complex, messy and infinite nature. Instead, the methodology foregrounds the richness of that complexity (Glaser and Strauss, 1978).

Key findings

- Youth research has an over-focus on urban experience. Reassessing constructions of the rural and its relationship with the urban produces a fuller understandings of youth experience.
- Working with visual and playful multimedia methods is a way to produce new knowledge of embodied/non-verbal/visual experiences of young people.
- Academic writing produces compressed narratives of qualitative research that hide the complex, messy, rich and infinite nature of

qualitative studies. Multimedia outputs challenge this compression and offer the chance for the reader/viewer to take an active role.

Introduction

Through the presentation and analysis of a series of participatory workshops that took place in the summer of 2017 in a rural town in the UK, the chapter aims to discuss the contribution that visual and playful multimedia methods offer to youth studies and, more generally, to qualitative research. In particular, the chapter shows how these methods allow for a deeper understanding of young people's experience, providing them with means of expressions other than words. Second, the analysis shows how these methods increase the possibility for young participants to exercise their agency during the research process, restructuring the relationships of power between them and the researcher. Finally, the chapter considers how multimedia methods can help qualitative researchers make their studies accessible to readers without hiding the complex, messy and infinite nature of qualitative research but, on the contrary, recognising in these characters the sources of its richness and of its meaningfulness (Glaser and Strauss, 1978).

The multimedia methods considered in this chapter include map making, walking, photography, writing and film making. These have been used as methods of research within a project focusing on young people in the countryside. The research was conducted in the rural market town of Green Mills,[1] during the summer of 2017. Green Mills is a small, post-industrial town with a population of 112,000 people (2011 Census). With 20% of the population aged 17 years and under, the demographic is in line with UK norms.

Through the use of multimedia methods in this specific focus of research, this analysis challenges the over-focus on urban youth that characterises youth studies by engaging with the way in which rural and urban research separate youth experience. The terms 'rural' and 'urban' are containers of meaning, construed through research and policy. Nostalgic conceptions of the rural as healthy and bucolic are practised and strengthened in how it has been described in sociological writing (Williams, 1973; Ward, 1988). Some theorists turn to the urban environment as a reason for our ills (Velarde et al, 2007; Grinde and Patil, 2009) and to the natural world for the solution (Rye, 2006; Louv, 2010). Accordingly, these concepts are often articulated through the ways in which government spending favours urban locations with higher populations, whereas in the countryside, statistics of social deprivation can be hidden by the distribution of wealth through rural regions (Secombe and Selby, 2017). Tom, a local youth worker, described the key issues for young people in the rural district (which covers an area of 460 km^2) as themes such as transport, planning, housing, anti-social behaviour, drug networks and child sexual exploitation, commonly identified in urban research and policy. These themes have also emerged during the research in Green Mills.

In approaching the study of youth, participation and inequality, this chapter seeks to avoid the often fragmented perceptions of youth reflected in institutional discourses on young people. These, as defined by policy documents, become fragmentary 'problems' such as 'academic achievement, obesity, tooth decay, screening for chlamydia, under 18 contraception use' (Gloucestershire Council, 2018). To combat this dislocating definition of young people, this chapter's analysis of youth is inspired by 'assemblage thinking', the layered, shifting collected self (Thrift, 2007). This thereby acknowledges how the local and the global work within the lives of young people.

The next section introduces the possibility for playfulness offered by the application of multimedia methods in research and how this relates to the analysis of citizenship. This is followed by an in-depth presentation of how multimedia methods have been applied in the study of rural youth in Green Mills. Findings point to how these methods have contributed in producing a more complete understanding and a deeper narrative of youth citizenship in the countryside.

Being playful in research

Through the exploration of a specific set of multimedia methods applied in this research, the chapter explores how we can understand forms of citizenship, other than the traditional forms of civic and political participation. Working with everyday activities such as walking and using phone cameras, the methodology utilises a pragmatic approach to civic participation in the rural through the everyday uses of public space (Bourdieu, 1990), shown through the playful interactions of young people in and with their locales. These 'micro-engagements' (Horton and Kraftl, 2009) are central to the shift in perception of what participation amounts to: through them, it is possible to show how citizenship emerges from the conscious and unconscious bodily practices of young people in the production of the landscape (de Certeau et al, 1998). Drawing on Horton (2010), this analysis aims to uncover the way in which place matters to young people, explored through their participatory place-based practices.

The research approach is invigorated by conceptions of 'play' as a form of possibility – a means to subvert and disrupt what is there and to adapt the world to one's own purposes (Bakhtin, 1984; Sutton-Smith, 2009). Introducing playfulness in research offers a way of creating an agile and responsive approach to research with young people. Playfulness is portrayed in these instances as ways to engage with research and research participants that are unconventional and creative. As the analysis shows, multimedia methods open up the possibility for playfulness within research – this kind of playfulness emphasises the care-free and creative aspects of play (Fink, 2016), rather than rule-bound playing of games or institutionalised play (Valentine and McKendrick, 1997). Play is central to the concept of 'embodied citizenship', which foregrounds the visual, non-verbal and embodied ways young people engage with where they live through multimedia practices. Children's appropriation and subversion of place (a form of playfulness) has long been recorded in sociological youth research (Opie and Opie, 1969; Jones, 2008) as a way to share their 'worlds', without having adult 'tidiness' imposed on them. To be playful in research offers openness to its outcomes and also reflects how young people are in the world.

By using multimedia methods, it is also possible to challenge the artificially finite nature of the research process (Travlou et al, 2008). A research project on the everyday must have a finite nature in order to be written up, even though life and the everyday continue beyond it. By acknowledging this, and exploring the use of interactive digital methods, it is possible to expand how we can understand the research encounter.

How can the research methodology open up these definitions and reconfigure how citizenship and civic participation are understood? Is it about allowing in the 'mess' to open up the dialogue? The example of a walk with the young people involved in the project helps to illustrate the richness of the research encounter and reflect on how much this gets lost in writing.

In vision:	Feet shots along canal – narrower path.
Harry:	'Look there's a dead fish.'
Hayley:	'Where?'
Harry:	'There's a lot of dead fish …'

In vision:	Walking behind Lucy (leg bleeding).
Claire [researcher]:	'Are you OK?'
Lucy:	'It doesn't matter.' [Raises hands in the air, seen from behind.]
In vision:	Empty shot of canal walking.
Lucy:	'This bit. Youths hang out, they sit on top of there and they hang out there.'
Hayley:	'I really hate this bridge so much'.'
Lucy:	'They go on there … I've seen them when we were running.'
Claire:	'Hayley, why is it scary?'
Hayley:	'I don't know. I just don't like it very much.'
Lucy:	'It's quite dodgy.'
Hayley:	'Yeah – if you're by yourself and you're in the rain, it's not very nice.'[2]

This fieldnote encapsulates much of the messiness of the research encounter: the meandering conversations while walking, the non-verbal communication, the jokes. This type of playful engagement can get lost in the structural requirements of academic writing. There is a

Figure 15.1: Walking along the canal, August 2017

Source: Maren Hahnfeld.

richness that is muted through the inevitable compression required to communicate the research to others. To counter this, experimenting with a range of methods, including photography and map making, helps to explore and undermine the narrowed focus.

Multimedia methods: a research approach

The research project on which this chapter is based involved eight young people (three male and five female). In 2017, they were aged between 13 and 18 years and lived in the town of Green Mills and the surrounding area. They were all members of the Green Mills District Youth Council. They went to different schools across the district and came from varying socioeconomic backgrounds.

The fieldwork described here comprises a series of participatory and playful workshops, designed to experiment with varied multimedia, visual methods. The goal was to create a participatory research project based on local places the participants care about, looking at how they make those places their own by way of multimedia practices. Their goal was to explore a place of their choosing and to produce a digital artefact that communicated their feelings about place. The chapter covers the structure of the workshop sessions and examines how the methodological framework engages with the conceptions of play as a means to disrupt the adult world. The illustrations from the field show how the research methodology has generated knowledge about youth experience and indeed where it has failed. The digital and analogue workshop methods used by the young people are also explored to further illustrate how including the complexity of the research encounter is integral to the understanding of how civic participation through those 'micro-engagements' is located in space and place.

Attending to the ethical aspects of research relationships was important: participants and their parents/carers gave written permission for the young people to take part in the research and the filming, and for their work created through the project to be shared. Consent is regarded as an ongoing process and it has been important to retain contact with the participants to let them know about progress of the project and to give them a chance to voice any concerns as the written and digital outputs develop (see Table 15.1).

In order for the project to engage and 'make sense' to the participants, it was designed using multimedia methods with goals within the allotted timeline, as shown in Table 15.1.

Table 15.1: Table of activity

Session	Activity
Pitch meeting	Pitch to group from Green Mills District Youth Council – session to explain the project and what it would involve if they took part
Session 1	Facilitated by Maren Hahnfeld (film maker/lecturer) Love and Hate game Research skills presentation and discussion Guided walk around Stroud (led by young people [YP]) with GoPro cameras for young people and Claire Levy filming Review of footage Collaborative map making Interviews Homework – YP to walk and research places that are important to them (begun in Love and Hate game)
Session 2	Facilitated by Mike Loveday (creative writing tutor) YP present their research/images/footage Writing examples and discussion Writing of reports based on research Interviews
Session 3	Facilitated by Claire Levy Finalising reports and reading each other's writing Adding to the map Recording the reports Interviews
Follow-up interview	Tom (Green Mills District Council youth worker)
Follow-up meeting	To share and discuss with the participants the progress of the production of the interactive documentary (iDoc) and written outputs and conference presentations

Table of activity

During the first session, using creative storytelling methods, such as the 'storycircle', the approach was designed to build trust through word games, visual stimuli and storytelling (Dunford and Jenkins, 2015). Participants were asked to focus on places they love and that they hate as the basis for a discussion (see session 1 in Table 15.1). Sampling different types of research methods, the aim of the project was to explore an important place for the participants and to produce a digital report using audio and visual media. The format for the final output was modelled on the BBC Radio 4 programme 'From Our Own Correspondent' with the aim of highlighting the local, and the participants as experts on their own locales. They were asked to plan and lead a walk around Green Mills that might incorporate some of these places.

Figure 15.2: Visual methods

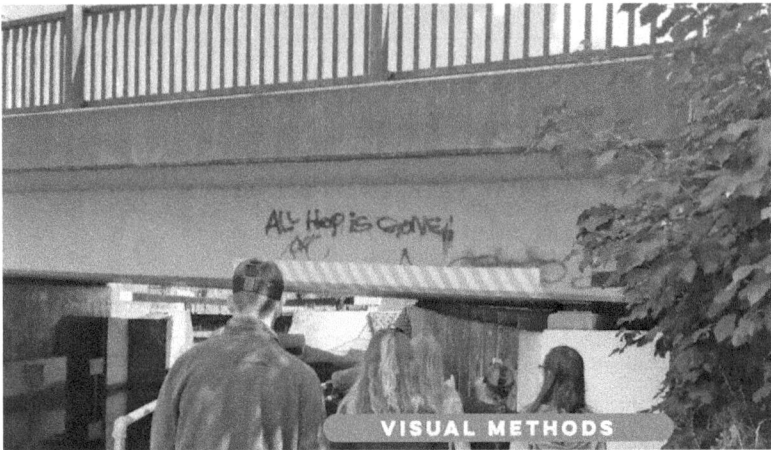

The walk was filmed by the researcher, as well as being captured by GoPro cameras worn or carried by the participants, so they could take video or images as and when they chose to. After this, we reviewed some of the footage and began creating a collaborative map, thinking about those places and others that were important. At the end of session 1, the participants were asked to choose and visit a place that could form the basis of their report, and to take photos and video exploring that place. They presented their research and discussed it in a group setting in session 2. The participants then worked with a writer to brainstorm ideas and start writing the report. Homework after session 2 was to finish writing the reports, so that in session 3 they could record them using a digital audio recorder. The participants learned how to use the audio recorder and helped to record each other's stories.

This type of approach followed a logic in terms of seeing how the methods might work towards a goal, but were designed to be flexible and to offer options to the participants, who might favour filming over writing, for instance. The material produced through the sessions is included in an iDoc, designed to allow the viewer to explore the material and the stories created in the sessions without a set, linear trajectory. Screenshots of the pilot iDoc follow.[3]

The fragmentary nature of the iDoc aligns with how the methodology is designed to engage with the everyday and to open up the ways we narrativise our lives, and indeed how we engage with the research. In its early guise as 'interactive hypermedia ethnography' (Pink, 2006, p 214), the iDoc offered an opportunity to deconstruct the research process, by including annotations and in-process material. This was

Figure 15.3: Walking

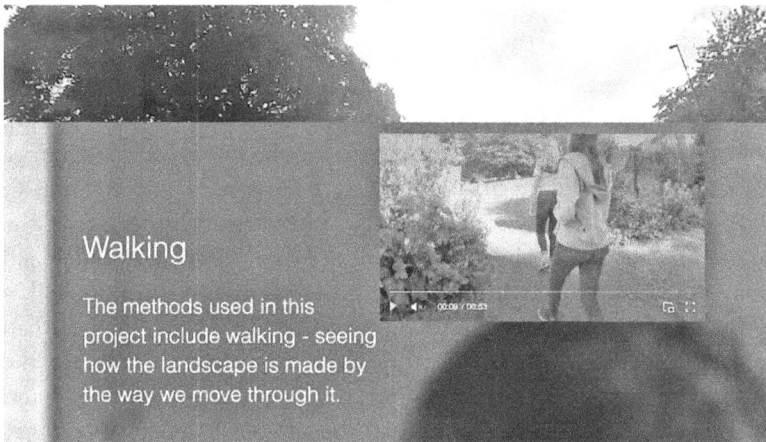

a form of resistance to the inevitable editing of text research outputs or linear film narratives. The fragmented, non-linear structure, which includes visual and auditory material, and its adherence to the ideals of co-production, also offers a continuation of the methodology in its presentation to audiences. The problematic nature of reflecting the true experiences found through research lies partly in the neatly packaged outputs required to report on those interactions. The 'filtering out' of anything problematic (Back, 2007, p 155) is not only at odds with research narratives of participation in the everyday, but also highlights the way that research gets condensed and edited in its written form. The 'messiness' of the research encounter often gets left out in the way it is subsequently conveyed (Law et al, 2011). The iDoc deconstructs the traditional documentary form and offers different ways to examine and interact with the material. In this instance, there is a diffusion here too of the researcher/producer's role. While it is inevitable that some selection and editing must take place to render the material accessible to its audiences, there is a freedom in how the viewer might choose and view parts or all of the material presented in this format. The 'live' nature of the iDoc format means it can be updated by viewers beyond the confines of the project. This is an articulation of the fragmentary nature of experience and the interactive nature of the iDoc expands how the research engages with the everyday, while working against the compression of written research.

Practice-led funded community projects are often construed as a means to access or encourage other forms of citizenship through creative work. Much of this approach stems from 'measures of impact' and 'value for money', implicit in the commissioning of this type of work (UK Research and Innovation, n.d.; Matarasso, 1997). The call by Alison Rooke (2013) for an open-ended sort of practice that starts with the community resonates. Hart's (1997) critique of the 'staging of participation' links place and evaluation frameworks when thinking about participatory work. To work with young people and encourage an articulation of place in their own terms means allowing things to happen, without predetermining the outcomes: 'letting go' of the process and acknowledging the value of 'mess'. Creating choice and opportunities to play within and with the research process, as well as with the output, has been part of the method's design. Rather than expecting certain outcomes, it has been important to embrace the unknown in a project that encourages autonomy of thought and practice. It has also been central to the project to encourage other ways to articulate experience aside from interviews, which have proved unwieldy or too formal to produce truly dialogic learning, which decentres the position of the researcher and opens up the research encounter as a reciprocal process.

The methodology sustains an open approach towards what can be considered a research outcome and how engagement can be understood, acknowledging that the 'inventiveness of methods for artists and ethnographers who operate not just as ways of knowing the social but also for engaging it' (Jungnickel and Hjorth, 2014, p 139). It is 'messy' in order to create openings for productive dialogue. Although the methods do not uncover a truth that is already there, they offer the chance to create understanding of people and place through a process of exchange. It is a 'becoming' of research, whereby the productive relations between researcher and researched 'change each other' (Coleman, 2008: 118). In this sense, the methodology can and will produce unexpected outcomes or indeed be disrupted by the participants. This is a rich aspect of the research process, which also aims to create a fluidity around the relationship between researcher and participant.

Multimedia methods as playful ways to disrupt power

Walking with the group around Green Mills and deflecting the focus from my own research agenda was possible by using a 'mobile focus group' approach (Clark, 2017). While working in this way, at the canal, which slices through the town from east to west, Lucy started to recount a memory of how she had previously been running down this stretch with her mum. By way of demonstration, she set off at pace

Figure 15.4: Lucy running, August 2017

down the towpath ahead of us, with little introduction to her actions. She found this action difficult to articulate later during an interview. The transcription of the exchange that follows highlights the difficulty Lucy had in expressing her reasons for running:

Claire: 'Tell me about the walk on the canal.'
Lucy: 'What do you mean? It's just a canal.'
Claire: 'What do you remember from your walk?'
Lucy: 'I have no comment. What do you mean?
Claire: 'What did you remember on the walk?'
Lucy: 'I just remembered stuff. What?'
Claire: 'Two things. Running with Mum and people under the bridge.'
Lucy: 'I remember lots of things. They are just topics. Not special.'
Claire: 'I'm interested in them. When you are in a space, you remember things.'
Lucy: 'Just telling friends about it. When you walk you have to say something. It's just making conversation …'

The interview process was not productive and aligns with Jackson's (2015) account of interviews with an individual participant sequestered away from others, causing difficulties and suspicion. In this case, I can only conjecture that Lucy was embarrassed about her spontaneous running. The footage includes sounds of the group laughing as she ran off, as though surprised by her response. Our exchange was painful because instead of being able to answer my questions, Lucy seemed bewildered by them and perhaps she felt 'put on the spot'. The design of the methods process is meant to have a logic and during this exchange it was clear it had failed. Instead of opening up the research dialogue, it had closed it down. Exploring a moment of performativity like this as an embodied experience that was seen and recorded offers ways to understand experience beyond the verbal. Methods of visual analysis are as important as the verbal expression. The failure of the methods at this point must acknowledge that sociological methods are neither neutral nor innocent (Law and Urry, 2011), but position participants in certain ways. Engaging with the performativity of the methodology suggests how the non-verbal is practised through this use of digital technology, and how these methods access the embodied ways young people participate in their locales.

The potential for the playful disordering of the research encounter was also evident during another moment of the interview. While the camera was running unattended, Lucy stuck out her tongue. I reflected on whether she was sticking out her tongue at me, or was it more connected to the opportunity to play with the device? What this playfulness indicates is how the research encounter is construed on the researcher's terms, rather than the participant's. Instead, the methodology provokes more (playful) action. This action uncovers how the seemingly 'flat' ontology of participatory projects masks the real power dynamic of the research encounter. Claims of a de-hierarchy of knowledge are undermined often by prescribed outcomes and fixed goals (Matarasso, 1997; Yúdice, 2004; Rooke, 2013; see also Chapter 14 in this volume). Acknowledging this can allow for moments of opening. Indeed, narratives of the non-verbal are shown through the analysis of this research to be a vital aspect of how playful research can bring forth different forms of understanding. These visual performative responses underline not only where the dialogue can be opened up, but also where dialogue is closed down. Exploring the everyday and how embodied citizenship can be figured means accepting that moments of opening and play can come when the researcher is not present. The researcher's absence might be as productive to the research findings, if not more so, in allowing the participants to explore ideas or methodologies on their own.

My findings suggest that using digital equipment such as phones that are not 'owned' by the researcher is one way to disrupt the power dynamic between the researcher and the participant, even within an institutional setting. By utilising their own mobile technologies in the co-production of knowledge, the participants have more ownership over the process and the methods are more closely aligned with everyday digital practices. Introducing the camera and exploring the non-verbal is a way to be alive to the other ways we communicate and to acknowledge the difficulties of the participant interview.

Keeping things complicated

> The places are what remain, are what you can possess, are what is immortal. They become the tangible landscape of memory, the places that made you, and in one way you too become them. (Solnit, 2006, p 117)

The complexities of everyday life and the fragmentary experiences we have of place were integral to the design of the methodology of the research for this chapter. Acknowledging the overlapping social spaces and the ways place and memory are connected was instrumental in the methodology's formulation. Through the process of walking, talking and map making, it was important to explore a translation of embodied experiences in the social places we construct, utilising the visual to help express 'what is going on'. The everyday was further figured through a post-walk map-making session (in session 1) reflecting on places that were important to the participants; this was added to periodically over the following sessions. It became a living document of the time we spent together, connecting us to the landscape from inside the council offices.

Reading of maps potentially involves much more than simply locating things in space; it is also about moving through the landscape (Travlou et al, 2008).

Figure 15.5: Map making, August 2017

This act of co-creation was a way to draw out ideas of the landscape within the group setting. Participants directed the process themselves, using drawing and collage. Conversation flowed through the process and the group worked together to help each other to plan and structure the map, according to their own criteria. Downs and Stea (1977) have pointed out that things get left out in this decision-making process of map creation and this reflects the fragmentary way we see place. The process also showed how, as Solnit (2006) describes, memory shapes those narratives, as the map included places the young people treasured or disliked from their younger childhoods. This process is about 'keeping things complicated', working against the simplification that the staging of participation can impose on young people. Instead, this approach allows for 'mess' in order to understand how we narrativise our lives. In this sense, Law's (2004) accounts of mess and the 'fixing' of writing apply not only to the way research is reported, but also to the research methodology itself and how our lives are recounted. It is a process that is 'interactive, remade, definite and multiple' (Law, 2004, p 122).

For Lucy, where she had found the interview process bewildering, the walk and map-making facilitated the exploration of several places. One place, 'Druggy Park', became central to her in the final stage of the process and she wrote about it for the audio report. As we walked through Green Mills, Lucy adopted a 'tour guide' style of narration, announcing to the cameras accompanying her that "the youths up here, they are dodgy", as we passed into the park. There was a working out, a fixing, that continued through the map production as she explained one of her contributions to the map:

Lucy: 'Finally we've got the park. The park is a very nice place, of course it has … some associations of being a bad place where thuggy youths hang out. [All giggle.] But it's just a place like if you're going to come to Green Mills, you've got to know Druggy Park.'
CL: 'Which is Druggy Park?'
Lucy: 'What do you mean?'
CL: 'Where is it?'
Lucy: 'Druggy Park, it's like …'
Hayley: Where is it on the map?
Claire: 'No. I mean where is it – what's it really called?'
Lucy: 'What is it really called? Is it Welcome Park?'
Rosie: 'No Lucy.'
            [Off camera – Green Gardens.][4]

Lucy: Green Gardens. Green Gardens. It's like, it could be nice, but it just isn't. People just go there. It's a good place, they go at night and they just do bad stuff. And I mean it could be a good place for Green Mills instead, it's not like surveillance or anything. So you can do what you like.'

Claire: 'That's a concern for you?'

Lucy: 'I'm not really sure. It's just Green Gardens.'

Amber: 'You get that everywhere though.'

Lucy: 'Yes it's everywhere, it's just got itself a bad name.'

Greg: 'It's got its associations.'

Amber: 'Every town has got a park where it has bad stuff to it.'

Lucy: 'Yeah.'

The working out of place through naming and description is processed via the walking, map making and discussion, both on-site and back at the council offices. This interactive fixing and remaking is channelled through the methodology, which encourages a working-out of ideas. While the research encounter is inevitably compressed through the writing, the process can still be shown and acknowledged. Detailing those stages is an opportunity to open up to the ways young people discern the world they live in. Using this kind of methodology enables choice and space for dialogue where the researcher–participant interaction is broadened and becomes a means for working things out. Revealing those processes produces a richness and contributes to how we can understand the ways the rural is processual and constructed.

The co-creation of the map is relational: it connects the participants and the researcher through the embodied experiences of place, which are processed and dissected through the making and the discussion. The video footage of the map-making process is punctuated by gossip, messages on phones, jokes. Part of the working-out of ideas is enabled through the relaxed, unfixed way the group produces the atmosphere in the room. Letting things happen and facilitating a space that is not 'controlled' in the manner of a traditional classroom contributes to how the 'illusion' of participation is reduced.

Conclusion

This chapter describes a methodological approach designed to engage young people and to capture how they interact with where they live. By using everyday practices of walking and phone photography, the method engages with the embodied experiences of young people in the countryside. Including and encouraging playfulness in the research encounter has also been integral to drawing out their experiences and being open to the learning shared through it. Attending to those playful practices is a way to incorporate the voices of young people to best represent that which is not fully 'knowable' (Wall, 2013). From its very beginning, sociology has critically reflected on the extent to which researchers can fully grasp the experiences of others. While not entirely solving this issue, such multimedia methodology can be instrumental in that understanding in as much as it can help to uncover young people's layered and interconnecting experience of place and possibility.

Using the landscape – in this case, the rural town of Green Mills – as a starting point and exploring it with a group of young people, the research offered the chance for a dialogical experiment (Freire, 1996). This is seen through the ways in which the participants produce knowledge in different forms, through the varied methodological tools the project employs. The power relations between researcher and participants are disrupted through the open-ended methodology. Approaching these encounters within a framework that respects and encourages adaptation, letting go and mess draws on my work as a practitioner/researcher. The opening-up of dialogue has been a key focus: looking at ways the research encounter can provoke this and also prevent it. Examining the ways in which the research encounter 'doesn't work' or is usurped by the participants has provided a rich seam of knowledge.

The project, carried out over individual sessions, was designed to build towards audio-visual outputs and create a trajectory for the participants. This sense of progression was important to help engage the participant group. The research encounter formed in this way allows a building of knowledge over time. It also offers the chance to accommodate and reference the complexity of the everyday, while acknowledging the inevitable compression of the written account. What the multimedia methodology offers is a window on to the continuing and mixed-up 'liveness' of the everyday, balanced against the need to deliver a completed written work. As part of that methodological argument, the final output is presented as an iDoc, which by its nature assembles myriad audio-visual materials into an open-ended organism. Efforts to incorporate this working-out within the inevitable compression of the research output go some way towards inviting new ways to understand participation through spontaneous, bodily practices on a multidimensional and microcosmic scale.

It is through multimedia participatory research processes that the key themes of youth, participation and inequality are explored. This is illustrated through the ways drug use is treated by the participants, and in particular Lucy, within the everyday of their own locale. This embodied form of citizenship is shown through 'micro-engagements' during the walk along the canal and then explored through the map making and discussions. What this methodology offers is a way to explore the (partial) world of these young people living in the countryside and how the digital incises that world. The methodology enables us to understand citizenship as a lived and morphable practice, embodied in the social spaces of young people that are explored and expressed through playful encounters. Such encounters were seen in the walks and discussions with Lucy; beside the canal; through the park; and around the map-making table.

Notes

[1] The name of the research site has been anonymised.
[2] The names of the participants have been changed.
[3] The iDoc is not yet available to view publicly.
[4] The name of the park has been changed.

References

Back, L. (2007) *The Art of Listening*, Oxford: Berg.

Bakhtin, M., (1984) *Rabelais and his World*, Bloomington, IN: Indiana University Press.

Bourdieu, P. (1990) *The Logic of Practice*, Palo Alto, CA: Stanford University Press.

Clark, A.J. (2017) 'Walking together: understanding young people's experiences of living in neighbourhoods in transition', in C. Bates and A. Rhys-Taylor (eds) *Walking through Social Research*, Abingdon: Routledge, pp 86–103.

Coleman, R. (2008) 'A method of intuition: becoming, relationality, ethics', *History of the Human Sciences*, 21(4): 104–23, https://doi.org/10.1177/0952695108095514

de Certeau, M., Mayol, P. and Tomasik, T.J. (1998) *Practice of Everyday Life. Volume 2: Living and Cooking*, Minneapolis, MN: University of Minnesota Press.

Downs, R.M. and Stea, D. (1977) *Maps in Minds: Reflections on Cognitive Mapping*, New York, NY: Harper & Row.

Dunford, M. and Jenkins, T. (2015) 'Understanding the media literacy of digital storytelling', *Media Education Research Journal*, 5(2): 26–42.

Fink, E. (2016) *Play as a Symbol of the World*, Bloomington, IN: Indiana University Press.

Freire, P. (1996) *Pedagogy of the Oppressed* (2nd edn), London and New York, NY: Penguin.

Glaser, A.L. and Strauss, B. (1978) *The Discovery of Grounded Theory: Strategies for Qualitative Research*, London: Weidenfeld & Nicholson.

Gloucestershire Council (2018) *Children and Young People and Families Needs Analysis Executive Summary*, Gloucester.

Grinde, B. and Patil, G.G. (2009) 'Biophilia: does visual contact and nature impact on health and well-being?', *International Journal of Environmental Research and Public Health*, 6(9): 2332–43.

Hart, R.A. (1997) *Children's Participation: The Theory and Practice of Involving Young Citizens in Community Development and Environmental Care*, Abingdon: Routledge.

Horton, J. (2010) '"The best thing ever": how children's popular culture matters', *Social & Cultural Geography*, 11(4): 377–98, https://doi.org/10.1080/14649361003774563

Horton, J. and Kraftl, P. (2009) 'Small acts, kind words and "not too much fuss": implicit activisms', *Emotion, Space & Society*, 2(1): 14–23.

Jackson, B.E. (2015) *Young Homeless People and Urban Space*, Abingdon: Routledge.

Jones, O. (2008) '"True geography [ ] quickly forgotten, giving away to an adult-imagined universe". Approaching the otherness of childhood', *Children's Geographies*, 6(2): 195–212.

Jungnickel, K. and Hjorth, L. (2014) 'Methodological entanglements in the field: methods, transitions and transmissions', *Visual Studies*, 29(2): 136–45.

Law, J. (2004) *After Method: Mess in Social Science Research*, London: Routledge.

Law, J. and Urry, J. (2011) 'Enacting the social', *Economy and Society*, 33(3): 390–410, https://doi.org/10.1080/0308514042000225716

Law, J., Savage, M. and Ruppert, E. (2011) *The Double Social Life of Methods*, CRESC Working Paper No. 95, Milton Keynes and Manchester: Centre for Research on Socio-Cultural Change, Open University and University of Manchester.

Louv, R. (2010) *Last Child in the Woods: Saving Our Children from Nature-Deficit Disorder*, London: Atlantic Books.

Matarasso, F. (1997) *Use or Ornament? The Social Impact of Participation in the Arts*, Stroud: Comedia.

Opie, I. and Opie, P. (1969) *Children's Games in Street and Playground*, Oxford: Clarendon Press.

Pink, S. (2006) *Doing Visual Ethnography: Images, Media and Representation in Research* (2nd edn), London and Thousand Oaks, CA: Sage Publications.

Rooke, A. (2013) *Curating Community? The Relational and Agonistic Value of Participatory Arts in Superdiverse Localities*, Swindon: Arts and Humanities Research Council.

Rye, J.F. (2006) 'Rural youths' images of the rural', *Journal of Rural Studies*, 22(4): 409–42.

Secombe, I. and Selby, D. (2017) *Health and Wellbeing in Rural Areas*, London: Local Government Association.

Solnit, R. (2006) *A Field Guide to Getting Lost*, Edinburgh: Canongate.

Sutton-Smith, B. (2009) *The Ambiguity of Play*, Cambridge, MA and London: Harvard University Press.

Thrift, N. (2007) *Non-Representational Theory: Space, Politics, Affect*, Abingdon and New York, NY: Routledge.

Travlou, P., Owens, P.E., Thompson, C.W. and Maxwell, L. (2008) 'Place mapping with teenagers: locating their territories and documenting their experience of the public realm', *Children's Geographies*, 6(3): 309–26.

Valentine, G. and McKendrick, J. (1997) 'Children's outdoor play: exploring parental concerns about children's safety and the changing nature of childhood', *Geoforum*, 28(2): 219–35.

Verlarde, M.D., Fry, G. and Tveit, M. (2007) 'Health effects of viewing landscapes – landscape types in environmental psychology.' *Urban Forestry and Urban Greening*, 6(4): 199–212.

Wall, J. (2013) 'Childism: the challenge of childhood to ethics and the humanities', in A.M. Duane (ed) *The Children's Table: Childhood Studies and the New Humanities*, Athens, GA: University of Georgia Press, pp 68–84.

Ward, C. (1988) *The Child in the Country*, Bury St Edmonds: St Edmondsbury Press.

Williams, R. (1973) *The Country and the City*, New York, NY: Oxford University Press.

UK Research and Innovation (n.d.) 'Pathways to impact', UK Research and Innovation, [online]. Available from: https://webarchive. nationalarchives.gov.uk/20200203113953/https://www.ukri.org/ innovation/excellence-with-impact/pathways-to-impact/ [Accessed 7 March 2018].

Yúdice, G. (2004) *The Expediency of Culture: Uses of Culture in the Global Era*, Durham, NC: Duke University Press.

16

Transformative participation in the lifeworlds of marginalised youth: learning for change

Mette Bladt and Barry Percy-Smith

This chapter contributes to discourses of youth participation by developing understanding about which forms of participation might make a difference for marginalised young people living in the context of structural inequality. The chapter critically reflects on some of the complexities and limitations currently at play in relation to enhancing the participation of marginalised young people and sets out key elements of a more critical epistemological framework. Drawing on youth participatory action research (YPAR) and critical utopian action research (CUAR), the chapter makes the case for a transformational learning approach to participation that involves learning and change at both an individual level and professional level in interventions with marginalised young people. The chapter is supported by case-study empirical material focusing on one project developed in collaboration with young people engaged in criminal and violent activities in Denmark. This case study provides an opportunity to reflect on the challenges and possibilities of using 'alternative', transformative, action-based interpretations of youth participation and empowerment involving social learning rooted in professional encounters with young people's lifeworlds.

Key findings

- Conventional, formalised approaches and interpretations of youth participation are falling short in terms of efficacy and accountability of policy and professional-led responses to youth marginalisation and inequality.
- Participatory action research offers an alternative possibility for transformative work rooted in the everyday lived realities of marginalised young people rather than professional agendas based on normative assumptions of youth.

- Reconstructing interventions using YPAR and CUAR reframes professional relationships with young people in ways that redress power imbalances and engender co-inquiry and mutual reciprocity in relationships of respect.

Participation of marginalised youth: contesting orthodoxies and assumptions

Austerity across Europe in the past decade has exacerbated the plight of large sections of the youth population already experiencing marginalisation and exclusion at the edge of society (Blackman and Rogers, 2017; Davies, 2019). In Europe, the current numbers of young people in the Not in Employment, Education or Training (NEET) category range from 7% to 24%.[1] At the same time, in the context of post-austerity, inequality has given rise to higher levels of crime, homelessness, poverty and mental health problems for young people in Europe (Horton, 2016) and decreasing levels of participation in education and the labour market (Andersen et al, 2017). As a consequence, at the European level there have been mounting concerns about how to enhance social, economic and political participation of young people reflected in, for example, European Commission funding priorities[2] research on youth representation and participation in democratic life (Cammaerts et al, 2013), and the forthcoming European Union Youth Strategy (2019–27); with an explicit commitment to adopt inclusive approaches towards youth participation. At the same time, the likelihood of the necessary policy commitment and reinvestment in social infrastructure to address fundamental inequalities appears somewhat distant, raising questions not only about political accountability, but also about what forms of participation (in decision-making and change processes) are meaningful and effective in response to youth marginalisation.

It is important to highlight the coexistence of two separate, but interrelated, interpretations of youth participation. The first considers the influence of young people in decision-making and change processes (Thomas, 2007). This is commonly taken to involve young people having a voice or being consulted about their views, needs and experiences to inform decisions made by professionals. However, increasing concerns about the limitations of voice in bringing about some kind of impact or change has given rise to an appreciation of the value of deeper processes of interactive engagement and joint learning that occur with co-production (Tisdall, 2013) involving dialogue and co-inquiry (Percy-Smith et al, 2019). More recently, the youth participation field has witnessed developments in understanding the significance of youth-led initiatives and manifestations of young people's own agency and activism as actors of change in the context of their own everyday lives (Kalio and Hakli, 2013; Caraballo et al, 2017). However, while these forms of participation are appropriate for responding to public issues, they are arguably less conducive to responding to issues concerning young people's own personal experiential lifeworlds. What is significant, however, is the shift towards a recognition of the agency and role of young people as actors of change.

The second keyway participation is understood in terms of young people's actual engagement in everyday social processes such as benefitting from education, securing employment, access to housing and other social goods, and contributing to public life (Walther et al, 2020). This explicitly concerns social status and inclusion, and the extent to which young people as citizens have access to social and economic opportunities (Ekman and Amnå, 2012). For young people on the margins with limited social capital struggling for participation as equal citizens, conventional forms of participation in decision making through consultation or youth councils are unlikely to have an impact in terms of bringing about changes to the life chances of marginalised young people and enhancing their opportunities to participate as equal citizens. Indeed, a recurring criticism of approaches to youth participation is the reliance on formalised structures and practices according to adult professional and policy agendas for responding to young people's lived realities (Percy-Smith, 2010).

There are two issues here. First is the assumption that policy will address the issues confronting marginalised youth. Even when young people do have an opportunity to speak out, policy frequently falls short of addressing the fundamental inequalities and injustices that marginalised young people face in their daily realities, as a result of a lack of political will and professionals failing to really listen and respond to what is going on in young people's lives (Percy-Smith, 2010; Tisdall, 2013; Bladt, 2013). Indeed, research shows that young people on the margins increasingly face difficulties with participating in formal political activities (Day et al, 2019; Hall and Pottinger, 2019), with Day and colleagues' study highlighting the extent to which young people have lost faith in mainstream politics and political parties across Europe. Instead, there is a growing recognition that, for participation to be meaningful, it needs to be relevant to young people's immediate realities (Walther et al, 2020).

The second issue is the assumption that youth marginalisation is the result of young people not yet having developed the skills to participate as normative citizens. This assumption is underpinned by a rationale that presupposes 'behavioural correction' in marginalised young people based on deficit constructions of youth as a threat, as vulnerable, as lacking ability or not yet learning appropriate skills of citizenship (Hall and Pottinger, 2019). Hence the underlying rationale for the great majority of initiatives rests on the assumption that young people must learn to fit into society, that is, social institutions, communities and the labour market (Tofteng and Bladt, 2017) and need (adult) guidance on how to do that. Little attention is directed towards understanding how young people's knowledge, experiences and abilities could be activated in response to their marginalised situations.

What emerges is a frequent disconnect between public policy and service systems and the lifeworlds of marginalised young people, with the result that the core issues in young people's lives remain unchanged. This disconnect, along with a lack of political commitment in addressing structural inequalities, raises questions about what forms of participation might be meaningful for marginalised young people. As a result, youth participation has experienced a shift towards 'alternative' forms of participation self-initiated by young people in everyday lived contexts (McMahon et al, 2018). This is giving rise to increasing acknowledgement of the diverse ways in which young people are exercising political agency themselves to engage in new forms of democratic action for change (McMahon et al, 2018) and in so doing are reshaping the architecture of youth participation. Percy-Smith and colleagues (2020) identify four dimensions that characterise young people's participation in everyday contexts: developing agency and capability through experience; having spaces for autonomy, experimentation and emergence; reflexive negotiation of context; and participation as relational practice. These are reflected in the case study in this chapter.

Towards a theory of transformative participation

In responding to challenges and criticisms of participation, the developments discussed in the previous sections signal a progressive move towards an understanding of participation that is transformative in terms of bringing about tangible change. Hart (2008) outlines three dimensions to transformative participation: transformation of those involved through developing skills, experiences and changed relationships between actors; changes that happen as a result of these activities; and the societal transformation that results. Key to these forms of participation is a focus on asset-based approaches and addressing issues of professional accountability through the development of new participatory relations (Fielding, 2006; Mannion, 2007; see also Chapter 13 in this book); both of which require different epistemologies of practice. Tisdall (2013) argues that co-production offers possibilities for activating young people's skills and experiences and challenging professionals and services in ways that can give rise to more transformative participation. In the context of this chapter, we extend Tisdall's theoretical assertion to argue that transformative participation requires the development of an alternative, youth-focused critical epistemology of participation focused on supporting young people themselves as actors of change, that involves the centrality of learning (in action) and reanimates professional worker roles. The revisioned epistemology of practice activated in this chapter draws on the developing discourse of YPAR.

Developing a critical epistemology of youth praxis

YPAR as an approach to youth participation (Torre and Fine, 2006; Cammarota and Fine, 2008; Rodríguez and Brown, 2009; Caraballo et al, 2017; Percy-Smith, 2018) has become increasingly more prominent in youth participation initiatives. Cammarota and Fine (2008) in their text 'Revolutionizing Education: Youth Participatory Action research in motion', argue the case for understanding YPAR as an explicit pedagogy of transformational resistance involving the redefinition of "knowledge as actions in pursuit of social justice" (Cammarota and Fine, 2008, p 6). Youth participatory action research (YPAR) offers a way of building individual capacity for action and self-determination through collaborative social learning and critical reflexivity to contest exclusion and improve young people's own lives and life chances through their own self-initiated learning in action and the formation of movements to reframe identity and belonging (Cammarota and Fine, 2008; Rodríguez and Brown, 2009 ; Quijada Cerecer et al, 2013). Lundy (2008) and Rodríguez and Brown (2009) among others, realising the limitations of voice as a tool for empowerment and social change, outline three essential features to YPAR, as follows:

- participatory – involving young people in self-determined activity as experts by experience in their own lives;
- situated and rooted in critically reflexive learning (Weil, 1998), supporting discovery and problem solving in responses to issues directly related to people's lives;

- transformative and activist – realising their own agency through actively reflecting on and responding to the forces shaping their lives.

In echoing these principles, one can argue that key to such an epistemology of practice is young people being able to exercise power and control over their participation through ownership and self-determination, as well as an emphasis on using critically reflexive learning as a foundation for action and change.

These developments we also find in Nielsen and Nielsen's theory of CUAR (Nielsen and Nielsen, 2006, 2007), which links participation to a higher level of social insight and learning for those involved. Social learning and imagination are important for the sustainability of participation with a focus on 'processes of democratic educational foundation in the shape of social learning for self-managed outlines for the future' (Nielsen and Nielsen, 2007, p 13, own translation; see also Wildemeersch et al, 1998) and key to young people being authors of their own lives. Various perspectives on participation are at play here. First, there is an educational perspective in which young people derive value and meaning from learning as participants. Second, the democratic perspective centres on thinking in terms of actual democracy – a redistribution of power – and presumes that the participants in the process have an actual influence on what will happen and how it will happen, focused by issues that have immediate relevance to their lives. Finally, the social change perspective centres on framing new proposals for the social reality of the future based (in this case) on young people's own ideas and dreams. In keeping with Freire's idea of conscientisation (Freire, 1996), through self-initiated participation, young people are able to engage in personal social learning, developing knowledge as authors of their own lives, as they take part in processes of transformation and claiming the authority and the right to make decisions and realise them in relation to their own and communal life matters (Nielsen and Nielsen, 2006).

Learning for participation in everyday contexts

Education is widely acknowledged as being key to social and economic wellbeing (Manstead, 2014). However, as Freire (1996) and Lave and Wenger (1991) have argued, it is situated social learning as self-knowledge that enables individuals to develop a sense of empowerment to participate as equal citizens. This involves having a space for creative exploration and experimentation and asking critical questions about the situation to develop knowledge and understanding of the factors that contribute to people's disadvantaged position in society and how that affects their lives and capacity to engage as active citizens. In this way, participation needs to involve transformative learning processes that enable young people to develop social and biographical capabilities in relation to the choices and actions they take in relation to their life situation (see also Chapters 11 and 14 in this book), as well as transformation of the context in which they seek to change. There are resonances here with the use of Sen's (1999) and Nussbaum's (2007) capability approach to understand agency and participation in childhood and youth (Hart et al, 2014).

The perspective is thus about learning and decision making that makes sense in the context of young people's lifeworlds rather than the logic, rationales and normative assumptions of policy systems (see also Chapter 3 in this book). For Weil (1998), this process involves critically reflexive action research that both challenges and changes the participants and the systems of which they are a part. In this approach, learning is not separated from action, but is intertwined as a dynamic process of 'learning for change' in the generation of actionable knowledge that has meaning and relevance for those involved. Hence, unlike conventional approaches to participation and research in which findings are reported to professionals who then act on them, in action research young people pursue reflexive learning according to their own agenda so as to equip them to take action to bring about change in their own lives (see also Chapters 5 and 15 in this book). This is not about individualising the problem of youth marginalisation; instead it is an asset-based approach that acknowledges strengths and seeks to divert power to young people to bring about change they see as meaningful. Transformative participation is therefore about bringing about change in people's lives as well as involving a transformative learning process to achieve change.

From educator to facilitator: the role of the professional

This approach in turn changes the role of the supporting professional from a traditional role as expert to a more interpretative and facilitative role working relationally with young people (Mannion, 2007). In such a role, the professional relationship becomes one of being 'a support, a resource and a facilitator, rather than a controller, of learning in relationships of mutual learning and co-inquiry' (Percy-Smith et al, 2019, p 267) focused by the rhythm, cultures and logics of the lived lives of young people (see also Chapter 2 in this book). Criminal activity and 'misdemeanors' that may occur are part of the picture of young people's lives and can become an opportunity for learning – an issue to work with, rather than an obstacle. This involves a focus on understanding individual contexts within a whole system in relation to structural issues, as well as social and professional resources through dialogue and co-inquiry. Addressing power issues in professional interventions with young people does not mean relinquishing a professional role, rather to redefine it by seeking a different balance between ensuring young people have the power to develop and exercise their agency through informal personal learning, and providing resources and input from the perspective of a helping professional. This may involve workers challenging young people to reflect on the implications of different attitudes and actions, but ultimately involves professionals listening to young people, to where they are in their lives and their perspectives on what might help. Professional (social) learning is therefore part of the participatory process by reflexively responding to young people, listening, learning and co-constructing practice to better support young people's needs (Percy-Smith and Weil, 2003; Percy-Smith, 2008).

In the following section, we draw on case-study material from a project with marginalised young people in Denmark to reflect on the realities and implications of adopting a transformative approach to participation in practice (for further readings on the methodological and ethical considerations for this research, see Tofteng and Bladt, 2020).

Transformative participation with marginalised young people: a Danish case study

In Denmark, work with marginalised young people is almost exclusively carried out under the aegis of the welfare state and its institutions. As in many countries, young people may receive piecemeal input and support from different organisations and services, each responding to a different aspect of young people's lives. In 2014, the municipality of Copenhagen, a large housing association and University College Copenhagen (KP) came together to develop a new approach to youth intervention, bringing different youth intervention projects under one umbrella 'All in' to engage in a series of action research projects (X-men 2014–16, Narnia 2016–17, Urban Dreams 2016–19, Sjælør 2018–19) with marginalised young people involved in crime. The projects were carried out in cooperation between researchers from KP and welfare professionals (for example, those working in local youth clubs and employees in the housing association).

The aim of these projects is to enable young people to make changes in their own lives, and therefore can be argued to be empowering and transformative in ethos. At the same time, the projects seek to use learning from young people and projects to bring about change in professional service systems to better align with young people's lifeworlds. The projects are located in deprived housing areas with young people from the area who are perceived as the most criminalised, uncooperative and most likely to arouse anxiety. The groups often number between ten and 25 young people aged 14–25 with a diverse range of severe problems such as struggling with addictions, showing severe aggressive behavior and having grown up in families with few resources. The young people have different ethnicities but tend to be from minority backgrounds, coming together in single- or mixed-gender groups. Project meetings with both young people, researchers and professionals are held once a week and most of the projects run for up to three years.

Methodologically the projects draw on the Future Workshop (FW) approach (Jungk and Müllert, 1984; Bladt, 2013, Bladt and Nielsen, 2013), the main concept of which is to work with the interplay between critique and utopias. The focus is on young people articulating their wishes and dreams as a basis for exploring the development of alternative life stories. In this way, young people, rather than professionals, are centre stage in responding to their circumstances (Jungk and Müllert, 1984). In these projects, a Theme Workshop (TW) approach was developed, involving 'free spaces' (Bladt, 2012; Bladt, 2013; Bladt and Nielsen, 2013) as a way of creating space for participants to develop their own critical analyses based on their everyday life experiences and to create visions of new futures where the everyday life perspective holds the key to the way they respond to the structural inequality they experience.

Although the TW approach follows the same analytical and action-based logics as that of FW in terms of working with the interplay between critique and utopian phases, the former is somewhat different as a result of the way the 'free spaces' are developed. The analytical process is captured on 'flip sheets' where the young people's experiences and opinions are written down and accompanied by videos, pictures, sound recordings, stop motion movies and so on. In TWs, there is no judgement of young people's behaviour, language, opinions or experiences, but workers challenge the young people to question their own actions.

The work starts with a critically reflective analysis of current conditions influencing young people's lives. One of the themes taken up by young people in all projects irrespective of social background is that they perceive themselves as having a problematic relationship with society, including their local area. They say: "I don't belong here", "You can't be yourself here", "We're always being kicked out", "I'd like to get to know myself and find out who I am, but I can't do that here." Young people are very aware of the mechanisms of exclusion that affect their lives and consequently their options in life and present themselves simultaneously on psychological, social and structural levels as they engage in a 'struggle for recognition' (Honneth, 1995; Thomas, 2012).

The young people describe a feeling of being 'wrong' no matter where they are. At home they are wrong by being 'too Danish', at the bus stop they are wrong by *not* being Danish, at school they are wrong by having 'too much attitude', on the street they are wrong by having 'not enough attitude'. They describe how it negatively influences their lived lives to grow up and live in overcrowded apartments, in so-called ghetto areas and to attend the most disadvantaged schools, and how the upshot of their cumulative life context is to perceive their access to the status of fellow citizen as being severely limited. As a result of their experiences of disadvantage, these young people see themselves as belonging to another reality characterised by inequality and alienation echoed in the following quotes from young people: "I can see that the old lady is afraid of me – but I'm not dangerous"; "When I take the bus, there is always somebody calling me bad things"; "I actually like to go to school but I'm always being kicked out." The importance of this process is for young people to come to terms with the reality of their situation and the extent to which their lives and opportunities are restricted and characterised by massive barriers shaped by structural influences, and at the same time to acknowledge their own views, options and choices in response to their situation.

The young people are then supported in exploring their utopian perspectives about how they would like things to be, reflecting a desire to feel valued and accepted, a desire for belonging, where they are not demonised for being different or dangerous – "a place to be, where nobody kicks us out". In several of the projects, work has progressed in seeking to develop these places in cooperation with local agencies. Young people are provided with a location – sometimes an old personnel carrier, a basement in their housing area or an annex next to a youth club – for them to use and develop. Finding facilities and locations for young people takes time and involves discussion and negotiation with local community members who are often worried and anxious about establishing these sorts of venues for young people. The work is led by young people in collaboration with the research team, welfare professionals and other agents such as architects, local organisations and housing associations. Young people apply for funding to develop the youth spaces, furnishing and decorating the space, and defining the opening hours and which activities should take place. In these ways, young people derive multiple benefits, developing skills, meaning and purpose, and a sense of value and self-esteem for their achievements that enables them to reposition themselves as something more than marginalised youth. Young people develop social skills as they seek to address conflicts and different perspectives in the group in response to decisions that need to be made – for example, about which young people should be allowed access, and about the internal design of the space. These conflicts and discussions are resolved by young people, played out in a democratic fashion.

Discussion

These projects are not unproblematic, and sometimes can 'go wrong' for many different reasons, but they become real-life situations that young people can learn and benefit from. When it is the young people themselves who assess the current situation, develop proposals to change things and then take part in experimenting with implementing their own ideas, an opportunity arises to gain experience and reanimate their marginalised youth identity as active fellow citizens able to make a positive contribution. This means that this type of participatory work creates a space for informal, situated social learning, shaped by young people themselves for the purpose of bringing about change in their immediate lived realities (see also Chapter 3 in this book). These processes are in turn characterised by transformation of the young people involved through enhanced skills and experience that develop their capacity to engage with the world differently, including how they relate to others and, as a result, become better able to bring about changes in their lives and community (see Chapter 4 in this book). As Tisdall (2013) argues, these changes may be small but are often meaningful for young people, valorising their new-found capacity for participation. Impacts from this work are reflected in a decrease in incidences of crime involving these young people and an increase in education and labour market participation. Albeit not constituting social change in terms of addressing structural inequalities, such changes contribute to social change from the bottom up.

Empowerment, understood as the ability of individuals to realise their own sense of agency and power to act, becomes central when talking about change in these contexts. Young people become empowered as actors of change in their own lives by challenging and transforming their own perceptions of restricted opportunities as they realise their abilities through wrestling with bringing their own ideas to life. This process of informal experiential learning is resonant with the action research projects in the EU PARTISPACE project that highlighted the extent to which young people participate in shaping their own lives by using creative ways of reflexively negotiating their lived contexts (McMahon et al, 2018). By adopting a more holistic, critical, epistemological framework for understanding participation as situated social learning in a context focused on young people and their immediate lived reality, participation becomes more meaningful for young people and more effective in terms of initiating transformation in their lives (see also Chapters 5 and 15 in this book). Such an approach stands in contrast to citizenship education and participation initiatives that are led by public policy and based on normative assumptions and negative social constructions about young people and youth transitions.

Through the projects, it became clear how the perspectives of the young people changed. In the beginning, the young people often adopt a strong oppositional stance to almost everything: "We'll just burn something down if we don't get what we want" or "They think we're psychos so we might as well be psychos" or "Fuck the system, the police, the school and the club – they do nothing for us." However, during the course of the project, the confrontational stance changes as young people start to reflect on and ask questions such as 'How do you in fact become a Danish citizen?', 'Why is it that there is no room for someone like me in this societal reality?' By asking questions, they pursue their own inquiries, and develop an awareness of options, often involving developing positive attitudes to learning. They go from wanting to gain an education to getting a study grant to pursue a new-found interest in education and actually completing that education. Personal achievement helps change young people's self-identity and creates a different way for the young people to interact with society. The work potentially entails the possibility that the young participants may linguistically, discursively, sensorally and thus also bodily experiment with what it is like to relate to society in an actively participatory manner. What this illustrates is the critical importance of active, critically reflexive 'learning' if participation, as a process of involvement in finding solutions to problems, is to be effective in realising positive (transformational) outcomes. Yet, situated, social learning-in-action of the kind that is central to participatory action research is so often missing from more conventional approaches to youth participation restricted to relatively benign forms of consultation and response.

But then what about societal change? While the focus in these projects is to empower young people through approaches to participation that involve transformative learning, enabling young people to realise their ideas and improve their immediate situation, the transformative logic extends to developing the scope for change at a societal level, by equipping young people to change the way they symbolically engage in relation to society. In these projects, the focus is on finding solutions to youth marginalisation in Denmark, building on young people's ideas as the basis for change. While structural change may appear a long-term process, the projects highlight how personal change can lead to incremental change in the short term. This includes measures such as changing the way facilities for youth are provided, changing modes of cooperation between young people and professionals and facilitating tangible changes in young people's immediate everyday realities.

Conclusion

There is a growing appreciation that, in order for youth participation to be effective in terms of bringing about outcomes for marginalised young people, it needs to be rooted in the everyday contexts of young people's lives focused around issues that are at the heart of their struggles to derive a sense of meaning and identity as equal and active citizens (Lister, 2007). This chapter has argued for participation to be understood as a critically reflexive learning process that supports young people themselves in looking critically at their own situation and, through that learning journey, develop a more heightened sense of awareness in practice, of how they can see and realise possibilities for inclusive citizenship. The projects discussed here provide a quasi-ethnography of using a different approach to youth participation, drawing on principles of action research that focus centrally on personal transformative learning as the basis for social change. In so doing, this chapter highlights some of the benefits as well as challenges in engaging young people in participation as inquiry that can bring about changes in their lives. Both of the authors have used action research to positive effect with marginalised young people (see, for example, Bladt, 2013, 2017; Percy-Smith, 2018). However, we do not argue that this provides a magic wand in bringing about an idealised form of emancipation of young people; instead, it offers an opportunity for positive work with young people that can bring about incremental gains in their lives. As such, what we present here echoes examples of good youth work and informal social education approaches (Batsleer, 2008) that can help young people to realise a sense of inclusive citizenship.

We started this chapter by acknowledging different perspectives on youth participation, in decision-making and change processes as well as social and civic participation. In these final reflections, we revisit this dual perspective by reiterating the mutuality and interdependence of these different perspectives. This article illustrates that by adopting a different – dynamic learning – approach to participation in which young people are able to exercise a greater degree of critical reflexivity, agency and power, rooted in everyday life contexts, possibilities for participating as active citizens can be enhanced.

However, we acknowledge that not all young people may be predisposed to participate in this way, with research across the EU highlighting the diversity of styles of youth participation (see also Chapter 5 in this book). Whereas some may be willing to engage actively in understanding better their situation and finding ways to respond, others may prefer taking part in activities with others, which can provide the foundations for change. Regardless of approach, this chapter has highlighted the importance of some key principles in the way youth participation is conceptualised and enacted as a transformative process. In order for young people to reclaim the power for self-determination, there is a need for a different enactment of youth participation that supports critical questioning and social learning and, in turn, enables young people to build skills and capacity as autonomous change agents in improving their own lives.

Notes

[1] https://data.oecd.org/youthinac/youth-not-in-employment-education-or-training-neet.htm

[2] See, for example, the European Union (EU) Horizon 2020 project Young 5a Youth Social and Political Engagement, http://partispace.eu/

References

Andersen, S.H., Jensen, B., Nielsen, B.W and Saksen, J. R. (2017) *Hvad ved vi om Udsatte Unge? Historik, Omfang og Årsager*, Gylling: Gyldendal.

Batsleer, J. (2008) *Informal Learning in Youth Work*, London: Sage Publications.

Blackman, S. and Rogers, R. (eds) (2017) *Youth Marginality in Britain: Contemporary Studies of Austerity*, Bristol: Policy Press.

Bladt, M. (2012) 'Frirum og værksteder', in G. Duus (ed) *Aktionsforskning – En Grundbog*, Copenhagen: Samfundslitteratur, pp 147–58.

Bladt, M. (2013) 'De unges stemme – udsyn fra en anden virkelighed', PhD thesis, Roskilde University.

Bladt, M. (2017) 'Socialpædagogikkens samfundsmæssige opgave om igen', in V. Larsen and G.L. Rasmussen (eds) *Social- og Apecialpædagogik i Teori og Praksis*, Frederiksberg: Frydenlund.

Bladt, M. and Nielsen, K.A. (2013) 'Free space in the processes of action research', *Action Research*, 11(4): 369–85.

Cammaerts, B., Bruter, M., Banaji, S., Harrison, S. and Anstead, N. (2013) *EACEA 2010/03: Youth Participation in Democratic Life, Final Report*, London: LSE Enterprise.

Cammarota, J. and Fine, M. (eds) (2008) *Revolutionizing Education: Youth Participatory Action Research in Motion*, New York, NY: Routledge.

Caraballo, L., Lozenski, B.D., Lyiscott, J.J. and Morrell, E. (2017) 'YPAR and critical epistemologies: rethinking education research', *Review of Research in Education*, 41(1): 311–36.

Davies, B. (2019) *Austerity, Youth Policy and the Deconstruction of the Youth Service in England*, Cham: Palgrave Macmillan.

Day, L., McGrath, C., Percy-Smith, B. and Petkovic, S. (2019) *Study on the Landscape of Youth Representation in the EU*, Brussels: European Commission.

Ekman, J. and Amnå, E. (2012) 'Political participation and civic engagement: towards a new typology', *Human Affairs*, 22(3): 283–300.

Fielding, M. (2006) 'Leadership, radical student engagement and the necessity of person-centred education', *International Journal of Leadership in Education*, 9(4): 299–313.

Freire, P. (1996) *Pedagogy of the Oppressed* (2nd edn), London and New York, NY: Penguin.

Hall, S. and Pottinger, L. (2019) 'Being seen, being heard: engaging and valuing young people as political actors and activists', in N. von Benzon and C. Wilkinson (eds) *Intersectionality and Difference in Childhood and Youth: Global Perspectives*, Abingdon: Routledge, pp 124–40.

Hart, C.S., Biggeri, M. and Babic, B. (2014) *Agency and Participation in Childhood and Youth: International Applications of the Capability Approach in Schools and Beyond*, London: Bloomsbury Academic.

Hart, J. (2008) 'Children's participation and international development: attending to the political', *International Journal of Children's Rights*, 16(3): 407–18.

Honneth, A. (1995) *The Struggle for Recognition: The Moral Grammar of Social Conflicts*, Cambridge: Polity Press.

Horton, J. (2016) 'Anticipating service withdrawal: young people in spaces of neoliberalisation, austerity and economic crisis', *Transactions of The Institute of British Geographers*, 41(4): 349–62.

Jungk, R. and Müllert, N.R. (1984) *Håndbog i Fremtidsværksteder*, Viborg: Politisk Revy.

Kallio, K.P. and Häkli, J. (2013) 'Children and young people's politics in everyday life', *Space and Polity*, 17(1): 1–16.

Lave, J. and Wenger, E. (1991) *Situated Learning: Legitimate Peripheral Participation*, Cambridge: Cambridge University Press.

Lister, R. (2007) 'Inclusive citizenship: realizing the potential', *Citizenship Studies*, 11(1): 49–61.

Lundy, L. (2008) ' "Voice" is not enough: conceptualising Article 12 of the United Nations Convention on the Rights of the Child', *British Educational Research Journal*, 33(6): 927–42.

Mannion, G. (2007) 'Going spatial, going relational: why listening to children and children's participation needs reframing', *Discourse*, 28(3): 405–20, doi: 10.1080/01596300701458970

McMahon, G., Percy-Smith, B., Thomas, N., Bečević, Z., Liljeholm Hansson, S. and Forkby, T. (2018) *Young People's Participation: Learning from Action Research in Eight European Cities*, PARTISPACE Working Paper D5.3 Evaluation of Participatory Action Research, [online]. Available from: http://doi.org/10.5281/zenodo.1240227

Nielsen, K.A. and Nielsen, B.S. (2006) 'Kritisk-utopisk aktionsforskning: Demokratisk naturforvaltning som kollektiv dannelsesproces', in B.T. Jensen and G. Christensen (eds) *Psykologiske og Pædagogiske Metoder: Kvalitative og Kvantitative Forskningsmetoder i Praksis*, Frederiksberg: Roskilde Universitetsforlag, pp 155–80.

Nielsen, K.A. and Nielsen, B.S. (2007) *Demokrati og Naturbeskyttelse: Dannelse af Borgerfællesskaber Gennem Social Læring – Med Møn som Eksempel*, Pozkal: Frydendahl.

Nussbaum, M. (2007) *The Frontiers of Justice: Disability Nationality Species Membership*, Cambridge, MA: Harvard University Press.

Percy-Smith, B. (2008) 'Revisioning professional practice with young people: a dialogical social learning model of participation', Paper presented at Reflective Youth Work – Linking Theory and Praxis Seminar, Helsinki, Finland, 2–4 July.

Percy-Smith, B. (2010) 'Councils, consultation and community: rethinking the spaces for children and young people's participation', *Children's Geographies*, 8(2): 107–22.

Percy-Smith, B. (2018) 'Participation as learning for change in everyday spaces: enhancing meaning and effectiveness using action research', in C. Baraldi and T. Cockburn (eds) *Theorising Childhood: Citizenship, Rights and Participation*, London: Palgrave Macmillan, pp 159–86.

Percy-Smith, B. and Weil, S. (2003) 'Practice-based research as development: innovation and empowerment in youth intervention initiatives using collaborative action inquiry', in A. Bennett. M. Cieslik and S. Miles (eds) *Researching Youth*, London: Palgrave Macmillan, pp 66–84.

Percy-Smith, B., Cuconato, M., Reutlinger, C. and Thomas, N.P. (2019) 'Action research with young people: possibilities and "messy realities"', *Discourse. Journal of Childhood and Adolescence Research*, 14(3): 255–270.

Percy-Smith, B., Thomas, N.P., Batsleer, J. and Forkby, T. (2020) 'Everyday pedagogies: new perspectives on youth participation, social learning and citizenship', in A. Walther, J. Batsleer, P. Loncle and A. Pohl, (eds) *Young People and the Struggle for Participation: Contested Practices, Power and Pedagogies in Public Space*, Abingdon: Routledge, pp 179–98.

Quijada Cerecer, D.A., Cahill, C. and Bradley, M. (2013) 'Toward a critical youth policy praxis: critical youth studies and participatory action research', *Theory into Practice*, 52(3): 216–23.

Rodríguez, L.F. and Brown, T.M. (2009) 'From voice to agency: guiding principles for participatory action research with youth', *New Directions for Youth Development*, 123: 19–34.

Sen, A. (1999) *Development as Freedom*, Oxford: Oxford University Press.

Thomas, N.P. (2007) 'Towards a theory of children's participation', *International Journal of Children's Rights*, 15(2): 199–218.

Thomas, N.P. (2012) 'Love, rights, and solidarity: studying children's participation using Honneth's theory of recognition', *Childhood*, 19(4): 453–66.

Tisdall, E. K.M. (2013) 'The transformation of participation? Exploring the potential of "transformative participation" for theory and practice around children and young people's participation', *Global Studies of Childhood*, 3(2): 183–93:

Tofteng, D. and Bladt, M. (2017) 'Det tværprofessionelle arbejde: et paradoks i skolens socialpædagogiske arbejde?', *I Tidsskrift for Professionsstudier*, 15: 14–23.

Tofteng, D. and Bladt, M. (2020) '"Upturned participation" and youth work: using a critical utopian action research approach to foster engagement', *Educational Action Research*, 28(1): 112–27.

Torre, M.E. and Fine, M. (2006) 'Participatory action research (PAR) by youth', in L. Sherrod (ed) *Youth Activism: An International Encyclopedia*, Westport, CT: Greenwood, pp 456–62.

Walther, A. Batsleer, J. Loncle, P. and Pohl, A. (2020) *Young People and the Struggle for Participation: Contested Practices, Power and Pedagogies in Public Space*, Abingdon: Routledge.

Weil, S. (1998) 'Rhetorics and realities in public service organisations: systemic practice and organisational as critically reflexive action research (CRAR)', *Systemic Practice and Action Research*, 11: 37–61.

Wildemeersch, D., Jansen, T., Vandenabeele, J. and Jans, M. (1998) 'Social learning: a new perspective on learning in participatory systems', *Studies in Continuing Education*, 20(2): 251–65.

17

Revisiting young people's participation and looking ahead: concluding remarks

E. Kay M. Tisdall, Ilaria Pitti and Maria Bruselius-Jensen

Introduction

Considerable policy and practice interest is currently promoting young people's participation, locally, nationally and internationally. It has become a popularised requirement for numerous domains, from community regeneration, to service planning, to policy making (Tisdall et al, 2014; Gal and Duramy, 2015). As discussed in this book's introduction, on the one hand, this popularisation is supported by the recognition of young people as current and not just future citizens, children and young people's human rights (including participation rights), and examples of young people influencing change. On the other hand, it is propelled by concerns about too many young people being disengaged with formal democratic politics, being potentially disruptive influences and changing demographics. Involving young people in decisions that affect them and their communities, and that address their concerns, both respects and binds young people's contributions to society.

Young people's participation is not new, from their contributions as family members, workers and leaders to their involvement in protests and strikes (Cunningham and Lavalette, 2016; Blakemore, 2018). What is new is a particular combination of discourses and trends, such as the decades that have articulated 'youth' as a separate (often transitional age- and stage-limited) category from 'childhood' and 'adulthood'; the rise of human rights, which has gradually extended to recognising both children and young people as rights holders and embedding a host of formal institutions and opportunities for participation; globalisation, which has arguably both connected much of the world's population digitally, economically and culturally, while also widening inequalities and creating new threats; and the 2008 worldwide financial crisis, which shook particularly the Global North and traditional welfare states, to the disadvantage of young people's future prospects. Further, simultaneously with this book's deadline, the COVID-19 pandemic has created a host of economic and societal changes with immediate and future effects on young people and their participation. Such a combination of discourses and new trends underlies and influences changes for young people's participation and requires subsequent reflection and conceptual development to support and challenge future practices. This book sits within such requirements, seeking to understand the changing practices of young people's participation and changing opportunities for youth engagement in society.

The book set out to revisit 'how, under what conditions and for what purpose young people – in different contexts – participate in making decisions and foster changes on issues that concern them and their communities' (Chapter 1, pp 000–000). The book draws on experiences within Europe, predominantly from Scandinavia and the UK, but also from the particular experiences of youth movements in Italy, digital participation in Estonia, and cross-national research. The book involves both young people as authors and young people as research participants, with a confluence of qualitative and quantitative methods. It does so with an interest in the interactions between the concepts of youth, participation and inequalities, in how they shape, weaken, support or lead to young people's participation. Here we explore learning from the chapters, to consider the changing landscapes of young people's participation both in practice and conceptually.

Where are we now – and where are we going?

The book's chapters trace an unease about the 'state' of young people's participation. The majority of chapters (for example, Chapters 10, 11 and 16) contain critical perspectives on the current 'status quo', sharing the dissatisfaction of both young participants and observers to conventional forms of young people's participation. They note that organisations such as youth parliaments or forums are too often opportunities for young people to practise citizenship rather than to enact it, so that young people have little opportunity to influence decision making. Chapter 11 demonstrates how young people with autism spectrum disorder, even though they have formal participation rights, seldom succeed in executing these rights when decisions are made by statutory caseworkers. Disenchanted with the formal mechanisms and institutions, there has been a growth of participatory projects. With various labels – from co-design, to co-production, to participatory action research – these projects support young people to participate and influence, and show some success in doing so. In Chapter 8, young people participating in a mental health project did influence the project's app development. Young people in Young Edinburgh Action (YEA) influenced local decision making (see Chapters 3 and 13). In Chapter 16, the action research projects led to incremental changes in youth facilities. But the 'logics', the ways the projects function, still made such influence a challenge and imposed limitations on the young people and their influence. Chapter 8, for example, traces how the mental health project's logics precluded young people from addressing some of the concerns that most interested the young people – their experiences with the mental health services. The Rights Respecting Schools project was even more limited: while the young people were appreciative of attending a cross-city workshop, Rights Council meetings and organising events, their participation made no substantial change to the schools' ethos and general practices of pupils' participation. Katherine Dempsie's and Myada Eltiraifi's experiences as young people being part of YEA were more positive, in that they felt that their views were respected within institutional decision making and by adult decision makers. But their experiences are presented as 'extraordinary', unusual, and being done despite the 'logics' of the institutional structures, within specially funded projects, and requiring particular efforts from funders, adult facilitators and young participants to ensure these constructive results. Thus the more formalised 'taking part' in something, and particularly taking part in civic and political activities, remains problematic for many youth participation initiatives, whether the more formal youth parliaments or the current trend of participatory projects.

Certain chapters find that the repositioning of young people from participants in projects to knowledge creators has the potential to disrupt and to transform. For example, Chapter 12 shows how supporting young asylum seekers to find collective ways to voice their experiences with living in a hostile environment led them to develop ways to practise politics 'differently' (p 195) by performing their play 'Faceless' to counteract what they felt as an imposed invisibility and silencing of their presence in UK society. Chapter 14 demonstrates how the method of journey mapping allowed potentially marginalised young people to engage in evaluation of participatory activities and express what made sense to them. Chapter 16, for example, discusses the Future Workshop methodology, where young people respond to their own problems and consider their own solutions. This draws them to an understanding of participation as social learning, and one with four dimensions in young people's contexts: 'developing agency and capability through experience; having spaces for autonomy, experimentation and emergence; reflexive negotiation of context; and participation as relational practice' (p 278). These dimensions trace on to Chapters 3 and 4, which describe the young people's own participation journeys. In Chapter 4, Barwago Jama Hussein writes powerfully of the collective, critical learning: 'We all discover that we all have stories and have experienced some things that we haven't dared to talk about, but we do now' (pp 000–000). The chapters demonstrate the young people's developing skills and experiences, from their initial, almost accidental, engagement to the increased breadth and depth of their involvement over time. In Chapter 3, Christina McMellon and colleagues discuss the spaces YEA and TRIUMPH created for and with them, which were highly dependent on the relationships and relational practices among peers and adult facilitators. This combination supported their engagement, and ultimately their influence, on matters important to them. Chapter 13 traces the power of young people being recognised as researchers, bringing both expertise to, and developing expertise, during the projects. This claim as generators of robust, evidenced knowledge gave a credibility and legitimation to the young researchers' projects and their views. At least in some contexts, the recognition and positioning of young people as experts, as having and generating knowledge, is ensuring meaningful and effective participation.

Further chapters argue for going beyond the formalised institutions *and* the participatory projects, to focus on young people's own experiences of civic and political participation. These chapters explore how young people engage in participatory activities outside formal settings and arenas. In these experiences, engagement develops from young people's uneasiness with the institutions' ideas about what participation should be – an uneasiness that forms a critique of formal participation's logics and practices. Chapter 7, for example, shows how access to digital information and political forms of expressions can have considerable democratic value to young Estonians, as their history as a former socialist country means low levels of trust in formal political channels. Several chapters look towards the cultural, such as critically considering the cultural industry (discussed in Chapter 2) and deliberately developing opportunities to disrupt, insert and influence the cultural conversations, performances and contributions as forms of (youth) participation. With this in mind, Alessio La Terra explains how he and peers have carried out their 'cultural activism' through cultural projects and events. Focusing on practices of self-organisation developed within occupied spaces, Chapter 9 discusses how young people in Italy have created their own structures of participation – alternative to the institutional ones – through self-managed projects addressing social and intergenerational inequalities. While in these chapters young people's engagement is understood and developed as an explicit political critique to institutions, other chapters focus on practices of youth participation that do not have a clear political stance. Chapter 10 charts how young people self-organised to construct participatory spaces in cultural events and for skateboarding. In Chapter 15, Claire Levy sought to support disruptive and transformative participation, developing methods that could respect young people's embodied and visual experiences in their rural setting and creating a documentary film with young people. These chapters display a disenchantment with more formalised participation and their associated institutions, leading to cultural expressions that may both better recognise and support young people's participation *and* exert the influence on attitudes that the young people want to achieve.

Throughout the book, the need to elaborate new understandings of young people and participation emerges. Some chapters challenge our understandings of the relationships between young people and participation, problematising classic assumptions and definitions. For example, Chapter 6 presents survey and interview evidence, suggesting that young people generally (and Danish respondents in particular) support conventional forms of participation, such as voting in national elections and joining a trade union. Rather than moved to participate actively in either conventional or unconventional forms (like social movements), Jonas Lieberkind finds the majority of Danish respondents concentrated on strategically navigating their own personal and social development in a complex society. In this chapter, he thus puts forward that young people may well be reflective, interested and personally engaged, but this does not necessarily lead to active involvement in either conventional or unconventional participation forms. Young people generally, then, may not be the disengaged group feared by some but nor are they necessarily eager to take up their participation rights actively to change society. Seeking to broaden existing definitions of youth participation, Chapter 5 engages with the concept of social participation to highlight the variegated forms and combinations in which youth participation can find expression, as well as discussing what challenges and what supports these different forms. Finally, the need to look for youth participation in spaces that are not traditionally conceived as participatory contexts is underlined by Chapter 7's study of digital participation, as well as Chapter 11's analysis of the possibilities of voice for young people with autism spectrum disorder in their interactions with statutory caseworkers.

While trying to assess existing concepts and methodologies, the book's chapters discuss the changing landscapes of young people's participation, from the concerns about more formalised institutions of participation, to the growth of participatory projects and accompanying activity, to the searching for alternatives that recognise young people's everyday participation and their critical learning. Rather than emphasising the 'taking part' in civic and political responsibilities, this move is towards 'being part' of something, being included in (or indeed creating and changing) a society with rights and possibilities.

Understanding the landscapes of participation

Two sets of ideas intersect with the changing landscapes of participation detailed in the previous section. One idea emerged from reading across chapters: the importance of space, place and time in young people's participation. The second was an intended focus of the book – inequalities – but its dimensions were unexpected, with less attention to structural and socioeconomic inequalities and more to other forms. These ideas are explored in this section.

Space is a recurring theme across several chapters. Human geography has given the wider academic community a rich combination of concepts that consider how the geographical combines with the relational and the material to create and recreate spaces and places (Holloway et al, 2018). Spaces are explained as more than a physical phenomenon, with reciprocal influences between people and space: 'At its simplest, the term "social space" can be seen as a way of recognising that space is produced by people (rather than pre-existing), and that spaces in turn shape people (rather than being inert and neutral)' (Gallagher, 2006, p 161). Places draw in social relations even further, often with deep-rooted meanings, distinctive activities and imaginings (see Campbell, 2018).

Attention to spaces and places can be traced through chapters. As presented in Chapters 2 and 9, Làbas and other social movements in Italy took charge of spaces, (re)claiming community buildings to develop ways of engaging and providing for their communities that would address structural inequalities and revolutionise their everyday lives and relations. Projects provide temporal as well as physical spaces for young people to meet together, to develop their collective agendas and – hopefully – to carry their agendas forward. Chapter 15 advocates for an explicit move from the formal spaces of young people' participation – which exclude and misrepresent young people living in rural areas – to the places that young people experience everyday. In Chapter 12, young asylum seekers felt invisible and excluded, and sought to find the space to express themselves. These and other chapters demonstrate the essential role of relationships and relational practices in creating and sustaining such spaces. Thus, recognising the 'work' of the relational and emotional, of attending to the spaces and places of participation, are at least as important for young people's involvement as more formalised concerns of discussion, development and organisation.

As Anne-Lene Sand writes in Chapter 10, attending to time, space and place is one way to change the 'logics' of participation. Recognising their importance to participation is powerful, as they foster and create the relations essential for participation to occur and to have impact. They can be radical, as young people's activism 'takes over' time and space, to create place and participation. They can be exclusionary, with young people moved on, pushed out or barred from entry, or more welcoming to some young people than to others. Whatever the forms of participation, attention to time, space and place is illuminating and potentially challenging.

The book set out to explore how inequalities influenced young people's participation. Across chapters, inequalities are demonstrated in myriad ways, from macro to micro levels. Chapters 2 and 9 on Italian young people's social movements are the most stark at drawing out how structural socioeconomic inequalities affect young people and – with the financial crisis of 2007–08 and ensuing call for economic austerity – have curtailed their planned trajectories. For these young people, realisation and reflection led to transformative action, where their participation sought to recast the cultural and other framings, to create environments and ways of being that could address, ameliorate and alter such inequalities. As suggested in Chapter 5, young people tend to engage in protest activities as a response to negative life experiences such as discrimination and social exclusion. Participation emerges as a way to react to the experience of inequalities.

For most book chapters, the focus is less on structural inequalities and more on other types of inequality. These can be grouped in two ways. First, the literature on youth participation is filled with concerns that young people are unequally involved in formal participation activities. The accusation is that only the elite participate – middle-class, educationally advantaged young people – further advantaging those young people and disadvantaging others. While that accusation may be valid in some circumstances, the empirical evidence regularly does not support this (see Chapters 8 and 13). Often organisations and projects are funded on particular bases that privilege the participation of certain groups of young people: for example, young people living in deprived areas (Chapter 4), young people involved in crime (Chapter 16) or potentially marginalised groups such as young asylum seekers (Chapter 12). Other inequalities that are less often considered can emerge. For example, projects require small groups of young people to work closely together over time. This privileges young people who have and can find the time do so, in their often busy lives and with competing demands. It may be the 'excluded middle', the quieter young person who does not get invited to or does not want to spend time in groups, who may not have their participation rights recognised. Together, the chapters underline that participation is unequally distributed, just not always by socioeconomic inequalities.

Second, the chapters show inequalities based on age. Social science literature rarely dwells on inequalities based on age, between children, young people and adults; they are framed as other issues, such as intergenerational hierarchies (Mannion, 2018; Punch, 2020) or rights' breaches (Haydon and Scraton, 2009; Taylor, 2017), if attended to at all. In contrast, Darpan Raj Gautam refers to inequalities based on age starkly in his participation journey: 'But the age thing is really weird in Denmark because you see age as something that determines how much you know, I guess, and not the maturity of the person' (pp 000–000). Such inequalities fundamentally play out in young people's participation. It is often because of young people's unequal claim to political power that they are 'given' spaces for participation, and funding to support their participation, as a panacea or training ground for their involvement. Children's participation, for those under the ages of majority, has been even more unacknowledged until the rise of the human rights agenda. Child and youth participation activities, literatures and theorisations remain unduly separated, losing their potential to join in intergenerational bonds and influence. Attending to the inequalities by age suggests that the inequities are neither inevitable nor fair; a sharper, systematic attention to them would provide a considerable challenge to policy and practice (see, for example, Wall and Dar, 2011).

For young people's participation, inequalities thus help shape the intersections of space, place and time – and space, place and time help shape the inequalities of participation. They create exclusions and inclusions, so that some young people are more likely than others to participate in certain contexts, on certain topics, for particular outcomes individually and on decisions. This suggests that noting these exclusions and inclusions is worthwhile, to minimise the former and maximise the later. Further, this suggests the need for multiple opportunities and ways of participation, supporting all young people's rights to participate.

Looking ahead?

The book demonstrates that those deeply interested in young people's participation – such as those writing the chapters, both young people and adults – are concerned that 'formal' participation for and by young people is inadequate. They do not argue for more engagement of young people in formal democratic institutions. They are distrustful of the capacity of formal organisations or projects to ensure that participation is meaningful and effective, to those involved as well as to others. The concern goes more deeply, to question the dominant narrative of participation. Wyness (2018) writes about the dominant narrative for children's participation, noting that it tends to be formalised and institutional, focusing on 'voice' and the expression of children's views, and aimed to develop and educate children into adulthood. He suggests alternatives that recognise the multidimensional nature of participation, the diversity of contexts where it takes place, and their embedded and relational nature. Chapters in this book too are searching for alternative narratives, seeking different forms of engagement. Chapter 16 emphasises critical learning, while a number of other chapters use theatre/readings/cultural events to generate and challenge ideas. Barwago Jama Hussein writes powerfully of a change in listening, the becoming more attentive 'to listening with our hearts', in her participation journey. Participation, then, to be meaningful must extend to include these other domains of performance, emotionality, and community and personal relations.

Such issues would be hard to read into the United Nations Convention on the Rights of the Child (UNCRC), as a legal document, and its participation rights. But, while they may not encompass all participation possibilities, the UNCRC and other human rights treaties have the advantage of law in their 'stickiness': they take time and negotiation to change, so that they stay firm in times of crisis and political turmoil where mere policies can be overturned overnight. Such treaties can provide a platform for the more expansive interpretation of rights, allowing for more radical and inclusive opportunities. This could include dramatically lowering the voting age (Munn, 2012) or requiring mental health services to learn with young people about their experiences of using them.[1] This could include the reclaiming of community spaces, for community benefits, as undertaken by young people in Italy (Chapters 2 and 9), but supported rather than hampered by local government. It can mean research and projects that facilitate the myriad ways in which young people contribute and communicate, to make these activities meaningful to a wide range of young people. The UNCRC has helped illuminate and scaffold young people's participation in particular ways. But the meanings of participation are not limited to it.

As the book developed and chapters were submitted, there were both familiar thoughts and provocative surprises, in the book's focus on the intersections of youth, participation and inequalities. It was not unexpected to know of the problems with young people's participation, the barriers and the challenges that many chapters outline. Some of these have newer dimensions, such as Chapter 10 on leisure spaces or Chapter 7 on digital participation, but these barriers and challenges have become familiar concerns in the participation literature. What was newer and intriguing were various authors' efforts to search out, and to learn from, participation examples that have been more meaningful, more influential or more transformative. This often led to recognising a wider range of relations, emotions and modes of participation, beyond the minimum requirements of the UNCRC. With young people's activism as well as participation now coming to the fore, from climate change to addressing the refugee crisis, our understandings of it will need to both keep pace and continue to challenge.

Thus, the book addresses but does not provide a final answer to the starting question of how, under what conditions and for what purpose young people – in different contexts – participate in making decisions and foster changes on issues that concern them and their communities. This book stresses the need continually to revisit the conditions and purposes of young people's participation. There is a need to reconfirm prevailing trends and persistent problems, but also to identify new limitations, as well new purposes and outlets, for young people to practice their participation rights.

This conclusion became even more definitive as the book was being finalised as the COVID-19 pandemic arose with considerable short-term and potentially long-term impacts on young people generally and youth participation specifically. This raises further questions. Will the economic crisis be reintroduced and place further pressure on young people, silencing them or leading to alternative movements? Will the crisis be the end to the growing climate movement, or will young people find new energy for their claims, new digital ways to express their stands or define new life and career paths less dependent on growth and global economy? Will young people be leaders in developing new paths for being social while keeping a distance? How will these trends have different expressions corellated with governments' different ways of addressing the crisis? All these questions, and many more, will be central in future research, further emphasising the ongoing need to address forms and conditions for young people's participation.

Note

[1] For an example of such a project, see www.scie.org.uk/children/care/mental-health/about-the-project [accessed 12 February 2020].

References

Blakemore, E. (2018) 'Youth in revolt: five powerful movements fueled by young activists', *National Geographic*, [online] 23 March. Available from: www.nationalgeographic.com/news/2018/03/youth-activism-young-protesters-historic-movements [Accessed 12 February 2020].

Campbell, C. (2018) 'Space, place and scale', *Past and Present*, 239(1): e23–45.

Cunningham, S. and Lavalette, M. (2016) *School's Out: The Hidden History of Britain's School Student Strikes*, London: Bookmarks Publications.

Gal, T. and Duramy, B.F. (eds) (2015) *International Perspectives and Empirical Findings on Child Participation*, Oxford: Oxford University Press.

Gallagher, M. (2006) 'Spaces of participation and inclusion?', in E.K.M. Tisdall, J.M. Davis, M. Hill and A. Prout (eds) *Children, Young People and Social Inclusion: Participation for What?*, Bristol: Policy Press, pp 159–78.

Haydon, D. and Scraton, P. (2009) 'Children's rights: rhetoric and reality', *Criminal Justice Matters*, 76(1): 16–18.

Holloway, S.L., Holt, L. and Mills, S. (2018) 'Questions of agency: capacity, subjectivity, spatiality and temporality', *Progress in Human Geography*, 43(3): 458–77.

Mannion, G. (2018) 'Intergenerational education and learning: we are in a new place', in S. Punch and R. Vanderbeck (eds) *Families, Intergenerationality and Peer Group Relations*, Singapore: Springer Nature, pp 307–27.

Munn, N.J. (2012) 'Capacity testing the youth: a proposal for broader enfranchisement', *Journal of Youth Studies*, 15(8): 1048–62.

Punch, S. (2020) 'Why have generational orderings been marginalised in the social sciences including childhood studies?', *Children's Geographies*, 18(2): 128–40.

Taylor, N. (2017) 'Child participation: overcoming disparity between New Zealand's family court and out-of-court dispute resolution processes', *International Journal of Children's Rights*, 25(3–4): 658–71.

Tisdall, E.K.M., Hinton, R., Gadda, A.M. and Butler, U.M. (2014) 'Introduction: Children and young people's participation in collective decision-making', in E.K.M. Tisdall, A.M. Gadda and U.M. Butler (eds) *Children and Young People's Participation and its Transformative Potential: Learning from Across Countries*, Basingstoke: Palgrave Macmillan, pp 1–31.

Wall, J. and Dar, A. (2011) 'Children's political representation: the right to make a difference', *International Journal of Children's Rights*, 19(4): 595–612.

Wyness, M. (2018) 'Children's participation: definitions, narratives and disputes', in C. Baraldi and T. Cockburn (eds) *Theorising Childhood: Citizenship, Rights and Participation*, London: Palgrave Macmillan, pp 52–72.

Index

Note: page numbers in *italic* type refer to Figures and Tables

A

abstract objectivism 200
access 130–1
ActionAid Denmark 43
  Part of the Community 43–50
    Barwago's participatory
      journey 43–7
    Darpan's participatory
      journey 47–50
activism 55, 59–60
  influencing factors 63, 64, 65, 66, 68,
    69–72
  and self-organisation 139–53
    case studies 142–3
    economic crisis as motivator 144–6
    position towards institutions 150–2
    research methodology 143–4
    social centres 146–9
  see also grassroots activism
Adorno, T.W. 19, 20
adult-led participation 157, 158–9, 160
adults
  perception of youth 4–5
  relationships with 39–40, 128, 133
advocacy 179–80, 182, 186–9
affect 242–3
age discrimination 65, 69, 300
age of entitlement 120
agency 55–6
  and life experiences 69–73
agents 120
Aliens Act 1905, UK 197
Althusser, L. 200
anti-racist mobilisation 198
assemblage thinking 257
assimilation 168
Asylum Act 2002, UK 198
asylum seekers 18, 195–208
  collective space 206–7
  hostile environment 196–8, 202,
    205, 207
  meaning of participation 199–202
  participatory research 203–5
  Refugee and Asylum Participatory
    Action Research (RAPAR) 199
austerity 276
austerity policies 140
authorities 57, 68, 150–2, 167
autism spectrum disorder
    (ASD) 175–89

advocacy 179–80, 182, 186–9
  communication 183–4
  recognition 182–3, 184–6
  research methodology 180–2
  statutory casework 178–9
Avant-Punk 26

B

Banaji, S. 101
Bangladesh 221, 223, 226, 227
Baobab Experience 143, 145
Barber, T. 160–1
BBC Radio 4 261
behavioural correction 278
belonging 58, 200
Bennett, W.L. 101–2, 112
Bhat, R. 101
Black, R. 120
Blair, Tony 198
Bologna 23–4
Boltanski, L. 122, 125, 133, 160, 166,
    168, 171
bounded agency 55–6, 72
Bourdieu, P. 20–1
Boylan, J. 179, 180

C

Cammarota, B. 279
capitalism 122
Casa Bettola 142, 152
Casa dei Beni Commi 143, 145
caseworkers *see* statutory caseworkers
Castells, M. 151
censorship *see* self-censorship
chaos 243–5
charitable work 60–1
Chiapello, E. 122, 125, 133
citizenship 203, 257–8
  embodied 258, 266, 271
  lived 120
  strategic 82, 89–92, *94*
    post-politics 92–3
citizenship education 286
citizenship models 101
civic broccoli 161
civic knowledge 83–4
civil society organisations (CSOs) 122
civilising process 161
climate change 3
climbing 170–1

Cohen, S. 202
CoLab 123, 125–6, 131
collective action 207
collective space 206–7
communication 36–7, 124, 183–4
communicative ability 177, 184
community 39, 58, 206, 245–7
concerts 163–6
conflict with authorities 57, 68
connective action 102, 112
connective logic 102
Conversation for Action 29–30,
    34, 35–6
co-production 279
co-research 202–3
  "Faceless" (play) 204–5, 206
  see also youth-led research projects
countryside settings 255–71
  map-making 267–9
  playfulness in research 257–60,
    264–7
  research activities 261–3
  research methodology 260–1, 263–4
COVID-19 pandemic 2
credibility 223, 224, 225–6, 229
Cuevas-Parra, P. 223
cultural activism see Quaderni
    Urbani, Bologna
cultural industry 20, 21, 296
cultural perspective 4
cultural reproduction 20–1

D

Dalrymple, J. 179, 180
Daniels, Robert Vincent 79
Day, L. 277
democracy 208
democratic perspective 280
Denmark
  autism spectrum disorder
    (ASD) 175–89
    advocacy 179–80, 182, 186–9
    communication 183–4
    recognition 182–3, 184–6
    research methodology 180–2
    statutory casework 178–9
  International Civic and Citizenship
    Education Study (ICCS) 77, 78
    conventional and unconventional
      political participation 86–9
    empirical findings 94
    knowledge, deliberation and
      involvement 83–4
    political engagement 81–2
    political trust and reflexivity 84–6
    post-politics 92–3
    strategic citizens 82, 89–92
  journey mapping

marginalised youth 236–47
  Part of the Community
    project 43–50
project-based participation 119–33
  as disembedded project
    bubbles 125–31
  findings 119, 132–3
  research methodology 123–5
self-organisation 157–72
  informal competencies 163–6
  organisational structures 166–8
  participatory place 169–71
  research methodology 162–3
  transformative participation 282–7
Derrida, J. 200
digital applications (apps) 124
digital divide 101, 110–11
digital participation 99–113
  context and data 103–7
  digital divides 101, 110–11
  opportunities for involvement 107–10
discrimination 61, 65, 69
  see also labelling
disembedded project bubbles 125–31
dispossession 207
diversity 48, 227
Downs, R.M. 268
dutiful citizen model 101

E

early years institutions 133
economic crisis 17, 139, 140, 141
  as motivator for activism 144–6
economic deprivation 26–7
education 57, 66, 180, 280, 286
educational perspective 280
efficacy see group efficacy; personal
    efficacy; self-efficacy
Ekström, M. 102
electronic voting 105
embodied citizenship 258, 266, 271
emotion 206
empowerment 285–6
Estonia 99, 100, 104–5
  digital participation 99–113
    context and data 103–7
    digital divides 101, 110–11
    opportunities for
      involvement 107–10
EU PARTISPACE project 286
evaluation practice 237–8
Evans, K. 55–6
everyday engagement 55, 60
  influencing factors 63, 64, 65, 66, 68,
    69–72
Ex-OPG "Je so pazzo" 143, 145
external collaborations 22, 25–6

F

Facebook 102, 111, 163
"Faceless" (play) 204–5, 206
facilitators 281–2
female surrealist artists 26
femicide 26
financial crisis 2, 139
  see also economic crisis
Fine M. 279
Foard, N. 57
Foucault, M. 200
franchise *see* Vote at 16; voting
Frankfurt School 20
Freire, P. 280
"From Our Own Correspondent"
    (BBC Radio 4) 261
Frontrunners Against Inequality
  Barwago's participatory journey 43–7
  Darpan's participatory journey 47–50
fun 128–9, 130
Future Workshop (FW)
    approach 283, 295

G

gender 227
gender-based violence 26
generagency 128
generational perspective 4
  see also intergenerational perspective
ghettos 45, 50n, 284
global financial crisis 2, 139
  see also economic crisis
globalisation 86
Goodwin, J. 206
grassroots activism 207–8
Great Recession *see* economic crisis
group efficacy 63–4, 69

H

Hanisch, C. 207
Hannerz, Ulf 163
hard individualization 237
Hart, J. 278
Hart, R.A. 133, 264
Healy, K. 178
helping behaviour 55, 60–1
  influencing factors 64, 65, 66, 68,
    69–72
Henn, M. 57
Hickey-Moody, Anna 250
homelessness 31–2, 148, 243–5
Horkheimer, M. 19, 20
hostile environment 196–8, 202,
    205, 207
household income 64
housing 23, 187
  see also political squats

I

Ida-Viru County 106
ideological engagement 78–81, *94*
iDoc 262–3
immigration 49
  hostile environment 196–7, 202
  see also asylum seekers; migrants
Immigration Act 1971, UK 197–8
impact 251
income 64
individual subjectivism 200
inequality 5–6, 44, 140, 299–300
  and agency 56
  and assimilation 168
  and asylum seekers 206
  and austerity 276
  and economic crisis 144–6
  and the internet 102
  in participation 227–8
  as political problem 153
  reproduction of 21
  and self-organisation 169–70,
    172
informal competencies 163–6
Inglehart, Ronald 80
institutional logic 172
institutions 150–2, 161
  see also authorities
intergenerational perspective 5
  see also generational perspective
International Civic and Citizenship
    Education Study (ICCS) 77,
    78
  conventional and unconventional
    political participation 86–9
  empirical findings *94*
  knowledge, deliberation and
    involvement 83–4
  political engagement 81–2
  political trust and reflexivity 84–6
  strategic citizens 82, 89–92
    post-politics 92–3
internet 101, 102, 103
internet voting 105
Internetisation 105
interviews 265, 266
isolation 240–2
Italy
  political squats 139–53
    case studies 142–3
    economic crisis as motivator 144–6
    position towards institutions 150–2
    research methodology 143–4
    social centres 146–9
  Quaderni Urbani 17–27
    project history 17–19
    project work and social impact 23–6

sustainability and militancy 26–7
theoretical assumptions, purposes
   and methodologies 19–23

J

James, A. 120
Johnson, V. 161
Jordan 221, 222, 223, 227
journey mapping 124, 125
   marginalised youth 235–51
   Part of the Community
      project 43–50
justification 160, 171–2

K

Kennelly, J. 57
Knowledge Leads the Way
   (KLW) 123–4, 126–7, 128–9,
   130, 131
knowledge production 222–3

L

Làbas 17–19, 24, 142–3, 145, 148, 150
labelling 56–7
   see also discrimination
language 206
language creation from below 200–1
latent class analysis (LCA) 59
Latour, B. 249
Law, J. 268
LaZecca 26
Le Borgne, C. 39
learning for participation 280–1
Lebanon 221, 222, 223, 227
Leccardi, C. 161
legitimacy 223–5, 226, 229
life circumstances 69–72
Lipsky, M. 179
listening 301
Lister, R. 55
lived citizenship 120
local connections 67, 69
logics 160
loneliness 240–2

M

map-making 267–9
marginalised youth
   digital participation 111, 113
   journey mapping 235–51
   transformative participation 275–9
      case study 282–7
      learning for participation 280–1
      role of professionals 281–2
      youth participatory action research
         (YPAR) 279–80
Matarasso, F. 251

material scarcity 26–7
May, Theresa 197
McMahon, G. 126
meaning 238, 251
meaningful participation 126
Mediterranea Saving Humans 24
memory 268
mental health services 37–8,
      123–4, 127
   see also Knowledge Leads the Way
      (KLW)
Metropolitan Snapshots 23–4
migrants 18, 143
   see also asylum seekers; immigration
migration policies 24
Mills, C.W. 202
Min, S.-J. 101
mobile focus group 264
Moss, P. 133
multimedia methods 255–71
   map-making 267–9
   playfulness 257–60, 264–7
   research activities 261–3
   research methodology 260–1, 263–4
music 163–6
mutualism 146, 152
MYPLACE (Memory, Youth, Political
      Legacy and Civic Engagement)
   context and data 103–7
   digital divides 110–11
   findings 111–13
   opportunities for involvement 107–10

N

Nairn, K. 228
NEET (Not in Education, Employment
      or Training) 249, 276
neoliberalism 133
Nielsen, K.A. 280
non-governmental organisations
      (NGOs) 24
   see also ActionAid Denmark

O

oligopticons 249, 251
online participation see
      digital participation
online petitions 109–10
open atelier 25–6
open workshops 22, 23–4
organisational structures 167–8
Ortika 26
ownership 250, 266

P

Part of the Community 43–50
   Barwago's participatory journey 43–7

Darpan's participatory journey 47–50
participation
  access to 130–1
  adult-led 157, 158–9, 160
  and advocacy 179–80
  challenges to 220–1
  definition 3
  dissatisfaction with 294
  future of 301–3
  inequality in 5–6
  interpretations of 276–7
  meaning of 199–202
  meaningful 126
  see also digital participation; political
    participation; project-based
    participation; social participation;
    transformative participation
participation workers 35–8, 39–40,
  41
participatory place 169–71
participatory research 202–5, 236
  see also journey mapping;
    youth participatory action
    research (YPAR); youth-led
    research projects
participatory spaces 126–8
Passeron, J. 20–1
peer mentor training 32
peer relationships 39
Percy-Smith, Barry 40, 278
performance culture 237
performativity 266
personal efficacy 53, 61–4
  see also self-efficacy
personal-political 207
petitions 109–10
Petrie, P. 133
photography 23
place 242–3, 258, 267, 269
  see also space
playfulness 255, 257–60, 264–7,
  269–70
police contact 57, 61, 68, 69
political choices 79
political collective see Làbas;
  political squats
political engagement 81–2
political franchise see Vote at 16; voting
political knowledge 83
political participation 203
  unconventional 87, 140–1, 152–3
  see also activism; digital participation;
    International Civic and
    Citizenship Education Study
    (ICCS)
political squats 139–53
  case studies 142–3

economic crisis as motivator 144–6
  position towards institutions 150–2
  research methodology 143–4
  social centres 146–9
political trust 84–6, 100, 144
politics 1, 30, 32, 47, 49–50
post-bourgeois leftists 80
post-politics 92–3
pragmatic turn 150–2
prefigurative politics 151
prepositions 247
private citizens 203
professionals 281–2
  see also participation workers;
    statutory caseworkers
project regimes 122, 125, 133
project society 122
project spaces 126–8
project-based participation 119–33
  as disembedded project
    bubbles 125–31
  findings 119, 132–3
  research methodology 123–5
PROMISE Youth Survey 53–73
  data and method 58–9
  social participation 54–5
    barriers to 56–7, 64–5
    enablers of 57–8, 66–7
    forms of 59–61
    and life experiences 69–72
    police contact 68
    role of personal efficacy for 61–4
psychiatric care 123–4, 127
  see also Knowledge Leads the Way
    (KLW)
public speaking 34
Putnam, R. 161

Q

Quaderni Urbani 17–27
  project history 17–19
  project work and social impact 23–6
  sustainability and militancy 26–7
  theoretical assumptions, purposes and
    methodologies 19–23
qualitative research 236
Quintelier, E. 102

R

recognition 182–3, 184–6
reflexivity 84–6
Refugee and Asylum Participatory
  Action Research (RAPAR) 199
refugees 222
relationships 38–40, 41, 296, 299
representativeness 226–8, 229
research 33–4

see also co-research; participatory
research; youth participatory
action research (YPAR)
Rights Respecting Schools
(RRSs) 120, 124, 127, 128,
129–30, 131, 295
Rooke, Alison 264
rural settings 255–71
map-making 267–9
playfulness in research 257–60, 264–7
research activities 261–3
research methodology 260–1, 263–4

S

safe space 41
Schlozman, K.L. 102
Scotland *see* Young Edinburgh Action
(YEA)
Segerberg, A. 101–2, 112
self-censorship 110
self-efficacy 84, 85, 86
see also personal efficacy
self-organisation
leisure time 157–72
informal competencies 163–6
organisational structures 166–8
participatory place 169–71
research methodology 162–3
political squats 139–53
case studies 142–3
economic crisis as motivator 144–6
position towards institutions 150–2
research methodology 143–4
social centres 146–9
semi-organisation 158, 162
sex education 34, 35–6
Shakespeare, T. 189
Simmons, R. 249
situated social learning 280–1, 286
skateboarding 161, 166–8, 169–70
social centres 142–3, 146–9
social change perspective 280
social class 6, 21
social exclusion 53, 56, 61, 64–5, 69
see also marginalised youth
social inclusion 101
social interaction 183–4
social learning 280
social media 99, 100, 101, 102, 103,
112, 113, 163
opportunities for involvement
107–10
see also digital participation
social mobility 4
social movement organisations
(SMOs) 142, 143, 153–4n
social participation 53, 54–5

barriers to 56–7, 64–5
enablers of 57–8, 66–7
forms of 59–61
and life experiences 69–73
police contact 68
role of personal efficacy for 61–4
social photography 23
social positon 69–72
social reproduction 20–1
social research 33–4
social space 298
social stabilisation 237
social trust 57, 67, 69, 84
social workers *see* statutory caseworkers
societal change 287
Solnit, R. 267, 268
space 40–1, 161, 298–9
collective 206–7
participatory 126–8
urban 163–5, 169–71
see also place
speaking bitterness 206
Specially Planned Youth Education
School (SPYES) 180
squatting *see* political squats
statutory caseworkers 175–6, 178–9
advocacy 182–3, 186–9
communication 183–6
Stea, D. 268
Stewart-Hall, Roz 235, 237–8, 251
strategic citizens 82, 89–92, *94*
post-politics 92–3
street photography 23
suffrage *see* Vote at 16; voting
supported housing 186, 187
surrealist movement 26

T

Tartu County 105–6
technology 236
see also digital participation;
multimedia methods
tests 160
Thatcher, Margaret 197–8
thematic readings 22, 24–5
Theme Workshop (TW) approach 283
Theocharis, Y. 102
Thévenot, L. 128, 160, 166, 168, 171
time 161, 242–3
Tingbjerg 45, 50n
Tingbjerg Youth Community 43–7
Tisdall, E.K.M. 39, 279, 285
tourism 23–4
transformative learning 238
transformative participation 278–9
Danish case study 282–7
learning for participation 280–1

role of professionals 281–2
youth participatory action research
(YPAR) 279–80
transition perspective 4
trust 104
see also political trust; social trust
Turner, D. 161

U

unconventional political
participation 87, 140–1, 152–3
see also political squats
UNICEF 120, 124, 125
Unite Against Facism 198
United Kingdom (UK)
asylum seekers 195–208
collective space 206–7
hostile environment 196–8, 202,
205, 207
meaningful participation 199–202
participatory research 203–5
Refugee and Asylum Participatory
Action Research (RAPAR) 199
multimedia methods 255–71
map-making 267–9
playfulness 257–60, 264–7
research activities 261–3
research methodology 260–1, 263–4
United Nations Convention on
the Rights of the Child
(UNCRC) 217, 218, 219–20, 301
urban space 163–5, 168–71

V

Verba, S. 86–7
vocabularies of motive 202
Voice against Violence (VAV) 221, 222,
226, 227
Voices for Mediterranea 24–5
Voloshinov, V.N. 200
volunteering 60–1, 146
Vote at 16 30

voting 105

W

walking 258–9, 260–1, *263*, 264–5
Walsh, L. 120
Walther, A. 122, 133
Weil, S. 281
Woodman, D. 161
World Vision 221–2
Wyness, M. 301

Y

Young Edinburgh Action (YEA)
29–42, 221, 295
Christina's story 35–8
Katherine's story 32–5
legitimacy and credibility 225, 226
Myada's story 30–2
relationships 38–40, 41
representativeness 227–8
space 40–1
young people, definition 9n
young researchers 222–3, 296
YoungRAPAR 199
youth 3–5
see also marginalised youth
youth council 49
youth mental health services 37–8
see also Knowledge Leads the Way
(KLW)
youth movements 79
youth on the edge 236–7, 249
youth participatory action research
(YPAR) 279–80
Danish case study 282–7
learning for participation 280–1
role of professionals 281–2
youth-led research projects 217–19,
221–30
knowledge production 222–3
legitimacy and credibility 223–8
see also participatory research

www.ingramcontent.com/pod-product-compliance
Lightning Source LLC
Chambersburg PA
CBHW070908030426
42336CB00014BA/2337